INSPIRED BY TRUE EVENTS

ENCORE...

HOW I SURVIVED AND THRIVED IN THE LOGISTICS BUSINESS

THE GOOD, BAD, and UGLY

TONY L HARRIS

Quantity sales special discounts are available on quantity purchases by corporations, associations, and others. For details, contact the publisher at the address above.

Orders by U.S. trade bookstores and wholesalers. Email info@ BeyondPublishing.net

The Beyond Publishing Speakers Bureau can bring authors to your live event. For more information or to book an event contact the Beyond Publishing Speakers Bureau speak@BeyondPublishing.net

The Author can be reached directly at BeyondPublishing.net

Manufactured and printed in the United States of America distributed globally by BeyondPublishing.net

BEYOND
PUBLISHING

New York | Los Angeles | London | Sydney

ISBN Hardcover: 978-1-637922-73-6

PRAISE FOR ENCORE...
WHAT SOME EXPERTS ARE SAYING

Encore is wonderfully written; the stories invoke fond memories of my 20+ years in the logistics industry. This is a must read for newbies or veterans like myself. Tony, I tip my hat off to you on a job well done.

Jack Hunt
Owner, Send It Express, LLC

Congratulations Tony L Harris for your courage to tell the truth and set the record straight once and for all. WOW! What a potential hiring explosion this book, ENCORE, could have over the next ten years, especially if the word spreads throughout the African American communities and people of color. This inspiring-humorous book represents a beautiful depiction of one man's grit and determination to succeed against all odds. I especially enjoyed reading about the hiring practices that young Tony was subjected to and endured back then, 40 years ago. As we have all heard, "if we don't learn from our past history, we are sure to repeat it." It is my sincere hope that you pick up a copy of this book and become inspired to seize the day, as we all embrace the change that we want and hope for in the world.

-Kelsye Jefferson
Solutions Specialist, Old Dominion

Whether you're one of the 10,000 baby boomers retiring each day, choosing to finally EXIT the workforce, or perhaps you're just graduating from high school or college and embarking upon the uncertainties and challenges of starting a new career, this book, "ENCORE," is a must read. Each story discussed is shaped with meaningful messages that are informative, uplifting, and entertaining. I highly recommend this book. Enjoy!

Greg Mercer
Director of Sales, XPO Logistics

Having served a lot of hard times in the logistics industry myself, I absolutely LOVE this book, loved hearing all the beautiful heart-warming stories and the powerful impact our logistic industry is making throughout the globe. Mr. Harris' illustrations of the characters and situations makes it seem as if you were there along with him. This is a great page turner for those of us still in the industry, it's highly recommended for those incoming and everyone in between!

Priscilla A Wilson, LCB
Corporate Customs Broker, Globe Express Services

This book represents a beautiful depiction of truth, honor, and legacy, and has become Tony L Harris' most urgent challenge and clarion call to all dreamers and forward thinkers, regardless of your occupation or career choice. To all conscientious truth seekers who are committed to serving and helping others, I encourage you to read this book for a daily dose of inspiration, laughter and courage.

Marc Weidner
Vice President of Field Sales, ArcBest

In this heartwarming, and humorous book, author Tony L Harris takes the reader on an exciting and memorable hero's journey through his powerful stories of struggle and ultimate success. Great read.

An amazing read for anyone seeking a career in logistics or perhaps someone who is simply searching. I had the opportunity to see Tony in action close up later in his career as a Corporate Trainer and reading his book now makes me appreciate both him and the incredible world of logistics even more. This book will have you asking for an ENCORE!

DEDICATION

To my wife Lora and my incredible sons Jacob and Joshua
who have given me unwavering love and support
throughout this journey.
May God bless you always with health, wealth, love, and a spirit of
happiness that comes with knowing that you truly make
a difference in the world.
I love each of you, today and always.

AUTHOR'S NOTES

This book is not intended to hurt, defame, or dehumanize anyone, but is merely an earnest depiction of my own experiences. It is a combination of facts and tales of inspired true events about my life's journey in the transportation-logistics industry. It is based on my best recollections of various events in my life. In some instances, the information should not be taken literally. I have strived to recreate events and conversations based on my memories of them. In other accounts, I have consulted my journals, friends, colleagues and work associates from that specific era.

To preserve anonymity, I have changed the names and identifying characteristics of the majority of the people mentioned in order to protect their privacy. In some instances, I rearranged and/or compressed events and time periods in service of the narrative, and I re-created dialogue to match my best recollection of those exchanges and my thoughts at that particular time.

Many of the stories were selected at random and represent only a fraction of my experiences. On occasion, I introduce a hypothesis or draw certain conclusions that have a limited basis in fact. In one form or another, some readers may find that I have unfairly criticized certain characters in the story. I recognize there are memories of events revealed here that are different than my own.

Bottomline, I encourage you to come with me on this hero's journey and allow the deeper message in this book to emerge with truth, fairness, and empowerment for all.

FOREWORD

Director of Sales, XPO Logistics

I am reminded of the poem by Maya Angelou that says, *"I come as one, but I stand as 10,000."* When I think of Tony L Harris, and even though I am 6'5" and much taller than him, clearly he is one of the many giants in the industry who's broad shoulders I am standing on today. I have a sincere appreciation and respect for the commitment and leadership that Tony has given to our logistics industry at large. His superb body of work speaks for itself as demonstrated by me and thousands of others that he's inspired to live the best version of themselves.

Tony's name is synonymous with *"servant caring leadership," in his daily work and as the role model he represents for so many of my colleagues, myself included.*

When he retired in March, 2020, the mayor of his city awarded him the distinct honor of declaring it **"Tony L. Harris Day."** Who gets such an award as this when they are retiring after 40+ years of continuous service? I challenge you to think about the last time you attended such an exuberant retirement celebration extravaganza.

Tony's unwavering inspirational coaching, and selfless acts of kindness have unquestionably made a tremendous difference in my life and career, which inevitably included the good, the bad and ugly of his memoir title.

So, I encourage you to open not only your eyes, but your heart as well, and really let the deeper message in this book, **ENCORE,** sink in. It will truly take you on a journey that highlights the power of faith, persistence, and dedication. My final words in closing, *"job well done."*

Greg Mercer
Director of Sales, XPO Logistics
2022

TABLE OF CONTENTS

INTRODUCTION

"Once you get in the trucking business, the trucking business gonna get in you. Be careful....May God bless you."

Bill *"The Magician"*
– My first mentor in Transportation Logistics

It's 6:05 a.m. on May 11, 1981. The speaker is Bill, a 65-year-old man, skinny as a greyhound dog, fast-talking, chain smoking, with a lifetime résumé dedicated to the trucking industry. It's also my first day on the job as a Management Trainee for Roadway Express, Long Beach, California. I've been on the lot since 4 a.m. and am already hungry, exhausted, and clueless. My brain and body are rebelling at this strange, high-pressure work environment that seems to come to life between midnight and daybreak.

"It's not normal, being up this early," I mutter to myself, "and everyone seems so hostile and upset." I wonder what on earth I've gotten myself into this time. In that moment, I knew that if it was going to be like this, it definitely wasn't for me. Nothing from my previous work experience compares to this situation, and certainly nothing has prepared me to cope. The rough culture, the fast pace, the hostile attitudes from the other workers – Teamsters, of course, all wearing garb that proudly states "*The International Brotherhood of Teamsters*" – and from management as well, feels foreign and strange.

If Bill has read my mind, at least he's nice enough not to mention it. He walks fast, talks fast, puffs his Prince Albert roll-your-own cigarettes like a fretful freight train, all the while keeping up a steady stream of information couched in unfamiliar slang and punctuated by loud expostulations aimed at me – his newest employee: "FOLLOW ME, KEEP UP! STAY OUT OF THE WAY OF THE FORKLIFTS! DON'T ASK ANY QUESTIONS YET!"

In between processing the shouts designed to keep me alive, I struggle with the unfamiliar language. What the HELL is a 48? A PUP? A GOAT? A YARD DOG??? Really??? No one I ever met in my life talked like this, and I wonder what it all has to do with transportation logistics. I'm in the middle of a surreal dream, wondering if I can survive it. Finally, my common sense takes over. Well, I'm here, and at least I can learn something before I completely give up.

I force my attention back to this fast-paced, skinny old man while struggling to keep up with him as he goes about his job. Between snatches of conversation and warning me to watch myself, he's simultaneously yelling to the dockworkers, giving instructions to other managers and supervisors on the dock via walkie talkie, darting in and out of the trailers, jumping down and back up from off the dock, to make sure trailers are properly blocked, and continually looking inside trailers to confirm what's in them. He's like Houdini or the magical wizard. Then and there, I christen him Merlin the Magician. He's a walking encyclopedia, a forerunner of today's Google. He seems to know the location of every trailer on the dock and in the yard, what's inside each and what to do with all this knowledge. I think it's safe to say that he has a photographic memory.

My attention is jarred back to the job when he suddenly looks directly at me and grunts, "Go tell the hostler to bring up Trailer 72395, put it in door 61, and switch out trailer 55647 from door 24 to door 67. Got that?"

"Yes, sir," I stammer, and I start walking in the direction he's pointing. I don't have a clue. I'm still struggling with the word "hostler" – or, I wondered, had he said "hustler"? What the hell is a hostler? Once I figure out the instructions with a little help from one of the friendlier dock guys, I am able to complete the assignment. When I return to Bill, he asks, "You got er' done?"

"Yes sir!" I reply.

Then he says "Okay. Now, try and keep up…we're getting into crunch time now, and we've got one hour to close out this shift before the daytime people get here."

If I was scared and confused before, it's worse now. He's walking ten times faster, and I'm having to jog to keep up with him. It's noisy, crazy fast-paced, and this old man is running circles around me. Imagine eight to ten guys on those noisy forklifts flying around like they're at the Indy 500, with everyone yelling and honking their horns. It's definitely starting to get to me.

As the greenest guy on the lot, I struggle with trust issues, especially with the guys who've been taunting me all night with things like, "Hey, Rookie, you won't last a week around here! We eat your kind for breakfast and spit you out." At some level, I can see that this must be some kind of initiation, and I'm determined to pass. This must be something like the Jimmy Hoffa era, which wasn't all that long ago. So maybe everyone thinks it's cool to do the Jimmy Hoffa imitation. After all, technically speaking, Hoffa's only been missing six years. Maybe he's not dead. Maybe he's going to show up again and reclaim his throne. One thing I know for sure, the International Brotherhood of Teamsters is alive and kicking at LBC-820.

Meantime, Bill continues talking circles around me. Certainly, I'm not used to all of this, nor working all night and being on my feet the whole time either. The only saving grace of this never-ending night is that Bill chain smokes all night long. Occasionally, he stops and takes a serious three-minute smoke break while contemplating his operational close-out strategy. These breaks are really good and proper smoke breaks. He takes a deep breath as he sucks in all that tar, nicotine, and carcinogenic flavor-filled smoke. What I don't realize at the time is that I am observing and sort of participating in a Master Class taught by one of the best ever. I'm observing a man in action who truly loves his job. And I am way too nervous and tired to appreciate it.

Many weeks later I realize that Bill doesn't have to come in four hours early to help the other four supervisors close their shift properly in accordance with his needs and his dispatch strategy. Bottom line, he's there to help – but also mainly to ensure that HIS trailers are loaded according to specifications. Bill's a perfectionist, and he wants to maximize the efficiencies of his Pickup and Delivery (P&D) drivers. What this means in real time is that Bill works fourteen-hour days. Dedication and sacrifice.

As the hours wear along, I feel like this is the longest shift I've ever worked at anything in my life. Watching Bill that first day, I notice that he doesn't look all that healthy. He looks frail and sickly, with his Prince Albert cigarettes cocked and loaded behind both ears, with one in his mouth. The one in his mouth seems to fit perfectly inside the gap between two missing lower teeth. I remember thinking, "Please God, I don't want to end up in 40 years looking like this man."

"Oops! Break's over!" Bill's voice breaks through my thoughts. He's already sprinting down the dock, barking out orders to the workers. I follow him, frantically trying to keep up, when he comes to a hard stop, turns around and looks me straight in the eye. He takes a deep drag on his cigarette and says, "Listen, son, once you get in the trucking business, the trucking business gonna get in you. So, be careful, and may God bless you!"

And before I can respond, he turns and is off again. For a moment, I'm paralyzed by his words, and then I'm up and following him again. But I'm also pondering what he's just said. Obviously, he's trying to tell me something important. I'm not sure if it's a warning or a welcome. I'd been ready to quit two hours ago, and now this. I'm starting to question my sanity. "What are you doing here, Tony? Are you sure you're in the right place?" Hmm…

★★★★★★★★★★★★★

That was 40 years ago to the day from 1981 to 2021. So, as I prepare to walk away from the industry I obviously fell in love with, I have a lot to think about. Don't get me wrong. There were many bittersweet days when I wanted to quit. But I survived it, learned from it, paid the price of sacrifice, and hoped it was worth it. Bill was right, you know. The trucking business does get into your blood.

As I prepared for my retirement party, people were constantly asking me the usual questions. "Are you counting the days?" asked one woman. "Are you looking forward to your honey-do-list and going fishing?" inquired another man. Truth is, I wasn't counting the days. I was actually sad, but also excited and scared, for me, because I kept hearing in my head, *Encore! Encore!*

And I know it's not over yet. It's time to begin again. It's time for a Second Act Career. It's time to pursue my CALLING! Yes, I'm ready to get my second wind and begin again. I refuse to walk away from this industry with all its opportunities to make a real difference, and not leave something of value behind. *ENCORE: How I Survived and Thrived in the Logistics Business…The Good, Bad, and Ugly,* is part of that legacy. Enjoy!

CHAPTER ONE

THE INTERVIEW

"Sometimes, we're tested not to show our weaknesses,
but to discover our strengths."
-Author Unknown

May 6, 1981. 8:44 a.m. Today's the day. I just know it. It seems like I've been trying *forever* to land this job as a Management Trainee with Roadway Express, arguably the most prestigious trucking firm in the country. I've gone through all their jumps, and now, I'm returning for the third – and hopefully, final – interview at their Los Angeles facility. The whole process has been exhausting, intimidating, and awkward from the very beginning. Like they need an entire army to sign off on my hiring contract. I wonder how that could be. After all, I'm just one person – and a well-qualified person, if I do say so myself.

The job description in the newspaper had detailed the requirements. "NO EXPERIENCE REQUIRED. MUST HAVE UNDERGRADUATE COLLEGE DEGREE." So, they wanted you "educated, but with no experience in transportation." "<u>You must have NO TRUCKING EXPERIENCE</u>." In the first interview, they'd made it crystal clear that this was non-negotiable. They'd told me that if I had even one day of transportation experience with a competitor, I'd be disqualified as a candidate for Roadway Express.

Before answering their advertisement, I'd done a little homework about the trucking industry. I'd learned that Roadway Express considered itself the crown jewel in the trucking business. Also, that it was indeed the best in the industry; one of the toughest, and it was one of the only companies that had a top-notch management training program. Rumor had it that if you got properly trained through the three-month comprehensive Roadway Management Training System and then worked for Roadway for at least two years, you could walk straight into a job with any competitor.

As a Roadway graduate, your status in the transportation logistics industry was likened to that of a Navy Seal. You were untouchable, and every competitor wanted you. If you worked for Roadway, you were viewed as a tough, smart, efficient, hardcore leader, who understood how to deal with Teamsters and union contracts. You had already suffered and paid a lot of dues, and if the competitor could successfully recruit you to join their team, most likely, it would feel like taking a breath of fresh air. Many people jumped ship after two or three years, if they survived that long, but many more made it into a lifetime career. (From my status as a 40-year veteran of the transportation logistics business, my hat goes off to anyone who survived 30 or 40 years at Roadway Express.)

Right now, though, I have no idea why this hiring process is taking so long. Immediately after my first interview, they had pushed me to provide proof of my work experience, along with my college transcripts from my Bachelor of Science program at Texas Tech (TTU), and from Stephen F. Austin (SFA), where I'd received my Master's in Education Administration. They were especially insistent that I provide proof of my master's degree. The transcript from Texas Tech had arrived immediately, but the grad school transcript was slow. It had taken almost two-and-a-half weeks longer to verify.

Bottom line, they wanted to know if I'd lied to them about my master's degree. For whatever reason, they didn't trust everything I'd put on my application, and the delay, according to them, was more my fault than theirs. At least, that's what they actually had said. They said I'd slowed down the hiring process simply by saying I had a master's degree.

I wondered how that could be. Here I was, trying to differentiate myself from the competition and stand out, and they saw my hard-earned master's as proof that I was a show-off, trying too hard to impress them. Disclosing the advanced degree from SFA was a strategy that had obviously backfired. Everything had been put on a slow burner until I could produce those official transcripts, no carbon or photocopies accepted. I was "officially under investigation". It felt like the FBI. During that last interview, intimidated or not, I had spoken up and challenged them.

"Why do you need me to wait before I start? You've already got my undergraduate transcript from Texas Tech, and I'm sure you'll be receiving my other transcript from Stephen F. any day now. Why can't we move forward with what you've already received?"

"You shouldn't have put down that you have a master's degree, Tony," responded Bob, my interviewer at the time. "Now we're curious to know if you really do, before we can move forward. Basically, we're wondering if you're just flat-out lying to us."

"WHAT?" I was astonished and insulted. "Why do you doubt what I put on my application?"

Bob looked me dead in the eye. "Look at you, Tony. You're 27 years old. You've been teaching and coaching in high school for the last four years in South Texas. You moved to California in August, just a few months ago. When did you have the time to get a damned master's degree? That's what I want to know!"

At that point, I realized it was no use to argue. I simply needed to relax and wait this thing out before I completely blew away my chances to get hired. For some routine reason, Texas Tech's transcript had arrived almost by return mail, but Stephen F. Austin was taking its sweet little time. That gave me pause. Still, I knew I would eventually have the last laugh, if this was all they were concerned about.

Years later, I would come to understand that I was being interviewed by men who were much older than I, most of whom didn't have a post-secondary education. In their experience, they had good reason to feel threatened by folks who had continued to pursue advanced education past high school. Many of these men were great leaders and would be great mentors for me, but they'd had to rely solely on their experience and networking skills to get promoted and move ahead. Indeed, in their experience, too much education would have been a serious handicap to their promotability. Some had 15 or 20 years of age and experience over me. They had skipped college and started at the bottom right after high school, creating their future careers in this world of transportation logistics.

So here I show up, with no experience, dragging along an advanced degree with very little value in the trucking industry of 1981, except maybe to get hired. It was still a "good-ole-boy" world, just beginning to change ever so slightly. While Roadway's forward-looking management trainee program was built to attract employees best suited to Roadway's internal culture, these old-school managers understood that choosing trainee candidates carefully could ensure good hiring decisions and minimize hiring mistakes that could become costly.

Interesting, I thought, that this whole job thing with Roadway had started out for me as a stopgap measure. I'd recently come to California from Texas, where I'd been a career educator, with a promising future as a teacher and coach. I already had the "firm promise" of a teaching job somewhere in the Inglewood Unified School District, but I hadn't actually signed the contract. However, I'd been around the teaching business long enough to know that until your signature is on the bottom line, you don't have the job. In any case, the job was a good four months away. In the meantime, there was no income. Three months of well-paid training, even in an industry I knew nothing about, was enticing. At worst, I could certainly learn something, and with Roadway, I had assumed that getting hired would be a matter of walking in the door and the job would be mine. So, what was taking so damned long?

Honestly, this series of interviews has felt more like interrogations. Always, when I was being interviewed to become a schoolteacher and athletic coach, it had always felt like the job was mine. In fact, the interview was more like an unofficial welcome into the teaching fraternity. We sat and ate breakfast and talked about what I would be doing in my new job. "Not in this new environment," I think, ruefully. "It almost feels like I'm the damned enemy, and they don't even want me. Like they're just going through the motions to try to run me off."

There was nothing in my 27 years on the planet that had prepared me for the earlier interviews, and today was a total unknown. Funny, though, the harder they pushed me, the more I was determined to get hired. If I did, I'd figure out later what to do about the teaching job. I thought I was well prepared for this interview and this job, and I was determined to see it through.

Driving to the Los Angeles offices of Roadway, I am mentally and emotionally preparing myself for the next interrogation. Between random thoughts, I loudly repeat my secret mantra over and over: "I am here to get the job. I am here to get the job! DID YOU HEAR ME? I SAID, I CAME TO GET THE DAMN JOB! YES, SIR, excuse me, but I came to get the job! I am here to get the job!" I'm having fun with it, but I'm deadly serious. I CAME TO GET THE JOB!

I shake my head to clear it and turn my concentration to my driving, but I can't stop running the whole scenario over again in my mind. "I should already be working here," I mutter. "At the last interview, they'd even said I was a good candidate, plus the fact that other guy, whose name I can't even remember, let slip that they are hiring a minimum of 150 Management Trainees throughout the country this time around. In fact, this is going to be one of the largest classes of Management Trainees they've hired in the last three years."

I wonder if they're gearing up for something really big this summer, since obviously, they need more people. I'm pretty sure I've impressed them enough. "So why can't we get this show on the road? Can't anybody step up and make a damned decision around here without having to consult five other people?"

My wallet is getting flatter, and rent is coming due. "I am so ready to get started, because I really need some money," I shake my head and chuckle as my dad's voice intrudes into my consciousness. "It's not all about money, son," I can hear him say. "I taught you better than that." Point taken. I return my concentration to the road.

Actually, there was some trucking experience in my immediate family. I remember that my ex-brother-in-law, Raymond, and his best friend, Leon, were both working for LEEWAY Trucking, a large trucking company based out of Oklahoma City. LEEWAY is pretty big in Oklahoma City. You would see their trucks everywhere back home, but come to think of it, I haven't noticed their trucks much since I moved to Los Angeles.

During his marriage to my sister, Pat, Raymond used to complain all the time about the hard work and long hours. He's a good man, tall and handsome, served in Vietnam, and was always good to me, but he never invited me to ride in his rig. Hell, I've never ridden in a big rig, not even as a passenger, and I can't even imagine having to drive one of those big-ass trucks. But, yet they're going to hire and pay me to supervise men and women, some as old as my parents, who drive those things as a career. Seems kinda crazy, but I'll let them pay me to manage these people – at least for now.

As I pull into the massive parking lot, I'm glad I'm wearing my best pinstripe dark brown suit with matching tie, and my long-sleeved white shirt is starched and spotless. I remember my last interview with Mr. Bob – damn, I wish I could remember his last name… anyway, he said they call this Los Angeles facility the breakbulk, one of the largest of their 444 terminals. Whatever a breakbulk is. Never mind, I'm sure I'll eventually understand all these terms and acronyms once I get the job.

The sight of the big rigs and the drivers make me remember when I was a kid and we used to listen on our walkie-talkies at night to those drivers talking back and forth on their CB radios. It was fun listening to all their rhetoric and chatter, and their alias names and handles. One lady had this crazy name like "Lonely Redhead", and all the guys would try to sweet talk her. It was all fun banter back then, or so it seemed. She sounded so cute and innocent, but I bet she would have whipped your ass if you bothered her. One guy sounded like he had a 30-year smoker's hoarse voice: "Breaker, breaker 19, this is Slim Dog checking in, what's your 20?" Whoa. Never in a thousand years did I think I'd graduate from college and end up here. It's amazing how your thinking can change based on your needs, and your life can change based on your thinking.

I park the car and walk inside the gate. Two or three drivers are coming through in their trucks, bobtailing. (Bobtailing, I'd learned on my last visit, is when you don't have a trailer hitched behind.) The trucks all stop for me. One of the guys honks his horn and beckons me to walk across. So, I do.

Reaching the building, I stand up a little straighter and take a deep breath. "Let's just get this show on the road," I murmur. In truth, I'm a little nervous about this interview. They had told me it was going to be in front of a board of four men, and Bob is the only one I've met previously. By the time I reach the interview room, I'm way past intimidated—in point of fact, I'm scared to death. I take another deep breath.

I will never forget that third interview:

The first thing I notice is that nobody is smiling. Everyone is standing up, looking like they're ready to fight. One of the four, dressed in his blue three-piece suit and a red power tie, is doing some hard-core staring, looking me up and down, obviously intending to be as intimidating as possible.

I try breaking the ice. "So, how is everyone? Nice weather today, isn't it?" Nice try, but it falls flat.

Two of the men nod their heads, but there are no smiles and no comments on my weather observation. And they remain standing. Two are smoking cigarettes and staring intently at me. It feels a lot like the time I was pledging my fraternity in college, surrounded by our "big brothers". Totally intimidated.

After a long, staring silence, one of the men, introduced as Paul, speaks: "You seem a little too damn nice and formal for this kind of work. Your niceness reminds me of a damned choir boy – too fucking polite for me!" Tossing my résumé and both transcripts on the table, he sighs and says, "Let's all sit down, fellows, and talk this out."

Everyone sits down, leaving me to wonder what kind of man would begin a job interview with a comment like that. (In 40 years, I've never been able to forget that interview. I've been on at least six dozen interviews since 1981, but never, ever did an interviewer begin with such a statement.)

I almost get up and walk out, but before I can do so, one of the other men, John, speaks up. "Let's just cut to the chase," he says. "Can you CUSS?"

Huh? "Excuse me?" I ask, politely.

"You heard me. Can you CUSS?"

"Uh, yes sir! That's an interesting question. But I'd like to think I can handle myself quite well with a few curse words every now and then. Let's just say that I know my way quite well around the curse world arena."

"Really? Why is that? Did your parents cuss, or your friends at school?"

"Well, I grew up with a pretty normal life, but sometimes my friends and I would sneak off and listen to comedians, you know, like Red Foxx, Moms Mabley, Lenny Bruce, and also Richard Pryor, and I know the lingo. Sir, I'm not from the 'hood', but I understand the 'hood.'"

I am starting to get more than a little pissed at the tone this interview is taking. I can't believe that they have the nerve to ambush me with this line of questioning. What are they trying to prove?

Bob takes pity on me. "LISTEN, Tony. We are dealing with hardcore Teamsters here. I don't think you really understand what that means. DO you know what that means, young man? Tell me what you think it means having to deal with Teamsters."

I take a minute to gather my thoughts. "Well, I know about Teamsters only from a distance. I can't pretend I understand the culture I've been exposed to in the last month, but I DO know there's a lot of pride in our country for unions, and people feel a certain security being part of a union organization. For example, my mother and aunts are all schoolteachers, and they belong to a teachers' union. In fairness, I will say that I've also heard some of the old stories about Jimmy Hoffa back in the fifties and sixties. But to be completely honest, sir, I don't really know what it means, especially from your point of view."

"Well, at least you're an honest sonofabitch," Paul says. Then he stands up over me and says, "Fuck all that! TEAMSTERS! Let me tell you about TEAMSTERS. Let me try to explain this to you, son. TEAMSTERS – see, it's like this: they don't like us, and we don't like them. Did you understand that? That they don't like us, and we don't like them. You got it? Now, if you don't understand that, you don't need to be working here. But somehow, in spite of our dislike for each other, we have to try to exist together and be productive and profitable. It ain't easy, and, frankly, nice guys finish last in this business."

"Oh." Suddenly the light dawns. "Okay. I got it, Sir, loud and clear." Truth is, I'm not sure if this is some type of game or if I'm on *Candid Camera*.

"Okay, here's your first test," Paul says. "You say you can cuss. LET ME HEAR YOU SAY DAMN!"

"DAMN!" I echo, with what I hope is appropriate firmness.

"Let me hear you say SHIT!" Paul continues.

"SHIIIIIIIT!" I yell, and to my horror, I find myself laughing out loud. I can't believe what is happening here. I just can't wrap my head around it. Out of the corner of my eye, I see the men exchange glances.

"Well, son," begins John, "let me tell you how this is going to work if you really want this job. Okay? Now, we're offering you the job, but before we'll allow you to accept the job, you have to observe a ten-hour operations shift WITHOUT PAY! You start tonight from 2200 to 0800. This is a ten-hour shift on your own dime. That's right TEN HOURS, on your own dime, and your own time. You got that?"

"YES, SIR! I'm ready!" I reply, realizing that my voice is louder than normal. Everything feels so intense, like I'm in basic training in the military. Deep down, I'm happy, because I feel like I could survive this ten-hour shift and get the job, no matter what.

But the men aren't done with me yet.

Dan has been quiet, but now, it is his turn. "Now, Tony, hear me good, okay? Tomorrow morning, once that shift is over, if you walk in here at 0800 and say to me and these other men, "I want the job, then the job is yours. It's just that simple."

"Yes sir," I respond, more quietly now. "Wow, this is so different!"

"Yes," Dan replies, "We don't want to waste your time or our money training you and then you quit because you can't cut it. We want you to know what you're getting yourself into, and if you don't want this life, well, no hard feelings. Because I'm telling you like it is – this business isn't for everybody."

"Yes, sir. I understand, and I'm ready for the challenge."

But down deep, I'm really not. I keep thinking, *Here they are, ganging up on me, trying to scare me and test my manhood.*

Bob takes over again.

"Okay, slow down, Tony. This is how it works: you come back here tonight at 2200 sharp and go see Ronnie. He's a good man, one of our lead Outbound Ops Managers. Just tell him you're from Long Beach 820, and he'll know what to do. We'll be here tomorrow morning about 0700. You come and see us at 0800 sharp and let us know your decision. Sound good?"

"Yes, sir. I'll see you tomorrow morning at 0800."

I am not yet dismissed, however. John speaks up again.

"When you meet Ronnie tonight, be sure and tell him that you're from Long Beach 820. Also, you must wear a long-sleeved white shirt and necktie. You might need a jacket because it does get a little chilly at night on that dock. But all our managers and supervisors are required to wear long sleeve white shirts and ties. Okay?"

"Yes sir. No problem. Why do I need to say to Ronnie that I'm from Long Beach? I actually live in Los Angeles."

"That's because 820 is where you'll be working, son, if you make the cut," Dan says.

"So, I won't actually work out of this Los Angeles location?"

"Hell no!" Bob said. "You aren't nearly ready for 821. This is HARDCORE UP HERE! ONE OF THE TOUGHEST TERMINALS IN THE SYSTEM. Plus, we need someone in Long Beach. If you make the cut, you'll be thanking us."

"Well, I want to say thank you right now for this opportunity."

"You can thank us tomorrow," Bob says. "Here's what you don't understand: We're about to move our break-bulk to Adelanto, California. That's about 100 miles from here, and all these guys who work here in L.A. are getting ready to move to the desert, and they are not happy campers. They just found out last week, so you'll be hearing the rumblings tonight!"

"Oh wow! Then I really do thank you. Thanks for putting all of this into perspective, and I look forward to seeing you all tomorrow morning."

"If you survive and make the cut, Tony, you are one lucky man," says Paul, with a big smile.

"Yes, sir! I understand, and I'd like to shake your hand right now and say thank you, because I'll be honest with you – I didn't come all the way from Texas to Southern California to be stuck out in the hot desert."

"Just one last thing," says Paul, with a serious frown. "STOP SAYING 'SIR'! You need to stop that right now. You can't supervise and lead these Teamsters calling them SIR. Understood?"

"Yes Sir. I mean YES, I understand. That's just my home training sticking out."

All four men laugh and shake my hand and wish me good luck.

That's the first time we all smiled together. As I make my way back to my vehicle, I am in a turmoil of feelings. Excited, confused, puzzled… I suddenly realize that they haven't asked me a single question in this interview except could I cuss! I wonder if I am being tested to see if I'd lose my cool under pressure. I have to say, it was a near thing! But on balance, I think I handled myself okay under the circumstances. I guess after they saw the official transcript from Stephen F. Austin, which cleared up everything, except whether I could cuss!

I WILL survive this ten-hour shift tonight, no matter what! I look around this huge facility with the giant dock the size of three football fields, and the long "drag line" with hundreds of orange steel mesh carts rolling round and round. No longer does this weird environment terrify me. It feels FINE. Dangerous? Noisy? Surely. Serious business? Definitely. Real? Absolutely. I can see a dozen ways to get killed if you aren't paying attention. These guys aren't playing. It is serious business, and so is the Teamster situation. Serious, and real, too. Deep in my brain, a new idea is beginning to emerge. God willing, this will be my destiny. The idea of once more being in the classroom – even a friendly classroom—is flitting right out of my head. I KNOW I will survive the next ten hours. No matter what. Tonight, my new journey begins! It probably would be smart to go home and get some sleep.

Well, I go home, but I'm way too wired to consider sleeping. What I seem to know, intuitively, is that somehow, after tonight, my life will never be the same again. In just a few hours, I will embark on a 40-year spiritual journey. One that will challenge me at every turn, starting with persistence and resilience!

CHAPTER TWO

THE DECISION

"Before you make a decision, ask yourself this question:
will you regret the results or rejoice in them?"
-Rob Liano

Well, daytime sleeping is harder than I expected. Just as I finally get into some serious sleep, the alarm jangles me awake, and it's time to get up. Obviously, so far, none of my efforts to fall asleep have been effective. I hope it will get easier. I won't have much time to figure it out. If all goes as planned, next Monday will be the first day on my new job, the one I am already claiming before I even see what the hype is all about. I remind myself to slow down. After all, I've got a good 12 hours before decision time.

It's 9:35 p.m. when I drive into the Los Angeles Roadway parking lot, and the air is electric with excitement. I'm fired up and ready to go, but I force myself to breathe and settle my nerves. It occurs to me that I'm not at all sure I can do this without some divine assistance.

"God, this moment is definitely bigger than me," I whisper, and I offer my thanks to the Deity for giving me this opportunity to try. As I enter the gates from the dimly lit parking lot, I'm literally walking by faith, but my self-confidence is back. It's a lovely, breezy evening! Perfect for an evening at the Santa Monica Pier drinking frozen margaritas, eating nachos, and listening to jazz and reggae. Well, Tony, that won't be tonight.

Once again, I feel the electricity in the air. This moment is much bigger than observing a ten-hour shift. It's my God-given opportunity to see a foundational design for my life's work – and I now know for sure it's no longer necessarily about teaching school. No matter how overwhelming and intimidating the next ten hours will be, I know in my gut I've already decided that I WANT THIS JOB!

It's immediately obvious that the Los Angeles dock is no joke. It's enormous and more intimidating than any high school football game or college track meet ever felt. An ant hill of Teamsters and managers is scurrying around and seems to be in rare form tonight. Everyone looks serious and hard core. Some of them are undoubtedly nice, friendly guys away from work, but my first impression is, in this environment, that they are "brotherhood first" with a bad-to-the-bone attitude and low tolerance for the rest of us.

It's also obvious that nighttime on this Los Angeles dock is a super-serious, fast-paced environment, not for the weak or the slow; a place with its own tempo and momentum. You keep pace or get run over and left behind. I notice that the managers are all wearing the requisite long sleeve white shirts and ties, as am I, so it's pretty obvious which team I'm on.

Hurray! The good guys with ties, I say to myself. That's my group, even though they don't seem very friendly toward me yet.

I had arrived early and checked in and had been told to "wait for Ronnie." Minutes tick by, and I'm still waiting for Ronnie. He sure doesn't seem to be anywhere around. I'm starting to wonder where the hell that prima donna is. Is he that important or busy, or just insensitive and lacking professional courtesy? Or is this part of the new guy hazing?

I know somebody has told him I'd be here at 2200. Hell, it's almost 2230. I'm starting to get worried. Maybe this is another one of those damn tests – like, they want to see what I'll do, or how I handle myself while I wait for Ronnie.

My rational mind takes over. Come on, Tony. Get a grip. They've already told you the job is yours if you want it. All you have to do is survive tonight and tell them in the morning you want the job. Besides, for all you know, Ronnie could be up there in those ivory towers, looking right at you.

I decide to be proactive, moving around and talking to the guys, asking questions. I'm naturally a friendly person, able to handle myself, and I understand that it's possible to learn something just by standing around, listening, paying attention, and trying to look busy.

A cool-looking guy drives up on his forklift.

"Hey, Terry," he says to someone in a manager's white shirt, "What do you want to do with this Atlanta headload? Six pallets, 12,000."

"Take it to Door 59. Let's start an ATL direct," says Terry.

"You sure? I've got a lot of southbound freight coming off my trailer," the other guy says.

"Would you rather rework your trailer and make Atlanta a header?" Terry asks.

"Yeah, I think we'll save time if I rework it, but that's up to you. I don't know what else you've got coming in tonight," the forklift guy replies.

"Nah, it's okay. Let's keep it all down there on your end, Mark. Do a rework with the ATL in the nose," says Terry.

Mark says okay and drives away.

"Wow," I think. "I have just observed a civil exchange between a Teamster and a manager. What's all this about they don't like us? That's not what I just saw. Obviously, these Teamster guys know their stuff, and surely, they aren't all trying to sabotage the company mission."

Right then and there, I vow that when I get hired, I'll develop a management style that will bring out the best in people. I'm glad I'd witnessed that exchange. Terry looks like someone I could emulate. I wonder again about the bad blood and the toxic attitude the managers had described.

I continue to watch the evening unfold. Here I am, front and center at the main office on the dock, near door 40. Right in the heart of the dock operations. Everything seems to flow from this central headquarters. Paperwork passes to a worker along with verbal instructions from the managers; and then, it returns after the job is done. Probably an over-simplification of a complex system, but it looks like this part of the business is pretty straight-forward.

Ronnie still hasn't made an appearance. I've kept my ears open, and so far, everyone is saying the same thing. Ronnie is "infamous" – the man, the myth, and the legend. They keep saying he's down on the far end of the dock, which is so far away I can't even see it. I sure as hell don't want to have to walk down there and find him – in the first place, it's his job to show up, and in the second, I've already walked the length of two football fields, and I just got here. Plus, they all keep passing on Ronnie's message to "just hang tight and wait." So that's what I'm doing. I hope this isn't my first test for the night, because I'm not in the mood.

So far, I've come up with one observation. The guys in the neckties would be kind of like my family. The guys in the blue jeans and work clothes are the workers. (Great guess, Tony. You're a genius. How did you get so damn smart? What the hell is wrong with you? Get your head out of your ass and stay focused!)

Just as I'm yanking myself back to reality, I'm hit with the biggest surprise so far. It's coming right at me. This fella is walking fast and yelling at different guys on the dock like he's the landlord. His necktie is half-cocked to one side, and his general aura reminds me of my high school football coach, L.D. Brown. Coach Brown's voice was so piercing and loud, you'd have knocked down a brick wall for him if he'd told you to. He was a "tough love" motivator, a born leader, and his training had changed my life. So, with that role model in mind, I have at this moment, a very positive view of Ronnie. That lasts about ten seconds.

"Hi. I'm Ronnie," the big man says as he shakes my hand. "You must be Tony." He's smiling, and his voice is deep bass and penetrating.

"Yes. I'm Tony Harris from 820. How are you?" I return the smile, but the next minute, I realize Ronnie's smile is gone and his eyes are flashing with anger.

"Long Beach? LONG BEACH? FUCK YOU! Long Beach.... Fucking 820! I can't stand y'all's asses!" he roars, looking me up and down.

Whoa! What's with this dude? So, to my horror and without thinking, I let my mouth run away with me.

"Fuck you back!" I reply, not too pleasantly.

"Fuck you, 820!" Ronnie matches my tone.

"Fuck you back, 821," I am wondering if this was going to be the extent of the evening conversation. I cannot believe I'm standing here cussing someone I've just met. Someone who's supposed to be my mentor for the entire night. I simply can't wrap my brain around this dance we're doing, but I refuse to be a punk and let him embarrass me. By now, every manager and supervisor on the dock is looking and laughing at us, and many of the teamsters are joining in the general merriment.

Wait a minute. This must be *Candid Camera*, so where's the damned camera? Here are two presumably intelligent adult men yelling back and forth like two fools—like we're representing some Los Angeles gang or something. 820 vs. 821? Seriously? What kind of shit is this?

Yet, part of my brain knows that any minute, we're all going to be laughing together. Is this my final initiation? Just as I'm about to give up, or cold cock him and walk out, the scene changes.

Ronnie pauses and takes a deep breath.

"Now that we've got that out of the way, Long Beach," he says, affably, "Let's do some business. Okay, first things first. As you can already tell, Long Beach, I don't like you, and it's not your fault. I don't like none of y'all sonsofbitches from 820. You motherfuckers fuck up freight every damned night and send it up here and expect us to fix your shit for you."

He takes a deep breath, and he's off again.

"Next thing, try not to get yourself killed, Long Beach, okay? Because as much as I don't like your ass, I don't need your blood on my hands. Not on my watch. You feel me? We just had some punk-ass Casual damn near kill himself last week because he wasn't PAYING ATTENTION!" He pauses and regards his wider audience with a jaundiced eye.

I remembered that a Casual is what they call a temporary employee who works out of the local union hall and is available to all union trucking firms.

Ronnie fixes his eyes sternly on me again.

"Got it, Ronnie," I reply, firmly, but cautiously, too. It's pretty obvious this is a guy who'll need careful handling. I wonder if he has a Napoleon complex. He isn't very tall, maybe about 5'4", and he acts like Arnold Schwarzenegger on steroids with a giant chip on his shoulder. Obviously, he seriously pumps iron. The dude is ripped with some big-ass guns. I seriously wonder if he's on drugs or steroids and prepare myself for the next outburst.

"You see this drag line, Long Beach?" he asks, sternly.

"Yeah, I've been watching it all night."

"This motherfucker never stops moving. You got that? It's gonna be moving around and around and around all night long. NOW, LISTEN UP! This drag line can seriously hurt you, and that right there—that forklift driver speeding past right now, or someone like him—will KILL your ass. As in DEAD. What I'm talking about right now, Long Beach, is survival, because this shit is going to be happening nonstop all night long and no one is going to be babysitting your ass. You got that? If you don't take this shit seriously, you can be a statistic. So don't say I didn't warn you. I hope you got plenty of rest last night, because you're gonna need it."

There is a brief pause, long enough for him to take a good breath, and he starts again.

"Rule Number Three: Don't get sleepy out here, Long Beach. These noises are constant and can put your ass to sleep. Seriously. Okay? If you start getting sleepy, go take a ten-minute break and get you some coffee. I know you're not used to this. You see these crazy fools – like those guys speeding through here on their forklifts – trust me when I tell you that not only are those sonsofbitches crazy, they don't give a fuck about us. Yeah, that's right. They don't like us, and we don't like them. I'm sure Bob told you about our relationship with these Teamsters, right? But – they do RESPECT us."

"They do?" I ask, warily.

"Not *your* ass, Long Beach. Nah, forget that shit. You don't even register on their radar yet."

Just then, Ronnie is interrupted, and I grab that interlude to collect myself. How can all this be? I personally saw Terry and the forklift driver, Mark, having a great strategic meeting without cursing or confrontation. They talked it over like two grown-ass men, made a plan, agreed, and kept moving. Is Ronnie maybe attracting the very chaos he's projecting onto his men? Here he is, literally getting back, like a boomerang, exactly what he's putting out to these guys, and he doesn't seem to even realize it.

I stop myself abruptly. *Hold up, Tony. You have no idea what you're looking at yet. So why don't you stop the Einstein stuff and just watch for a while. Good point.*

Ronnie's attention is back full bore.

"See this?" he says, holding up a pen. "This is our weapon. We've got the power right here between our fingers, which we can use if we want to, and upset a man's livelihood just like that. Don't get me started! Yeah, they win their jobs back 90 percent of the time when we fire them. But, like I tell them all the time, y'all might win nine times out of ten when we go to grievance hearings, but that one time when we win, your ass is out of a job with Roadway Express for life. So, we'll take those odds, because we can afford it. They can't. We don't mind spending money to scare the hell out of these scumbags and troublemakers, even if we know they'll probably win the grievance. It upsets their livelihood, their family budget, their wife gets upset because she can't pay the bills on time. No money is coming in til this is settled, and they don't know for sure if they'll win back their job. Every time they go before the board, it's a big ass risk and disruption anyway you look at it. Meantime, we get a few weeks of peace and quiet before the decision is made. If they win, we'll start up again, plastering their walls nonstop with warning letters and suspensions until they submit.

"They write my name on the bathroom walls because they know I don't play. I've got major rock star status around here. Why? Because my name is on the bathroom walls. I'm a damn legend, and my bosses love me. Ain't that right, Mark? Don't give me no shit tonight. I see you over there, Oscar. Y'all know what time it is."

For once, I am smart enough to keep still. This guy is on a roll and it's his bully pulpit, aimed as much at his audience as at me. Better to just get through it. I still can't believe we'd just been yelling cuss words at each other like gang members claiming our sets.

"Anyway, Long Beach," Ronnie continues, more calmly, "this is just one night for you. But I'll be honest with you. They're giving very low odds on your survival. They say you're not going to make it."

Suddenly, I've had enough. "So, is this how it works?" I demand, hotly. "I have to beat the odds by proving myself to a Teamster?"

"Hell yes, you have to prove yourself. No one's gonna give you shit around here. You're fresh meat, man. If they can break you before you join us, they've got you. So, you best be watching your back, cuz these motherfuckers will test you and try to scare the living hell out of you, to see if they can make you quit. You wanna quit?"

"Hell no," I said.

Then, for just a second, everything inside me is dark and numb as I try to process what I've been hearing. Maybe Bob and his buddies were right—maybe this isn't for me. Now, I understand why I'd been given that quick lesson in profanity as a tool. Apparently, cussing is part of your professional certification in this industry.

"Okay," Ronnie says, winding down, "Keep your eyes and ears up and open and try to stay alive. Also, try to keep up. I'll be moving super-fast all night. You follow me everywhere I go except the bathroom. Are we clear, Long Beach?"

"Yeah, we're clear," I mumble.

For the rest of that night, Ronnie continues to call me Long Beach, but I no longer resent it. In fact, it's kind of a badge of honor.

Long Beach is in the house! Fuck you, motherfuckers, I think, silently.

As the night wears on, I start watching Ronnie more closely as he walks fast and talks trash. Behind those wire-framed glasses, he's probably about my own age, even though he acts a good ten years older. Actually, we are contemporaries, and under other circumstances, we might even be friends; maybe over a couple of cold beers, discussing the women of Los Angeles.

"Listen, these L.A. women are some of the finest, prettiest women I've been around in all my 27 years. They're everywhere, just constant beauty in any direction you look."

For a brief moment, it occurs to me we could make a damn good team out partying. *Hold up a minute, Tony. Better scratch that thought.*

During that never-ending night, so many conflicting thoughts run through my head. *What kind of world is this? Or is this just a really bad dream?* This shit is insane, and the strangest part is that the crazier it gets, the more I'm grooving on the energy. I like the fast pace; it gets the blood pumping and the heart racing. I almost think I'm getting the hang of it.

The rhythm of the work assignments I'd observed earlier is playing out. Obviously, there's more to it than I'm in a position to see, but equally obviously, this is something I can actually learn to do. So far, the only drawback is the night shift. Despite the cussing and their general state of high alert, these men, overall, are very professional. I realized that they also have made it their collective mission to mess with my head all night, and they have been both successful and highly creative.

"Hey, Rookie, do yourself a favor, man," says one Teamster. "Call it off! Leave now, before you get hurt. This life ain't for you, dude. Come on man, go home. Quit now, man. This shit ain't for you!"

"Nah, I think I'll stick around."

"Why? You know how this is gonna end."

"Nah. It's time for a change. I'll let you know how it turns out."

The more shit they talk, the more I start to feel a fire well up inside me. "Fuck these guys. They can't make me quit. This is my opportunity, and my money they're messing with. I'm about to make the biggest paycheck ever, starting next week. All I have to do is make it through tonight, walk into that office tomorrow, and claim the job."

Coming from a teacher's household, that isn't saying much. Everyone knows teachers are grossly underpaid, but here, in this new world, I have a burning curiosity – this need to understand the world where other people earn their money doing different things. Just one single headline burns inside me: Can I do this job? Can I manage grown men and women? Can I instruct an older person, as old as my parents, to do a job they already have the knowledge and understanding to do better than I can? I had always thought my college degrees would provide me with full authority to compete with tenured, skilled professionals, but this world is completely different from managing high school teenagers.

"Hey, Long Beach," Ronnie interrupts my reverie, and this time, he is making a polite request. "I need you to go out in the yard and locate trailer 55828. Open it up and tell me if there's a header in there."

"Okay, but that's a big yard. Where should I start looking?"

"Start on the east side with the first trailer you see and then walk north til you find it. I know it's out there, so take this walkie talkie and call me when you find it."

I find it in less than 15 minutes, so I call him.

"Hey, Ronnie, I found the trailer. It's got about 20 feet of room left in it."

"Cool, man. Thanks. You're a lifesaver. What's on it?"

"A bunch of Huffy tires, all bundled."

"Huffy tires."

"Yeah."

"Damn, Long Beach. Okay. Now I need you back to the dock. Go down to door 77 and walk inside that trailer. Go all the way inside to the nose and tell me if it's got a headload. I'm looking for a one biller, approximately 10,000 pounds going to Miami. Go check it out for me and let me know what's in there. I'll be down near door 35 when you get back."

"Okay. Will do."

"Thanks, man."

Walking down to door 77, I'm wondering what the attraction is, the fascination, the hook into this mysterious, complex, new world. It's like a secret society I never knew existed. Why didn't I know? Still, I remind myself, I'm actually only here for the money, the immediate attraction, and the commitment. All there is to it. I can take it or leave it.

And there's door 77. I go inside the trailer and start slowly walking to the front. It's really dark in here, and I can't see where I'm going, and my damned flashlight has stopped working. I use my cigarette lighter to put a little light on the subject.

The next thing I know, while my back is turned, someone slams the roll up door down tight and locks it. Then I realize that the yard dog is under this trailer and quickly starts moving it out from the door.

"HEY! HEY! STOP! STOP! THERE'S SOMEBODY IN HERE. STOP!!!"

The trailer keeps moving. "HEY, SOMEONE'S IN HERE! STOP!"

I'm yelling, sweating, and beating on the wall. Helpless and more than a little scared. What the hell is going on? Just when I was starting to relax and feel at home. This guy is driving like a bat out of hell, and I'm being tossed back and forth, side to side. He keeps making hard right turns, causing me to slam into the side walls and almost fall. I struggle to keep my balance. I can't even steady myself enough to use the walkie talkie, so I slide to the floor, hoping to stabilize myself. What if something falls on my head? I could die in here, and I don't even know what's in the nose of this damned trailer. This is scary as hell, but it's also funny – or it would be if I wasn't so damned scared. After about 12 minutes of this nonsense, I feel the trailer bump the dock, and it stops and settles down.

Someone opens the door. I pull myself together and as the door goes up, I walk out, trying to look cool and composed. The first thing I notice is that I'm back at door 40, where I spent the earlier part of my day.

Ronnie is coming toward me shouting, "What the hell, man? Why are you playing around in the trailer?"

"I just got tricked. I think…"

"What do you mean you got tricked? Where the hell have you been?"

"I think you know where I've been," I say, fixing him with my meanest stare.

"Yeah, well, did you find my Miami header? What took you so long?"

"No, there's nothing in the trailer. You can take a look for yourself. It's right there in door 40. And what took me so long, let's just say I went for a 10-minute joy ride around the yard to clear my head, and now I'm back."

"Man, if someone did that shit to you, they've got to pay. That's not cool. On the other hand, it may be a good sign. I mean, they either did that because they like you, or they did it because they don't like you. Take your pick, but it's a good sign, I think." Ronnie smiles.

"Oh, really? Well, you could have fooled me."

So that's how my night of unpaid observation went. Nonstop thrills every moment. Then, surprisingly, this ten-hour shift is suddenly over so fast I can't believe how quickly it ended.

Just one thing left to do. Go upstairs and give those four men my decision. Do I still want this job?

Truth is, I never wanted any job so badly. I'd never seen anything like what I've experienced tonight. I loved it. I'm not sure why, but by the end of the shift, it has been added to my list of my Top Ten Things to Love. The excitement and fear all rolled together remind me of playing football. Kinda like Teamsters versus Managers.

Still, I have no idea what the Los Angeles vs. Long Beach thing is all about. Ronnie had called me Long Beach the entire night but wouldn't elaborate on the feud. Months later, I finally learn that it was more about his anger over his denied transfer request and wasn't about Long Beach and their damaged freight. Plain and simple, Ronnie just didn't want to move to Adelanto. He had been seeking a transfer to one of the satellite terminals, but nobody was offering it. He was personally upset with anyone remotely tied to Long Beach or other satellite terminals, because he believed he was a valued employee who deserved a chance. In retrospect, I think he might have been actually too valuable to their break bulk operation, and they didn't want to replace him.

The management seems to love him, and although I don't personally care for his attitude, I can see that he is valuable to the company, and also why he took it out on me. Brand new, no experience, and I don't have to go to the damned desert. Ranked almost as low as a Teamster but saved from moving to the desert.

I figure that wound will take a while to heal, but right now, what I know for sure is this: I'm not going to quit. I have to see what's in it for me, and what's on the other side of sacrifice and hard work.

I say my goodbyes and special thanks to Ronnie, Terry, Vince, and some of the other managers, and head toward the main office. On the way, I notice a long line of identical fleet automobiles – fleet cars, and I wonder who they're assigned to.

Inside the double door entrance, I see a large sign on the wall at the very top of the stairs. The words on it literally take my breath away: "NOTHING HAPPENS UNTIL SOMEBODY SELLS SOMETHING."

Near the sign is a room I hadn't seen before, so I take a moment to check it out. It's the sales staff's headquarters. I wonder if they know what we'd been doing all night, because we'd definitely been making things happen. This room, though, looks like the fun room. I realize I'm staring when one of the occupants notices me and actually takes a minute to greet me.

"Hey there, man, you work here?"

"Yes," I reply, "I'm Tony from 820."

"Well, alright! I'm Greg. Nice to meet you."

I notice that there are twelve or fifteen men in that room, all dressed the way I always wanted to dress: immaculate in dark blue suits and red power ties. The epitome of polished cool. Also, probably the lucky drivers of the company cars I'd seen parked outside. Immediately, I know I belong in that room. The men are taking their ease, some smoking cigarettes, drinking coffee, chatting with other salesmen, or customers via the phones. My kind of world. All men. No women.

Wait a minute, that's interesting. Where *are* the women? This is a whole room full of men. When I was teaching school in Texas, I was surrounded by 20 or 30 women teachers and administrators every day. That teachers' lounge was a melting pot of diversity.

I look again. All. White. Men. Okay, this industry obviously marches to its own drum, even though it sure could use a little color and a pretty woman or two. For the moment, however, I decide to christen them "The Men in Blue" because of their choice of clothing. Thus, for me, before there was the movie *The Men in Black*, there were The Men in Blue. Who are these prima donna salesmen, how did they get there, and what would I have to do to join them? Because that's where I want to be as soon as possible.

I decide I would put my energy in learning everything about the business, but especially about the part of the business this elite crew represents. I intend to figure out how I, too, can qualify for membership in this elite fraternity. In fact, I want in as badly as Tiger Woods wants to play and win at the Masters.

At that precise minute, it is clear to me that whatever Roadway has to offer me, getting into that room will be my ultimate destination, and there is no doubt in my mind that I can achieve that goal. I know in my gut that eventually I am going to have that "golden boys' career".

Turning away, I walk around the corner to my final destination, and there they are, three out of the four men in the big conference room, awaiting my answer. I realize that two minutes ago, I'd claimed the job when I met Greg and proclaimed that I worked for Roadway LBC/820.

"Good morning," I say, "I'm here to tell you I want the job and I'm ready to get started." I tell them how much I appreciate everything I've seen and learned. But internally, I also realize that the most excitement comes from my introduction to the Men in Blue, and the job I am being offered is only Step One. I have just seen my future, and it looks great.

Bob and Paul quickly pull me back from fantasy land. In perfect harmony, they both ask, "Are you sure?"

"Yes, I'm sure." I look each man in the eye with the conviction of someone ready for war. The men nod at each other, and then Bob says, "Alright. You will start this coming Monday."

Then, Paul picks up the phone, dials the Long Beach terminal, and hands me the receiver. Dan Dixon, the terminal manager, greets me, welcomes me to Roadway and the Long Beach family, and reminds me we'd met in my first and last interview. Right, suddenly I realize, that's the man who everyone says is becoming a major rock star!

He tells me to show up on Monday at 0400 and ask for Bill.

"Bill's a good man. He'll take good care of you, and I'll meet you around 0700."

I thank him, hang up the phone, and thank the other three men. We shake hands, and I say my goodbyes. They assure me we'll meet again.

I walk out of the building into that bright morning, feeling happy and relieved, even though my mind and body are totally conflicted. I am exhausted, but also so overjoyed that I want to go out and celebrate. It's 9 a.m. and I'm starving – but breakfast isn't what I crave. Got to find me a soul food restaurant with some fried catfish and black-eyed peas and greens, and my favorite mixed drink – bourbon and coke.

Is this what happens when you start working the night shift, I wonder? Looks like my world is about to change forever – and me along with it!

CHAPTER THREE

IN SEARCH OF WHY

"Those who have a why to live can bear with almost any how."
–Friedrich Nietzsche

May 11, 1981. I can hardly believe how my life has changed in just five days, once I got through that surreal final interview. Here I am on Day One, officially at LBC/820! A new life, a new beginning.

The night shift started hours ago – and it's obvious I've way too much to learn about the company. For the next two weeks, I'll be working from 4 a.m. to 2 p.m. Each day, I start out working with Bill on the Inbound dock, and then transition into the office, where I'll visit the various departments, including the sales department. I've already learned that there are three main Operation shifts: Outbound, Inbound, and Dispatch. The Outbound shift's hours are 5 p.m. to 3 a.m., Inbound starts at 11 p.m. and runs to 9 a.m., and Dispatch starts early morning, around 7:00am, and won't ever stop before sundown. Best I can tell, it's controlled chaos, like nothing I ever imagined. So far, the worst is trying to stay "alive, awake, alert, and enthusiastic" in an unfamiliar and possibly dangerous world. So far, though, I think the worst part of this job will be my inability to sleep in the daytime.

In my trainee's introduction with Bill at the Long Beach Terminal, I'd gained a limited idea about the job conditions and the work atmosphere typical of an Inbound shift. Now, on my first official day, after three-and-a-half hours on the job, morning is here. The sun's up, and the weather's going to be pleasant. I don't have much time to appreciate it, but I take a minute to enjoy the gentle dawn breeze. Part of my mind, though, remains stuck on Bill's memorable words.

"Listen, son," he'd said, very seriously, "Once you get in the trucking business, the trucking business is gonna get in you. So be careful, and may God bless you!"

The more I replay his words, the more I realize he was trying to tell me something important. Time will tell if it was a warning or a welcome. I'm already feeling tired out of my mind. Two hours ago, I'd been ready to quit; wondering, and not at all sure, what the hell I was doing in this crazy new world.

So far, I know I haven't performed too badly, despite enthusiastic hazing from the Teamsters in the back row church pews. At least the trash talk isn't as vicious as 821 during last week's endless ten-hour unpaid shift. On one level, I'm grateful that Ronnie had demonstrated some of the dark side of the business, although his intent might have been to do his best to break me. I've already noticed that Bill is different. He walks the walk and talks the talk of a seasoned professional. He's all business, but he obviously respects the men and gets the most out of everyone.

God, I think, fighting sleep and trying to ignore my sore feet, I definitely know I'd partied a little too much over the weekend. And because of that memorable – and late –party weekend with some new guy friends and an assortment of lovely Los Angeles Ladies, I've started this new career unnecessarily fatigued. Still, it *was* a great party… Ruefully, I realize that I really must want this damned job if I've agreed to put myself through this chaos and sacrifice – on a never-ending shift that's not even half over.

Just then, Bill's worried voice on the walkie talkie jerks me back to the work at hand.

"Tony! I need you to go out into the yard and find a 48-foot empty trailer – ASAP! It has to be completely empty. You got that?" The slight nervous tremor in Bill's voice immediately puts me on guard.

"Yes, I got it," I reply.

"I desperately need this one right now, Tony, so get on it right away! I've got to go inside and start dispatching my drivers. You call me as soon as you find it!"

"Right, Bill, will do!" I exclaim, and take off full blast into the huge yard, and begin opening up every trailer – all of which seem to be in use. I wonder briefly if this is the prelude to another "Door 77" trick, that well-played hazing prank that now seems laughable. In today's hindsight, it seems more like a high-spirited initiation, a perfect ending to my ten-hour unpaid shift.

"Hey, Tony, you found it yet?" Bill's voice on the walkie talkie is urgent. "Don't come back on this dock til you find it! I needed it ten minutes ago, so get with it!"

"Working on it, Bill," I reply.

This sounds serious. I'd better get my butt in gear and find that damn trailer. He hasn't been wrong about anything all night. He's given me time to learn, but now I understand what he means about crunch time. Everyone's moving at warp speed, closing out one Pick-up and Delivery (P&D) trailer after another. Those P&D drivers need to start their day on the streets making deliveries, and Bill needs to transition to the front office as lead dispatcher.

For the first time, I feel pressure in my chest. My heart's pounding and my breathing is fast and shallow. I've got one, and only one job: find that damned trailer. I don't want to let this man down. I know that if he'd been the one looking, he'd have found it in a New York second.

"Help me, God," I pray, "Don't let me screw this up!"

No sooner are the words out of my mouth than the answer comes! HERE IT IS! Right in front of me! Found it! The relief almost brings tears to my eyes when I open up the double doors and find it empty. To think, 20 seconds ago, I was ready to give up, but I heard something in Bill's voice that let me know the empty trailer was here, somewhere – I just needed to keep pushing harder until I found it. I can't believe that finding a damn 48-foot trailer could be so emotional. Thank God nobody was paying attention. Quickly, I get on the walkie talkie.

"Bill, good news – Trailer 53511 – that's your empty, my man!" I say it loudly with the confidence of a rookie rock star in the making.

"Alright! You're a good man, Tony Baloney, and I'm gonna tell Dan you're definitely a keeper."

I hear the relief in his voice, and I realize that this consummate professional wants me to succeed. His confirmation, with a hint of comedy, is worth a million dollars to me, and the best part is that he didn't follow up with, "Now, I need you to go to Door 77." It's beginning to look like I'm being taken seriously here. Wow! I just went out into this giant yard and found a needle in a haystack in less than six minutes. And Bill the Magician just told me I'm a KEEPER!

Eventually I would learn that, at this hour of the morning, finding an empty trailer can be a real challenge. Every trailer is being used and already either full or assigned. So, metaphorically, God and I just pulled off a small miracle.

As I make my way back to the dock, I tip my hat once again to tough guy Ronnie and his band of brothers, who've helped prepare me for today. I sense that I'm becoming a different man, growing some tougher skin. I'd felt almost like a pro, hopping in and out of those trailers, quickly opening and slamming trailer doors down as I confirmed each trailer's status. I'd kept good notes, too, carefully writing down each trailer number and location, to make sure I hadn't skipped any. That wasn't something I'd been told to do – it just made sense, in case I had to demonstrate that I'd checked every trailer.

Now, with fresh eyes, I'm observing the facility more carefully, processing what I'm seeing. As a satellite terminal, Long Beach is different from the Los Angeles breakbulk. For one thing, there's no drag line. I wonder why but realize that its absence eliminates one way I could get killed in this man's workplace. It's obvious that management has given me a break by assigning me to a satellite branch where there would be a little time to get my bearings. I know in my heart that I can do this job, and if I can use this time to learn as much as I can about the business, I can reach my ultimate career goal of becoming, not just a Man in Blue, but a Top Salesman in Blue.

I find myself continually preoccupied with my glimpse of the sales department. I wonder what kind of sales team this satellite terminal would have. All males? How many? What about the women? In fact, where are the women? Best I can tell, mostly missing.

So far, the only Black people I've seen are dock workers or drivers. I've been told that there are a few other Black management trainees like me, and a handful of Black dock managers and supervisors around the Los Angeles Basin. In sales, though? Realistically, probably not. Elitist jobs like this tend to have the names of white guys or somebody's brother-in-law already on them. But things are changing, and personally, I intend to be one of the faces that the Roadway customer gets to see, know, and trust. The hell with school teaching. Been there, done that.

I've heard tales about the sales department lifestyle from outside and caught a glimpse of its perks. So far, all I've seen for sure is that exclusive row of brand-new fleet company cars parked in a prominent section of the parking lot. I can't wait to investigate that further when I have a chance to meet the sales guys in person. I've heard stories of success, and the incredible perks of their jobs: company car, unlimited expense account, credit card, trips with customers to exotic places, total access to every professional sporting event in the area and around the country, not to mention every major musical concert or theater act, swim party, ski party, happy hour, fine dining at great restaurants, boxing matches, strip tease bars, you name it. Sometimes even luxury trips abroad. Gorgeous women, young, beautiful, ready to fully enjoy the California lifestyle, and where better to meet them? How better could a young man new to California learn his way around and partake in the good life, with enough income to fully sample and enjoy its delights?

I'm aware that the exotic lifestyle must necessarily result from high-dollar new business for the company. At the bottom, the sales game has to be about results and return on investment (ROI). Hell, that would be no problem for me. I know about hard work, and I also know I have a salesman's personality. Based on my limited experience with Roadway, this is an industry I can learn to love, especially if it has an open career path leading to the sales department.

I know I've got a lot going for me: a strong family background with a very good education and reasonable professional success; unbounded ambition, and demonstrated qualities of leadership throughout high school, college, and in my previous profession.

I also firmly practice that old adage, "If you dream it, you can have it." I know I'm "born to sell", and I intend to put myself in a position to be ready. I know all about breaking barriers, and being "the first one, or the only Black man in the room." I'd been the first Black captain at Texas Tech University in track and field back in 1975. Hell, I was one of the captains in high school in all three major sports (football, basketball, and track) and the first Black student council president at my newly desegregated high school (Hugo High School in Oklahoma (1971-72). There remains many unanswered questions, but no matter how the future plays out, this is my new "why?" Or rather, perhaps, my new "why not?"

I suddenly realize I'm no longer sleepy. I'm filled with new energy. For the first time since I got here, I feel alive just thinking about those sales guys and what they do for the company. I'm pumped, with a return of what I'd felt in Los Angeles when I discovered the Men in Blue. Today, I'm looking forward to meeting the front office daytime staff and learning what they're about. And I'm definitely more than ready to meet the women of Roadway and the Men in Blue.

"Tony!" The walkie talkie has come to life, and I'm being paged. I snap to attention.

"Tony, turn in your walkie talkie to Don, and come on inside and meet the day shift."

Just what I've been waiting to hear. Walking toward the office, I see Dan Dixon, the terminal manager, at the back door, waving me in. I wonder if Bill has already told him I did a good job and I'm a keeper. But I KNOW I've done a good job, and it was observed. Dan is smiling and waiting for me. We shake hands, and I recognize him at once from my last interview as one of the men on the hiring team.

"Let's take a walk inside," he says. "I want to introduce you around." I follow him into the office while he continues to talk. "Did Bill take good care of you last night?"

"Yes, indeed. He really knows his stuff."

"He's one of the best in the game. You've been working with a real freight master today. I don't know how he keeps track of everything. He's old school, doesn't even need to write anything down. He's just damn good."

"I believe it," I reply, silently thanking God that his style is nothing like Ronnie's. I never want to be like Ronnie!

Dan starts introducing me to each person in the office. There's David, the assistant dispatcher who helps Bill. Good looking, dressed for success, and obviously eyeing his next rung on the promotional ladder. Next, there's Kim, a stunning Asian woman, drop dead gorgeous—petite, slender, with long, dark hair and a smooth, gorgeous, dark brown tan. I had no idea I liked Asian women until this very moment.

Moving on, I meet Mary, a sweet, cooperative workaholic, cute as a button, married with photos of husband and kids prominently displayed. Barbara is serious, rough around the edges, and a chain smoker like Bill, who apparently enjoys complaining. Dan can't get a word in the whole time. Can we get to the sales department, I wonder?

Except for Kim, these office women are my mom's age, and Dan's giving me their entire life story. It's great meeting them, but then I learn they are all Teamsters, including the gorgeous Kim. All of that suggests they're "off limits" for any kind of personal relationship. Besides, David, Bill's intense-looking assistant, is eyeing me and her – possessively. I wonder if they've got something going on.

I take in a bit of the paperwork system, which Dan proudly shows off. Dan explains in detail that the same paperwork management system is used throughout the company, something rare in the industry of 1981. I realize that this systematic management is probably what led them to develop the outstanding management training program that is giving me a chance at a career.

As we continue our tour of the offices, Dan emphasizes the pitfalls and practicalities of dealing with a super-active Teamster union.

"Now, you've been told, Tony, about the fact that this industry is definitely built on relationships between labor and management and governed by air-tight, die-and-go-to-hell contracts that set out rules by which we all live. As a practical matter, and you MUST internalize this: Management – that's you – does one kind of work, and labor – that's them – does union work. For example, under NO CIRCUMSTANCES can I do union work. If I do, no matter how good the reason was, the union employees, including these women you just met, are obligated to file a grievance, and we will end up paying a penalty with possible back charges and salaries for the mistake.

"As much as they may like me, I cannot take advantage and violate the work rules. If they do win the grievance, we may also have to hire additional workers, especially if we continue to perform union work – because each time we do that, we are, in essence, saying that we need to hire more union workers to get our work done in an eight-to-ten-hour shift. It's just that simple.

"The bottom line – is that if I, as the manager, keep performing union work illegally, the company will have to pay and, ultimately, hire additional help. The same rules in reverse apply to them. If they abuse company time or create a work slowdown, I can use that infamous pen as Ronnie describes it, to write them up with warning letters that may result in termination. All of this gets worked out at expensive grievance hearings – but this is how we communicate and learn the rules of respect, so we can work together in harmony, to get the job done. You have to understand that these hard-core rules between Teamsters and management have been created over the last 50 years, and they are not easily broken down. So, as you are learning the ropes here, that's something you must learn well – and never forget!"

"I understand," I reply, realizing that this is a serious conversation that will take some attentive processing. Also, it will divert my attention from the gorgeous Kim – but then, Dan announces that our next stop will be the Sales Department!

And, *Oh shit! There they are! There they are! The Men in Blue!* They don't look much different than the group in L.A., so they must represent the type of men Roadway chooses. Some look like ex-athletes, slightly gone to seed. A couple of them look like they're getting ready to do a *GQ* magazine cover. Seven or eight men, confident, laughing, dressed to the nines, just entering the sales department, smoking cigarettes and laughing. I remember that one of them had brought in ten dozen donuts for the office women, dispatchers, and dock workers. I had also heard he planned to provide donuts for his 8:30 drivers' meeting, and maybe take some to customers afterwards. I am so in awe of these men and their apparent freedom. THIS IS WHERE I BELONG! I AM IN THE WRONG GROUP!

Dan interrupts my reverie. "These guys make it all happen," Dan says proudly.

I look up and there it is again: the same sign I saw in L.A. I read it out loud. "So, 'Nothing happens until someone sells something.' Right?"

"That's right," says a new voice. "I'm Eric, the sales manager, and this is our Long Beach sales team. Hell, you guys introduce yourselves! This is Tony, our newest management trainee. He'll be working the Inbound and Outbound shifts once he completes his training. I'll be setting up a time when you'll hang out with us for a few days, Tony, and learn all about the life and sometimes the death of a salesman. In the meantime, y'all try and help him out if he has any questions regarding sales. Would you care for some coffee and donuts, Tony?"

"Yes, thank you," I reply politely. Then, I continue. "I've got just one question. What do I have to do to become a salesman?"

"Well…" Dan seems taken aback. Then he says, slowly, "You gonna have to pay some dues before we can have that conversation. Right now, let's start showing you the ropes, the basics in the operation before we get too far ahead of ourselves. Sales has a lot of finesse with a technical side to it. I'll be real with you, Tony. Not everyone can be a good salesman. It looks pretty on the outside, but there can be some sleepless nights. Ain't that right, Mark?"

"You better believe it," Mark said.

I laugh and smile but press the point just a little. "I understand I've got a lot to learn, but I'd be lying if I didn't admit that this department here looks like the place where I ultimately plan to be."

They all laugh pleasantly, and so do I.

The talk drifts off to general introductions – one white man after another, each graciously introducing himself. I vow that I will become one of them. I put the image in my mind that they are welcoming me into their fraternity of brothers. Little do I realize that it will take four long, hard years to realize that dream, and it won't be with Roadway, either.

Soon, I walk over to the other side, into the more secluded dispatch office area, where I'm assigned to observe Bill for the rest of the morning, watching him dispatch all those loads he'd built earlier. I watch David, his assistant, and note that he seems a little too wired, like maybe he's taken some type of legal medication or a hit of cocaine. He seems to frustrate easily, while Bill remains cool as a cucumber. I hope I won't have problems with David, but it feels like we might clash. With his swaggering good looks and fancy clothes, I'm sure he'll wind up in sales.

Dan shows up about 11:00 and announces that I'll spend the rest of my shift studying. I follow him back over into the main office area, passing through, and saying "Hi" to all the office women. WOW – there's Kim looking even better than I remembered from my first glance.

Dan takes me over to a secluded area in a corner with a desk and plenty of workspace. I sit at the desk he indicates, and he hands me a huge book. A "bigger-than-the-typical-family-Bible" book. He tells me it contains everything I need to know about Roadway Express and informs me that I will need to study it from cover to cover.

Then, he looks me in the eye with a stern glare and says, "Now, Tony, you hear me good, and don't forget I told you this. This book is literally the Roadway Express Bible, and there will come a day when you are going to be tested and be responsible for knowing everything in this book. Don't forget that today I'm telling you this.

"There will come a day – maybe in three months, might be next year, might be two years from now, but there will come a day when you will be held responsible to know everything in this book, and you will take a test that will determine your future career at Roadway Express."

"A test? Tell me more."

"Well, it's a pass/fail test. If you make 70 percent or better, you pass. If you score below 70 percent, you fail, and that means you're out. It's just that simple," Dan replies.

"What do you mean, I'm out?"

"Just that. You heard me right the first time. Here's the deal. We fly you to Akron, Ohio, to our home office for four or five days, and while you're there in class, you will take this exam, which covers the information in this book. On the final day, your grades are announced, and you'll be confirmed as to whether you have a career with Roadway Express. It's pass/fail. You're either in or out. So, don't say I didn't warn you, because sure as I'm standing here, that day is coming." Dan finished this little lecture with a smirk.

"Okay, thanks," I respond. "I do understand."

And that was that.

For the next two hours of my shift, I study that big Roadway Bible. It opens doors I never knew existed. There is a whole new language to master: acronyms, strange combinations of ordinary language that mean something entirely different in the industry. The different sizes of trailers. The number of doors in a satellite location vs. a breakbulk. And what a breakbulk actually is. The strategy of where to place each facility and why. Shipping and managing hazardous materials. The types of fines and penalties the company can be charged if you don't adhere to the rules. I cannot believe how much there is to learn – and besides, it's interesting. I never realized how the continuous flow of products affects the economy, and the way the pulse of an economy is measured by the flow and quantity of supply chain and transportation.

At times, I would get bored and sleepy and start to drift off, and then, I'd remember I'm being paid to learn, so I'd shake myself and keep reading. Kim and Mary are sitting nearby, not only nice to look at, but smart and helpful when I have questions.

I learn that Kim is taking a class to learn Japanese. That surprises me. I had assumed she'd grown up speaking the language. She says she'd never learned it and now is planning a trip to visit Japan and is ashamed that she never learned to speak her parents' language. Wow! Who knew? So much for a little cross-cultural understanding!

At 1300, Dan stops by and invites me to lunch. So, off we go to a little sandwich shop around the corner, where he fills my ears with tales of the past. He talks about wildcat strikes, crossing picket lines, and the dangerous times he'd seen with the teamsters back east during the Jimmy Hoffa era....

He's been with The Big R for 15 years, since high school. One thing for sure: he loves this company and has made sacrifices, which, he reminds me, are the kind of dues you have to pay to grow and be promoted. You might have to move to another state, take a job you don't want, and you may lose a wife or two along the way. He's been married three times and divorced twice. He continues his long litany of sacrifice and pain, and I'm thinking, *Man, I don't want to do that. Too much work. Too much sacrifice*…and I'm back to square one in my head.

"Dan, here's what I really want to know, though," I try one more time to get through to him. "Seriously, what does it take to get promoted into sales?"

"Now, Tony, what I've been telling you *is to just slow down*. You just got here. Let me just tell you what I said earlier. It will take you maybe two or three years to learn what you need to know, to pay the dues of experience. But, if you do that successfully, at the end of that time, we could seriously think about giving you a shot. But not now. Put that out of your head right now. First things first. You've got to master the operation. How are you going to sell our services if you don't know how our system works throughout the country? You learn first by doing just what you're about to start doing. Nobody goes right into sales. Nobody. And you start paying your dues in Operations."

"Thanks, that's what I needed to hear," I reply. Taking him at his word that I've got a fair shot at the prize, I can manage to settle down and learn the business first.

I check my watch and realize I've been here since 0400, which means nine-and-a-half hours, and I'm sitting here having lunch, as if I'm going back to work. However, we finish eating and Dan drives me back to the parking lot. He tells me to gather up my things and call it a day, but be sure and report to work in the morning at 0400 sharp.

I thank him for lunch, and we say our goodbyes.

In that moment, and for some time after that, I trusted and believed Dan with all my heart. He seemed to be a straight shooter, no-nonsense man, and was, by far, the coolest and smartest guy in the room. I was ready to follow him into war. I also loved the way that Bill handled his job – effectively, but respectfully, and not one curse word. Maybe there would be problems—perhaps problems that would eventually surpass 821, but at that moment, I didn't see them. I felt like I was home. I was all in.

For a long time, I kept my eyes on the prize and remained hopeful. I was determined to become one of The Men in Blue, even if I had to leave Roadway to do so. All of us who have made this kind of career know how we were first introduced to this industry – but the bigger question that often remains un-answered is why. As in Why Did You Stay?

For me – I stayed in this industry for the next 40 years because I'd found my Why. I found it that first day when I saw The Men in Blue. And that became my WHY.

CHAPTER FOUR

TIRED, SLEEPLESS, AND CONFUSED

"If you can't fly, then run. If you can't run, then walk.
If you can't walk, then crawl. But whatever you do,
you have TO KEEP MOVING forward."
– Martin Luther King, Jr.

The last six weeks have been a complete blur. I've been observing and working in every department inside and outside the Long Beach terminal. I'm fitting right in, catching on easily, and creating value that makes me shine. During this training period, I've also begun learning my way around the terminal facility and understanding the purpose of the layout design.

For example, the dock area facilitates the storage, loading, and shipping aspects of the business. It's basically a big open-space warehouse under a protective roof that shields workers from the rain, but not much else. The warehouse area is shielded and complemented by a series of standard-sized loading dock doors about 15 feet apart, to safely accommodate several standard-size trailers strategically parked side-by-side. The warehouse doors can be pulled down for security reasons, as well as to protect the commodities and employees from the weather.

Connected to this long, extended, open-spaced dock is the office building headquarters, which is very modern and typical for the times. It is your basic modern, temperature-controlled administration facility designed to house and accommodate supervisors, dispatchers, office staff personnel, the upper management hierarchy, as well as the sales department and visiting guests. Also, the dispatch office is located in the building, but quite separated from the other departments, due to the constant volume of noise and communication between drivers, customers, and office staff.

Being a dispatcher has got to be the toughest job in the building. You're dealing with irate customers, disgruntled drivers, and the constant ringing of the phone lines all day long. The phones will not stop ringing, and the drivers are on their CBs in between phone calls. Oftentimes, it feels like everyone is complaining at the same time, mainly to two or three people: especially Bill and David. It's a thankless job, and I admire Bill and his calm demeanor. He is "Cool-Hand Luke," a.k.a. Merlin the Magician in my book.

David isn't cut out for this. He gets rattled about the least little thing, and so do I. I knew we would eventually clash, and so we have. He yelled loudly at me one day to "come over and help answer the damn phones" when I was clean across on the other side of the building, studying the Roadway Bible, as I had been instructed to do by Dan. For whatever reason, David seemed to feel that I should have taken the initiative and simply stopped what I was doing and come over to help answer the phones. At that point in my career, I wasn't aware that I could – or should. Dan had never suggested that I stop and help out if the phone lines got overwhelming. I wish he had, because David and I were ready to take it outside.

I immediately yelled and cursed back at him. Ronnie's spirit, all the way from LAX/821 kicked in like a pit bull, and I let him know that we could take this SHIT outside right now and get a better understanding. I don't know if my response was a good thing or a bad thing, but David never spoke in that tone or yelled at me again.

In retrospect, I had not yet been shown how to be a team player and what that spirit looked like in this context. I was still new and uninformed about how to be graceful under fire. We were young and acting out, trying to model what our superiors had shown us. They wanted us to be tough, and we tried our best. Before the end of the business day, I'd made a point of burying the hatchet with David, because I realized that, ultimately, we needed each other. We were on the same team, and we needed to find a way to work together.

Don't get me wrong. David isn't by himself. I'm not cut out for dispatching either. I would be as uptight as he is if I had to do that job every day. In fact, if I had to choose between the dock and dispatching, I'd choose the dock, and you already know how much I hate the dock and those night shift hours! So, what does that tell you? In my humble opinion, being a career dispatcher ages you just like the president of the United States will age. It's already quite noticeable to me how quickly one's hair can turn gray, and how hostile one's attitude can get, being in that hot seat every day. People die of strokes and heart attacks doing that job if they don't take care of themselves. It was a tough job back then, and it's a tough job now.

The drivers generally don't come inside the dispatch office but pick up and return their paperwork at a walk-up window. Then, they go back outside, crossing via the dock to go down the ramp to get into their respective trucks. They usually check their trailers and the way their shipments are loaded before driving off.

Even though I'm aware that my first permanent assignment will be working on the Inbound or Outbound dock, by the time I complete the management training program, I will have spent a sufficient and fair allotment of time in all the departments, learning the business from the ground up.

Some of the departments are quite interesting, but the more I see, the more I know that, although there will be interim jobs I'll have to endure as I "pay my dues," my ultimate permanent destination is sales. The truth is, as I look back over my life, in that year of 1981, I didn't start out with a vision or belief beyond going into transportation sales. Over time, though, my vision will continue to expand to embrace and believe in it as my true purpose and calling.

I've found the inside work to be both monotonous and boring. I mean, who wants to answer a phone all day long and deal with one customer complaint after another? These customers are calling non-stop all day, and most are mad about this or that. "Where is my shipment?" "What's my pro number?" "You promised me it would be here today." "You all damaged my shipment again and denied my claim. Tell Huckabee (the sales rep) he'd better get his ass over here and make this right, or I'm cutting you guys off as of today." The list of customer complaints is endless, and the complaints must be resolved with courtesy and efficiency.

Then, there is the Brotherhood of Teamsters, who, for the most part, are good, hard-working people. Still, there is that five percent of bad apples who are angry at the world about something all the time for no apparent reason. They see me as being part of their problem by default, simply because I wear a long-sleeve white shirt and tie. I don't even know these people, and they already think I'm the enemy.

I often wonder who I should sympathize with the most: the customer or our beloved Teamsters. It all seems like a movie playing out in real life. We all have our lines to read. My script says: "Walk into the dispatch office and stare the dock worker down. Look serious, like playing hardball, and hand him his paperwork with his work assignment instructions. Afterwards, pause, but don't speak. Just stare." Then he stares back, as if to say, "I will whip your ass!"

Wow, it's such a damn game. I can't let them think I'm afraid of them, but I really don't like how I'm starting to change. I still envy the sales guys and want to be in that department, but I've calmed down and taken seriously the entry level job in front of me. I feel as if they're cutting my training short by two weeks. Perhaps I've progressed too fast. Dan is talking about letting me run the Outbound dock all by myself if I keep this pace up. Maybe I should slow down. Clearly, he's impressed with my progress, enthusiasm, and engagement with both our staff and the Teamsters.

I'm a team player; always have been. I think my commitment is becoming obvious, but truthfully, I'm just playing the game to get ahead. But what do I really know? First, I need to become a student of the game. I'm so new at this, but Dan says you've gotta pay your dues if you want to get ahead. So, I'm committed to doing just that. I'm willing to make certain sacrifices, but I'm *not* going to get married three times and divorced twice!

So far, my favorite department is OS&D, which stands for Over, Short, and Damaged. Well, the truth is, I love working with Kim in OS&D. Kim's job is to locate the distressed freight. She's one of the OS&D clerks, and she has a floating schedule that changes from mornings to afternoons, depending on the workload. Previously, she was classified as a "Casual," a term used to distinguish part-time union workers who are not guaranteed work, but instead are on call, unlike "regular" union workers, who have seniority status, guaranteed work, and health and welfare benefits. She's just become a full-time employee for Roadway, and I truly look forward to seeing her every day.

She often asks me to help her locate distressed shipments, which turns into innocent fun almost every time. I like walking outside with her during midday and early afternoon when it's quiet and no one else is around. We've got the entire dock to ourselves to play and act like silly kids. We'll laugh, flirt, and smoke cigarettes together. And we also work to find the distressed freight, which is either damaged, short, or lost. Out there on the quiet dock, I get to check Kim out without her really noticing. She's very pretty with her long, black hair and light brown, tanned skin, but damn, I had no idea until I was walking behind her, just how shapely her figure really is.

One day, I asked her to speak to me in Japanese. Wow! She's good. It's not quite as sexy as Spanish, but it'll do for now, coming from her cute little face. It's safe to say that I'm smitten with her, and if she were willing to keep a secret, I'd date her in a heartbeat.

I know David would, too. I don't care what Roadway's rules say about management and Teamsters. When I get started with my new position as Outbound supervisor, she won't be working directly for me anyway. (Sorry for the distraction…just keeping it real!)

Aside from OS&D, I've also sampled other departments like Billing, Early Pickups, Filing Delivery Receipts (DRs) and Bills of Lading (BOLs), sorting the paperwork, customer service – and I've even spent a few days riding with the local P&D drivers. I like talking with those drivers and meeting customers from their vantage point. Many customers seem very comfortable and quite familiar with our drivers. Some seem to have great relationships with them that extend outside work. I can easily see how some are not only friends during work hours, but might go fishing or hunting together or hang out on the weekends and drink and party together. I wonder how all this plays out, since the sales reps are also vying for customers' time and attention all the time. Now, I see what Dan meant when he said that our drivers can make or break us. Truth is, some of these drivers know the customers better than the sales guys.

If you ask me, when I finally make it into sales, I'm going to be schmoozing our good Teamster drivers, the 95 percent good guys, as well as our customers. I can easily surmise that I would do well as a salesperson, talking with these customers, helping them work out solutions to their problems, and deepening my relationships with these men and women.

The last two weeks, I've been working strictly on the dock in Operations; Outbound for one week and Inbound the next. I don't hate the work, but working on the dock puts one outside in the elements, where the full effect of American industry hits you in the face. If it's hot, you fry; if it's cold, you freeze; if it's windy or smoggy, you're right in the middle of it. And then there are the odors that go along with heavy industry. In this neighborhood, the meat processing plant is the worst. You can set your watch by its predictable, timely, daily intrusion. It happens every morning, and the stink of rotten meat being cooked penetrates the pores of your skin, burns your eyes, and penetrates your clothing. The only way to escape the odor is to go inside the office, but its presence coincides with CRUNCH time, and it's all-hands-on-deck outside! We're trying to finish up and close out the Inbound shift in time to get the P&D drivers on the street at their designated start times. So, by the time the shift is over, my heart, soul, and body feels violated by that overwhelming inescapable odor—and added to that, by the end of the shift, I'm dead tired and barely functional.

I really do hate the long nighttime hours. I can't sleep well, and my body is dead tired all the time. With the Inbound shift, around midnight is the absolute worst. I can't sleep in the daytime, and as evening creeps in, I finally get sleepy and start to doze off, and then it's time to wake up and get going. I'm so exhausted that my mind and body don't agree on what day it is and don't want to cooperate.

I'm so tired I'm even yelling in my sleep, "HIGH AND TIGHT!" That's a term in trucking that encourages the dock worker to be quick, agile, and absolutely efficient in utilizing all available space on the trailer. It's probably the equivalent of a basketball coach yelling to his star player to, "TAKE IT TO THE HOLE!", which would mean to the player with the ball to dribble and drive directly to the basket and score.

The cardinal sin in transportation is when an Ops Supervisor sends a half full 48- or 53-foot linehaul trailer to its destination. Financially speaking, that's a loser and a bad decision by the supervisor. Imagine an airplane with only 50 percent of the seats filled. Loser! Bottom line, you've got some explaining to do in the morning when Dan and the rest of the crew arrive.

Oh, how I crave soul food in the morning. That's never happened before – craving food in the morning that I typically enjoy in the evenings. It's like my body has flipped upside down. I'm craving fried catfish in the morning with black eyed peas, turnip greens, cabbage, and cornbread. I even prefer my favorite mixed drink in the morning: Jack Daniels and Coca-Cola, instead of pancakes, bacon, eggs, and orange juice.

My mind and body are so exhausted and confused that my relationship with Cynthia, my new girlfriend, is already in trouble and suffering big time. I didn't even know I was the jealous type, but working these crazy nighttime hours has my mind playing tricks on me. I imagine all kinds of things going on at 2 a.m. in her bedroom while I'm at work. I'm accusing her of stuff, and she's denying it, but I don't believe her. I'm ready to quit the relationship because I don't trust her anymore. If I only could catch her in the act, but hell, she knows my schedule and when I'm working. Thing is, I don't even know if I really love her like that, and at times, the relationship seems doomed. It's becoming very obvious that I'm not happy – but I'm still jealous and can't let go. This job has me co-dependent on a toxic relationship I'm totally unhappy with. This is just plain bullshit. My mind is on overload… totally confused.

I don't even know what's real anymore. Maybe it's me. Maybe she's the most honest person in the world and it's me and my crazy exhausted imagination. I'm walking around like a zombie strung out on No Doze and deeply suffering from sleep deprivation.

Oh, and there's another thing. On my last two weeks working on Outbound and Inbound shifts, there was this Black supervisor named Earl who helped train me. We worked together for two solid weeks, and I saw him every night. He was the Outbound Supervisor, and Jim was Inbound. They worked together in tandem quite well, since their shifts would overlap and merge at times. I like them both, but Jim was definitely more assertive with the dock workers and linehaul drivers.

Earl was very helpful in showing me the ropes. What I liked most was how unselfish he was. He literally showed me everything he could to help me. One day he said to me, "I've survived five years with Roadway, and that's not easy." At the time, I wondered what he meant.

Jim was a little standoffish and ruled the Teamsters with an iron fist. He was totally no bullshit when it came to the teamsters, but was really easygoing when he talked with me and Earl. He told me he'd been with Roadway for ten years and had started back east in Akron. He wants to be Dan's assistant as Ops Manager, and maybe he's going to get it. Earl doesn't think so, though. I asked him why, and he repeated, "You and Jim are going to be working together."

"What? Where are you going?" I asked.

Earl had started prophesying in a joking manner on the second night we worked together. He'd said, "You know you're here to replace me, right?" Each time I was quick to reply, "Nah, man! No way. They're going to keep both of us and have us handling the night operations together. Me and you going to be running this thing together." I would laugh, and he would say, "What are they going to do with Jim? Where's he going?" I would reply, "Jim will probably go into sales, or better yet, get promoted to Dan's assistant."

Earl would laugh at my naïveté. He'd say, "Nah, you and Jim will be running this dock together. Watch what I tell you."

I'd answer, "Nah, man, this is going to be a Black thing – you and me running it together."

Turns out Earl was right. On my last night before I returned to the day shift, Earl didn't come in. I asked about him, and Jim said he'd decided to take some vacation time to deal with some personal family business. Then, after a few days, Dan told me Earl had decided to quit and move on. They made it sound like he was unhappy and wanted to change his situation.

I hadn't detected any of that kind of drama when I was talking with Earl, and I wondered, but I didn't have his phone number. As fate would have it, I ran into him three weeks later. He was with his wife and two young kids at the Long Beach Pier. He told me that he'd not been on vacation, and he didn't quit either. Instead, he was fired, just like he had predicted.

"Dan fired me before I started my shift," he said. "He escorted me out of the building and off the premises. He told me I was fired, and it happened just like I told you it would."

I was speechless, but he went on to tell me he was already working for Yellow Freight, and life was ten times better and easier. So, it would appear that as of now, I'm the token Black supervisor at LBC/820 after all.

Right after that encounter, I learned that the next week would be my ride-along with the sales boys, so in my anticipation, I put the Earl situation out of my mind and life moves on. I'm so happy and excited that I will finally see the sales department in operation. I call this my "Oh Happy Day!"

I learn that I'll be riding with three different sales guys this week and picking their brains. This is my tenth week of training, and I can't wait to see what these guys do, and how someday, I will be joining this elite club. So, needless to say, there's no time to mourn the loss of Earl, even though I was profoundly shocked when I heard it on Saturday. I guess I've decided I'm all in for the next two years, no matter what – but this coming week is going to be the pinnacle of everything I've experienced so far.

I've got my three-piece, brand new blue pinstripe suit and red power tie ready to go. I look good, if I do say so myself. "Move out of the way, Denzel! I'm the man up in this piece. This is the week I've been waiting for!"

CHAPTER FIVE

TRANSPORTATION SALES

*"Great salespeople are relationship builders
who provide value and help their customers win."*
– Jeffrey Gitomer

Monday morning is here at last. I'll be riding today with Larry, one of my favorites, a cool, good-looking guy who looks like he might have been a model a few years ago before going into this business. He's tall, about 6'3", and probably played Division 2 college basketball at one time. He has a son in junior high who practices every day with a personal trainer, preparing to become a point guard for high school and college. Wow, they start these kids dreaming early about an NBA future these days.

Anyway, I'll ride with Larry first, and for the next five days, I'll ride with someone different each day. This will be my life. The life of a salesman! Wow! I am stoked!

"Ready to go?" Larry asks.

"Absolutely!" I reply.

As we walk toward the terminal door, Larry turns to Eric, the Sales Manager. "Should we include Tony on our outing tomorrow?" he asks.

"Sure, why not? It'll be fun," Eric says.

"Hey, Dan, are you going tomorrow?" As he's about to step out the door, Larry yells at Dan. I can't hear the reply, but I think Dan has said yes.

Inside the car, Larry checks his itinerary, determining where we'll go and who we'll see. "Hey, Tony," he says, almost as an afterthought, "Starting right now, you're going to see a lot of stuff this week, and you need to promise me that whatever you see and do is all confidential. Okay?"

"Of course. Absolutely," I reply, wondering why this is such a big deal. "You don't have to worry about me. Whatever happens this week, I'll take it to my grave, baby. Now, let's do this!"

"Alright," Larry replies. "But understand, if you do talk, we'll deny, deny, deny, and you'll have blown your chances to ever go into sales! The Teamsters and even some of our managers are always poking at us, saying we don't do anything but go out and spend money entertaining customers. I assure you that we do more than that, but entertaining our customers is a HUGE part of the job."

"Hey, you don't have to tell me twice. My lips are sealed!"

Larry then whispered to me in a soft tone, as if he were about to tell me a top secret, "Well, just remember this: in this business, relationships are king and queen."

Damn, I'm super excited that these guys are saying I'm cool enough to be trusted with their secrets. Oh yes, I am. Thank you, God, I'm home.

The first thing we do is drop off some donuts to two different customers who are appropriately appreciative. Also, Larry reminds each of them about Casino Night. Nothing hard about those two stops.

Next, we see this old guy, Al, who looks half hungover from a night of drinking, and now here's Larry taking him more booze to drink this evening.

"You got my Crown Royal?" Al asks.

"What kind of question is that? Are you showing out just because I've got company with me today?" Larry chuckles.

Al laughs and turns to me. "How are you doing, young man?" he asks. "I'm Al… Don't believe a word this guy says about me. He's full of it."

"Really? I thought he was one of the good guys," I reply in kind.

"Not until he shows me my bottle of Crown Royal."

"Now Al, you know it's in the car. Come on, man, how's business?" Larry asks.

"Ah well, it's a little slow today. But I got you about ten shipments right now, ready to go, and it's not even ten in the morning. I might need you to send ole Tommy Boy in early today."

"Alright, we'll take care of it. I'll let Bill know," Larry says.

"Now, no bullshit. Y'all be messing up my evenings when you get here after 6:00. I got me a new girlfriend that I need to tend to. You know what I'm saying?" Al continues.

"Okay Al, we'll handle it! I'll call dispatch and tell them."

Watching this morning's exchanges, I'm thinking, *Man, this is going to be easy. Passing out donuts, pizzas, liquor, and going to happy hour Casino Nights. What the hell is Casino Night? Shit, I can do this all day long!*

But then, Larry takes a brochure that looks like a map of the United States out of his briefcase. "Now Al, he says, we're starting a new program you need to know about. We're launching a new air shipment program in the next few months."

"What? Air freight? That shit's way too expensive," Al says.

"I know, but if you ever have a shipment from hell that you gotta move quickly, just keep us in mind, okay Al?"

"Alrighty…. Now, let's walk out to your car and get my Crown before I start kicking me some Royal ass," Al laughs.

I follow them out to the car. On our way, I ask Al how long he's been working in this job. He replies that he's been there 33 years. "I started back when I was just a little whipper snapper like you. It's been a good gig. They treat me good, don't really bother me – you know, kinda let me do my own thing."

I notice that Al's skinnier than Bill. He looks sick, like a puff of wind could blow him clean over. He's got that smoker's voice, too—the one I hope never to have.

"By the way, Larry," Al says, "The other day, Consolidated Freight stopped by and offered me a 15 percent discount next week. Said your little 5 percent was an insult to me."

"Al, c'mon, man. I told you we're trying to get a handle on this discounting stuff. Just bear with me a little bit. We really don't know what we're doing quite yet with all this deregulation stuff, but I'm going to be taking a class real soon on discounting. But, hell, I can give you 15 percent—okay? So, hold your horses, man!"

"Nah, you best start getting on it and head 'em off at the pass. I've got appointments with PIE and Yellow next week."

"Don't worry Al, I'll get 'er done," Larry says, firmly, opening up his trunk and pulling out the Crown Royal in its cute little purple sack. He hands it to Al.

"Thanks, Al, I really appreciate you for all you do for me," he says.

"Hey, like I always told you, you scratch my back, I scratch yours."

Then, to my amazement, Al opens the damn bottle and takes a big swig right there in the parking lot. Putting the top back on, he takes the bottle over to his pick-up, opens the front door, and puts it under the seat. Then, he shakes both our hands.

"Good luck, Mister Tony," he says to me. "I wish you well in your career. Larry's a good man. He'll treat you right."

As we drive away, I notice that Al could care less about that 15 percent discount. He really only cares about that Crown Royal and his close relationship with Larry as someone who understands his real needs.

Larry rolls down his window and yells, "Al, if I bring my boss by and he asks you about our air shipment program, don't you be acting like I never told you about it, hear?"

"Don't you bring that sonofabitch around here! You know I can't stand Eric's ass," Al replies, angrily.

Larry laughs and keeps driving out of the parking lot.

Next call is to a woman named Naomi. Larry and I are sitting in the lobby waiting for her, but she is clearly visible through the glass window. She's talking on the phone to another freight company, sounding tough, just like a hard-nosed man would sound. This is definitely not her first rodeo. If she wasn't so pretty with her Farah Fawcett hairstyle, I might believe her bluff. She's not my type, but she's definitely pretty.

"Listen Jeff, you guys better find my shipment, or I'm cutting y'all's asses off. Do you hear me? You've got 24 hours to find my shipment."

Without another word, she slams the phone down.

The secretary looks up and says, "Larry, Ms. Bryant will see you now."

Now, it's our turn to go in. Larry smiles and thanks her. He hands her a couple of our Roadway notepads and ink pens as we head toward Ms. Bryant's office. For the first time today, Larry doesn't look his happy self.

"Larry, you guys are killing me," she begins, without so much as a hello. "Why can't you get my proof-of-deliveries (POD) back to me sooner? I can't get paid from my customers until I get proof of delivery to attach to the invoices. You know that. I've got unpaid invoices two months old sitting here on my desk for my customers!"

"I know, I know," Larry says apologetically. "I'm doing all I can to expedite the situation." Wow, Larry is damn near on his knees with this one. Maybe her bite is bigger than her bluff. Larry hasn't even introduced me to her yet.

"It's taking you guys three and four weeks to get the PODs back, and then, I still have to attach them to my invoices and mail them out to get paid," she continues, warming to the subject.

This argument rages for another ten minutes, and then, Larry finally interrupts to introduce me, apologize again, and promises to correct or improve the problem. I never hear how he plans to fix it. Lastly, he tells her about the air shipment program, gives her a brochure, and reminds her about tomorrow's Casino Night.

She laughs and says maybe she needs to start shipping everything via air and then maybe the PODs would get back sooner.

"Think about this, Larry. You're taking seven to ten days to deliver my shipment and then another seven to ten days to get me a POD, and then—and only then, can I bill my customer and get paid. This is ridiculous! You guys have got to do better."

Finally, she smiles, and I can tell that they're really good friends. She asks me how I am liking Roadway so far. I tell her I'm loving it; it's intoxicating, but I truly want to do what Larry's doing.

"Well, you just keep going. It can happen, you know. Larry's been my rep ever since he started in sales seven or eight years ago." Then, she wishes me good luck.

"Now don't forget, I want to see you in the place tomorrow night," Larry interjects, flirtatiously, trying not to sound too demanding.

"Maybe, if I can find a babysitter in time," she replies.

"Oh, how is Little Susie doing?" Larry inquires.

"Little Susie my ass. She's good, 14 going on 40. Oh, she's a handful. Got the nerve to ask me if she can start drinking and taking birth control pills when she turns fifteen!"

"Are you serious?" Larry asks.

"Hey, these kids today are growing up way too damn fast, watching all this crap on TV. It's got them going crazy. She's already sneaking around trying to smoke cigarettes," Naomi shrugs.

We all take a deep pause for a moment to suck in on our respective cigarettes, without giving a single thought to the lasting impression we're making on Little Susie's generation.

"Hey, I gotta go to a meeting now, but I'll probably be there tomorrow. Are you going to be there?" she asks, looking directly at me.

"Yes, I am. I can't wait," I say.

"Well, if I get there and Larry is too busy to give me the proper attention I require, maybe I'll hang out with you," she says.

"Sounds like a plan," I grin.

Oh shit, I think I just changed my mind. *Maybe Ms. Farah Fawcett look-alike is my type after all. WOW, that just happened!* I can't make this stuff up.

Next call, we take six large pizzas and a bunch of sodas to a group of guys in the back of a warehouse. All nice guys, but we don't hang around to fraternize. Larry reminds them about the Casino Night and gives them the air shipment brochure, and then we're gone.

Next, we stop for lunch at his favorite restaurant. He's a cool guy, a true native Californian. The restaurant is equally cool, filled with local sports memorabilia – Dodgers, Angels, Rams, Raiders, Lakers, and a little bit of the Clippers. At this point, I am feeling a little uncomfortable, now that it's just us at the table, but Larry is a great host. He seems to know everyone inside, and he makes me feel welcome and important. The whole thing reminds me of a *Cheers* restaurant and bar.

I ask Larry how long he's been in sales, and he says ten years.

"Did you start in sales or in operations?" I ask.

"I started on the dock in Operations with Transcon, just like you, but it was short-lived for me," he replies.

"Oh?" I hope he will give me some straight answers.

"Well, they had an opening and needed someone as soon as possible, so in less than six months, I was promoted to sales."

"Was Eric the sales manager back then?" I ask.

"No. It wasn't at Roadway Express when I started in the business. It was a local Los Angeles-based trucking company, Transcon Lines Trucking – a really good company, and we had a guy at the time named George Merson. George was good, really good, but old school. We loved him, and the customers loved him, too. Nah, I started with the competition. Man, we did everything back then. We had big fun."

I can't even imagine what big fun was like then, based on what I've seen today. I hope Larry will elaborate.

"Well, today it's getting to be cutthroat and rigid, especially now with deregulation. Just like Al screaming about a 15 percent discount. Hell, I'm not doing that. Roadway doesn't do that. We're the market leader, and we won't bow to these pricing wars. Roadway is probably the toughest company to work for, but if you survive two years here, you can get hired by any trucking company in the industry. I mean any of them would love to have you – especially management trainees like you. So, keep your nose clean and your head up, because you'll be getting options if you hang in there. Seriously, companies will be calling you and offering you a job. It'll happen for you. I've seen it."

Larry pauses and sips his drink. "You know that's what happened to Earl, right?" he asks. I nod. "We let Earl go on a Friday and he was hired by Yellow Freight the following Tuesday. Really, and he's told me he's happier than ever!"

Well, that seems to answer that question. All I need to hear at this point.

After our final call for the day, and as we are returning to the terminal, Larry asks if I have any other questions.

"Yes. I noticed that you avoided telling Al about tomorrow's Casino Night, yet you told practically everyone else. Did you forget to mention it to him, or was that on purpose?"

"Al's too much baggage to handle in that type of situation. His drinking is a serious liability. I'd be worried he'd indulge too much and have an accident on his way home. I've taken him out before, and he's a handful. Fortunately for me, he doesn't like crowds, so I don't have to worry about him getting his feelings hurt if he happens to hear about our outside events. He's happy with a visit and a bottle of booze every two or three weeks. That's our agreement."

"So, what about the 15 percent discount he says he wants?"

"Oh please. I'm not giving that man shit, but a bottle of booze, and he'll be happy. Like I said, Roadway isn't budging about doing this pricing war. I just said that to appease him."

Wow. I'm definitely getting an education today.

"One last thing. Was Naomi flirting with you and me?"

"Oh, hell yes. That woman was flirting. Don't you think she's hot?"

"Hey, I'd be lying if I said she wasn't hot, but what do you do if your customer tries to go too far?"

"Well, that hasn't happened yet. I'll let you know if and when it does. Yes, she's a single mom without a lot of support from her ex-husband, and she's raising a teenage daughter alone. You damn right she was flirting. If I wasn't married, I would probably…well, you know what I mean."

"So, what are you going to do if she shows up tomorrow and starts flirting with you again after she's had a few drinks?"

Larry laughs. "I guess we'll cross that bridge when we get there, huh? What about you, do you like her?"

"Sure, but she's really not my type."

"So, what is your type?"

"Well, I kinda like my women like I like my coffee, if you know what I mean."

"Oh. You're one of those brothers that's loyal to your soul sisters, huh?"

"I guess so," I replied, thinking that was about enough of this conversation.

The truth is, I've seen so many beautiful Black women since I moved to Los Angeles, I haven't really thought about dating other women outside my race – except for Kim, of course. I mean Kim's the exception to any man's rule. She's got a nice, brown tan and could almost pass for Black, a forerunner to *Wayne's World*'s Tia Carrera, plus she's Asian, so in my world in 1981, as far as I'm concerned, Kim's damn near one of the sisters.

Larry isn't done with the subject yet. "Well, good luck, because your loyalties may change after tomorrow night when Ms. Naomi comes strolling in, wearing one of her tight red miniskirts."

We laughed together. I thank him, and we say our goodbyes right there in Roadway's parking lot.

As I walk to my car, I know I am more than ever sold on the notion that I want to be in sales. Instead of going straight home, I drive to Barnes and Noble's bookstore and buy me three books on salesmanship.

One of those books is to become the one I've kept by my side and lived my entire career by. Since that fateful day in 1981, I've read hundreds of books, but *The Greatest Salesman in The World*, by Og Mandino, changed my life forever. It's the story of a poor, destitute camel boy, Hafed, who rose from poverty to become the richest man and the greatest salesman in the world. He faced many struggles of survival and challenge in his uncompromising motivation to become wealthy. His WHY was simply this: he wanted to become successful and rich, so that he could marry the king's beautiful daughter, Alicia.

Not only is it a beautiful love story of how he earned both respect and his bride, but the second half of the book includes ten scrolls for success to live by. The reader is challenged to read and live for the next ten months by each scroll, and it is suggested that the reader focus on each scroll by reading it three times a day for thirty days. Read it in the morning and afternoon silently, and at bedtime, read it out loud.

As I ponder the story, I realize that my deepest and most profound desire at this time is to become a salesman for Roadway Express. That goal is my WHY, and I know I need a secret weapon to achieve it. I start that very evening to live by those ten scrolls.

The next morning when I report to work, I am assigned to Brett. We do pretty much the same thing that I'd done with Larry the day before. I'm starting to see just how valuable these relationships are to Roadway's success, and how much money they spend to cultivate and nurture these relationships with gifts and favors. Maybe that ubiquitous sign is accurate: "Nothing happens until somebody sells something."

It's the same routine, different day. Donuts, pizza, ballgame tickets, baseball caps, and selling the service flavor of the month – the program that's supposed to become available "soon". This air freight business is a brand-new concept, completely foreign at this point in our LTL industry. We don't even have the infrastructure set up yet, but they're busy getting the word out to customers that it's coming – and if Roadway says "It's coming" – believe me – it's coming. "The air shipment program is coming. Give us a try."

Meantime, Casino Night is here. This should be fun. Roadway has its own private suite inside the hotel, and customers are starting to show up and mingle. I'm introduced to many of the customers and then, the games begin.

Everyone is given thousands and thousands of dollars of play money to use for gambling. Cocktail waitresses in sexy clothes are walking around serving drinks all evening. I'm in heaven! We are having so much fun, laughing, drinking, and playing games. Gifts like televisions, stereos, and a grand prize weekend trip to Las Vegas at the Hilton are among the prizes. Other similar items, compliments of both Roadway and customers are available as well. Roadway has hundreds of personal giveaways: baseball caps, ink pens, t-shirts, and flashlights are on the tables for the taking. All I keep thinking is: *This is the life. I want it. I can do this job.*

Oh, in case you're wondering, Naomi doesn't make it to the party. She can't find a responsible babysitter. Thank you, God!

By Friday, I'm still excited. It's my last day with sales, and what a way to conclude the week! Once again, I'm with Larry, and we're going to a swim party. It's a total secret, even from Dan and Eric. I've come to understand that Eric and Dan are birds of the same feather, and the sales guys don't necessarily like or trust them. Both are very strict and rigid, and some customers, like Al, aren't too fond of Eric. I can't believe these sales guys are going to trust me with this swim party secret. I feel as if I'm already being accepted as one of them now. I've got a brand-new pair of swimming trunks in the back of my car.

And we're off. Next thing I know, we show up at some Roadway employee's house in Huntington Beach, just a block from the ocean. It's a beautiful home and the party is already jumping at 1:00 p.m. I am totally shocked when we walk into the house and see so many people who work for Roadway. I'm meeting guys in sales and operations from surrounding areas. I even meet a couple of guys from 821, and they remember me. Thank God Ronnie isn't here, but maybe he's on the way.

This is crazy. I can't believe how many people are here on a Friday afternoon at a swim party. However, a lot of these guys work seven days on and seven days off, and this could be their 7 off, which would explain a lot. But who are all these beautiful women? There are some gorgeous women parading around in bikinis here, and people are drinking and partying everywhere. Also, I'm not the only Black person at this party. There are two beautiful and fine Black women here and three Black guys plus me. I can't believe it!

Well, actually, there are two other Black guys and one brother who isn't sure if he's black or white. Ha – I'm sure the LAPD could provide this brother with a clear answer in less than a minute regarding which ethnicity box he should be checking. Anyway, far be it from me to judge this man any further regarding his ill-informed confusion. Today is a great day, as I take in this secret little melting pot all tucked away in Huntington Beach, in our secret little oasis of a playground on this cool Friday afternoon. If Naomi shows up today, she is in big trouble, because

I just had a paradigm shift and my horizons have been expanded for life, to be more inclusive of all people.

Hello Southern California!

I would say that 50 percent of the attendees are from Roadway, and the other 50 percent are friends of people who work for Roadway.

Wow! Look who is just walking through the front door! David, the assistant dispatcher. He was at work earlier today, and now he's here at 1:30 p.m., on the busiest day of the week in our dispatch office. He casually walks in and immediately spots me and comes over to say hello.

"Hey, David," I say.

"Hey, Tony. I took off a little early to start my weekend."

"Who's helping Bill today?" I ask.

"Oh, Bill's fine, got two of the office girls helping him manage the phones today. But come on Tony, let's be real. You know Bill doesn't really need me. The only thing Bill needs me for is to empty his ashtray and maybe grab a couple of phone calls." We both laugh.

"Yeah, you're probably right," I reply. "I was just asking."

"Well, how's it been going?" he inquires.

"Great, I'm loving this life!"

Next thing, ten minutes later, in walks Kim. David and I both see her at the same time, and he comments first. "Oh, there's Kimmie. I guess she took a vacation day today, because I didn't see her at work. I think I'll go and say hi to her."

My heart sank. I just stared. *Who the hell is Kimmie? Do you mean Kim? My Kim?* I silently stage a huge protest inside my head. Damn, they must think I'm stupid. They planned this whole thing, and now the nerve of them, coming in ten minutes apart, as if they aren't together. Look at them over there on the other side of the pool acting like they barely know each other.

Now David is inviting her to come jump into the pool with him. They have their swim clothes underneath their regular clothes. Kim sees me, waves, and gives me a huge smile from across the pool as she takes off her blouse. I wave back, but I'm so jealous I can't see straight. They are an item. A real couple.

All this brings me down for a moment, but I still try to have fun. I even try to talk to one of the Black ladies, but she and I aren't vibing at all. I am still having a great time, but when Kim takes off her blouse, shorts, and reveals just what she's working with – that sweetly curved, tanned body and her bikini lines as she jumps into the pool—I almost lose it. David is submerged under the water for several seconds and then slowly comes back up right in front of her, attempting to pull her in closer and closer. She pulls away and laughs as she sprays water in his face with a water gun.

I can't believe how jealous I feel. All those special moments we'd been sharing on the dock looking for distressed freight. I thought we had something special. Ha ha.

Larry, Brett, Huckabee, and two other guys walk over, and Larry whispers, "Remember, you've been sworn to secrecy."

"I know. I know, man," I reply.

All six of us eat BBQ ribs and burgers together, and later, Larry and I get dressed and leave. Larry has to make two more calls before 5:00. He takes four Disneyland tickets to one customer, and delivers a case of Budweiser to another, and we're through for the day and the week. We don't talk any more about Kim and David, even though he knows I am visibly upset.

"Come on, Tony," he says, "get it together! She's not your woman. You do have a girlfriend, remember?"

Oh yeah. Cynthia. I'll see her this weekend and finally meet her son, Jamal.

Back at the office, Larry drops me off at my car, and we call it a day. I wonder if it would be okay for me to go back over to the party on my own and try to talk to Kim, or if I was only an invited guest of Larry's. After thinking about it, I decide to head home.

Well, this week in sales will remain a lasting memory. It definitely has solidified my desire to go into sales. I am feeling like I am a part of something so big and so special, and proud that they had allowed me to witness up close and personal the real life of a salesman. As upset as I am about Kim and David, I also realize that I didn't have to see it – not any of it. I wouldn't even have known the truth if Larry and the other sales reps hadn't invited me into their world. I would still have been as naïve as the schoolteacher and coach from Orange, Texas.

Bottom line. Now I know for sure that not only can I do this job, but I will enjoy doing this job. I can't wait to get home and wash away the memory of Kim, in that damn sexy hot pink bikini with David right there next to her, swimming and playing – oblivious to me and others, without a care or a worry in the world. It's time for me to regroup and continue my study of *The Greatest Salesman!*

THE FIRST SCROLL

"Today, I begin a new life. Today, I shed my old skin which hath, too long, suffered the bruises of failure and the wounds of mediocrity. Today, I am born anew, and my birthplace is a vineyard where there is fruit for all. Today, I will pluck grapes of wisdom..."

CHAPTER SIX

A DEFINING MOMENT

"I am not a victim of the world I see."
– A Course in Miracles

My exciting introduction to the world of sales has left me plenty to think about, but I was surprised, as I replayed that week over and over in my mind, how fixated I was on that pool party. It wasn't just the glamour, excitement, and general good fun, but my unexpected negative reaction to Kim and David as a couple. I kept wondering about my naïveté at seeing them together. Moving into the weekend, I can't let it go. That is unfortunate, because this weekend, I'm finally invited to spend it with Cynthia and her young son in her beautiful home. It will be my first meeting with Jamal.

In an attempt to somehow return to my normal cheerful sanity, I begin the weekend by continuing my regular basic spiritual practices. I know that, at one level, I'm suffering from hurt feelings; but at another, I am ashamed and angry that I had allowed myself to be diverted. It is past time to take myself to the woodshed. Probably the guest bathroom in Cynthia's lovely home is not the best place to do it. But…here I am.

"I am not a victim!" I yell softly, yet muttering out loud underneath my breath. "How dare you allow yourself to get distracted by the exotic and beautiful Kim?" I ask myself. When I first arrived in Los Angeles, my landlord, a retiree still moonlighting as a part-time player and "O.G." from Chicago, had warned me not to be fooled by the expensive eye-candy around town and not to fall for the "Okie doke". For some strange reason, I respect and admire him for his straightforward perspective. Even though he's long retired, he still seems to know everyone in the entertainment world, including Muhammed Ali, Barry White, Diana Ross, Marla Gibbs, Lionel Richie, Stevie Wonder, Smokey Robinson, Mr. T, and many others. Yet, here I am, totally ignoring his advice and falling for that crap.

"She was never yours, Tony, nor was she promised to ever be yours," I tell myself, firmly. "She may be a good person on the inside, but she's still an 'expensive, exotic piece of eye-candy' that men will pay to be with, and she knows it."

Then, I become as quiet and still as a hunted mouse while I continue to stare at myself in Cynthia's guest bathroom mirror. I take three deep breaths, then slowly close my eyes while I stand and perform a quick self-inspection from head to toe, using the memory of my last visual snapshot to imagine and recall each body part. Just as I drift off into deeper relaxation, I close my eyes and silently tell each body part to relax and let go. "Relax and let go. Relax and let God. From the top of your head to the bottom of your feet, RELAX." I continue to repeat the mantra silently inside my head.

Wow! This meditation stuff is really starting to make a difference, I sigh, feeling my body start to melt and relax. I literally feel the tension oozing down and out. Only two months ago, I was introduced to transcendental meditation by Charles, an older guy from church, but I must say, as weird as it seemed at first, I am becoming a big fan of the process and its fantastic benefits.

Still, my jury is still out on this New Age approach to enlightenment. It's way too soon to tell for sure if I am in the right camp, even though they say the practice of meditation is safe and over 5,000 years old. *If it's so damn old, why do they call it New Age,* I wonder. But, after all, this is Southern California, you know, 'LALA Land', and a lot of people out here are saying a lot of shit. Sometimes, you don't know who to trust. I don't want to end up being tricked into following some Jim Jones cult leader back to Guyana and have my life end horribly like that awful tragedy two years ago.

Shaking my head, I refocus again, acknowledging and allowing those momentary thoughts to pass, ever so gently, across the plains of my mind. And all of a sudden, there's Kim in that damn pink bikini and her beautiful, tan body.

"This is some bullshit, and you know better! You are better than this, Tony!" I mutter, blinking away the flashbacks of Kim and David playing Marco Polo in the swimming pool. *Get her out of your mind, NOW,* I scream inside my head. Yeah, I am having a serious "come to Jesus" moment.

Over the course of the weekend, I keep talking to myself silently and intermittently, trying to find peace of mind – while attempting also to be the man, and entertain Cynthia and Jamal, her 13-year-old son. Mostly, I'm able to keep my private cussing and fussing to myself, my emotions in check, and my head on straight during this special weekend. Still, the Roadway management staff would be so proud if they could hear just one fifth of my weekend deep-dive rants of cursing.

On the other hand, Cynthia is definitely not amused, and isn't having it. After all, this is her first attempt to introduce me to Jamal, obviously her pride and joy. And to be honest, I'm blowing it big time, and I know it. I can tell she's starting to wonder if I'm losing my mind, and I know Jamal has already told her privately that I'm a "strange bird", after he overheard me talking to myself in the bathroom.

I've been trying to be respectful of the fact that they might hear my rants – and after all, I am a guest in their home for the weekend. I am trying to be present in the moment, but I'm not processing quickly enough, nor am I clicking on all cylinders. I'm feeling lethargic, as if I were on drugs – but I'm not. Instead, I'm a house divided, and my spirit is broken.

This should be so simple for me, I wonder. *Hell, I know how to handle kids, and I'm good at it, too.* I reflect on my days in Texas as a schoolteacher and athletic coach, remembering how much my student athletes used to love me and my last year of coaching them to the Golden Triangle 9th Grade District Basketball Championship. Yeah, we did that, with a winning season of 19-1.

What's so hard about just hanging out and having a good time bonding with Jamal and Cynthia? I wonder if my torment could be more about my commitment to my relationship with Cynthia. This is a package deal any way that I look at it, and, in many ways, I feel trapped, out-of-my-league, and clearly not ready to take on the responsibility of the inevitable next steps. If I'm being honest, this is a ready-made-family, and I'm scared to death. Cynthia had warned me early on, before anyone said the "L" word, that she was looking for a serious relationship. Ruefully, I remember that I'd answered her with shit like, "Yeah, me too." But now I'm becoming anything but Mr. Serious. (*Shame on you, Tony.*)

I'm not sure that I'm the guy for this job, even though I like the perks and benefits, many of which are new to me since my arrival in Los Angeles – her great cooking being just one of them. I'm also concerned about giving false hope to Jamal and negatively impacting his critical teenage years. That's definitely a deal breaker, not something to play with. If I earn this young man's trust and respect and then disappoint him, I won't know how to live with that, and I certainly don't know how it will affect him long-term. I've got so many unanswered questions. I do not want to play that game with a child, especially a young Black man growing up in Los Angeles. *Help me, God!*

Maybe this is the bigger problem this weekend, rather than my disappointment and bruised ego about Kim. Perhaps I'm really afraid of this situation with Cynthia and her ready-made family, and seeing the carefree Kim and David is my way of dealing with "buyer's remorse". *You are a selfish and greedy prick, Tony, and should be ashamed of your thoughts and intentions.*

Steve Harvey's book *Act Like a Woman, Think Like a Man*, instructs women to put their man on a 90-day plan before having sex. No sex for 90 days! Maybe that's my problem. Cynthia, by accident or by choice, has put me on such a 90-day plan, and I've ended up buying the cow. What I really wanted was to simply drink the milk and only when I was thirsty.

Wow! What does that really say about me?

It says, "You are so immature Tony!" I need to focus. I should only have three main goals for the week-end – (1.) bond with Jamal, (2.) have lots and lots of fun creating beautiful memories with Cynthia and Jamal all weekend, (3.) fulfill one of Cynthia's wildest romantic fantasy requests later on. I nod my head, agreeing that's my task for the weekend, but before I can pull myself together, Cynthia gives me a look that could kill.

The three of us have been attempting to watch Saturday morning's *Soul Train* with Don Cornelius, and she is not amused by my inattentive and distant stares out the front door. Concealing that I'm distracted and not having fun isn't working. I am definitely not present, and finally, she has had enough.

Firmly, but very politely, she asks me to come out to the garage with her to help her look for a hammer and some nails. Once in the garage, her manner turns to ice, with an edge that suggests she just might hit me with that hammer. In my face, she confronts me, and tells me off like a drill sergeant.

"How dare you come to my home and act so distant and strange? What the hell is wrong with you, man?" she asks.

I stumble an apology, agreeing that she definitely deserves better from me, and promising it won't happen again. But I am partially lying, blaming my actions on a bad week at work, and the fact that next week I'll start working the night shift. The second part of that statement is true. I really am getting the Sunday night jitters.

"Frankly, I'm worried," I say. "I'm not sure I can manage these Teamsters. Most are older than me and these people ain't no joke—they're hardcore. If you think I'm strange, you haven't seen strange. I've never had to take on such a challenge. Lately, I've been yelling in my sleep. I'm yelling and arguing with people and saying shit while asleep like, "High and tight dammit, high and tight."

She smiles, and then she hugs me and assures me that I'll do just fine – and that she will do whatever it takes to support me. It is almost a mother and son moment, and I'm ashamed to admit it, but I need that assurance. She is so sweet, and she seems so relieved that my problem isn't about another woman that she begins to cry in my arms.

Man, she cries about everything. The truth is, though, it really is about another woman, but not the way she's assuming. At least, not really like an affair with another woman. If it is an affair, then it's a one-sided thing, happening only in my mind. I'm not sure that counts as cheating. Suddenly, it's very plain. Kim was just a fantasy of my dreams. Very similar to the movie *The Woman in Red* or that song by the Temptations, "it was just my imagination, running away with me."

I learned a valuable lesson that weekend. They say there are only 3 things that we can control, (1.) our thoughts, (2.) our imagination, and (3.) our behavior. Well, that weekend right there in Cynthia's garage, marked the beginning of me truly learning how to control consciously and intentionally all three. A few minutes later, after regrouping, I went back inside with a new attitude and did just that. I walked back inside and became the life of the party. I was "locked in", like Magic Johnson. Soon, we were all laughing and dancing to *Soul Train* and creating our own dance moves and soul train line. Oh yeah! It was showtime, and I was the Master of Ceremonies. When I went back inside that house, I became a different person with a Patty LaBelle new attitude.

How did I do it? Well, I invited my alter-ego (King An'Thony) to kick in and do the driving. The next thing I knew, I had Jamal and Cynthia laughing so hard, they were in stiches on the floor. Hell, I could dance my ass off back then! They didn't know what hit them, and they loved it. We all loosened up and started to have fun, and the rest of the weekend was magical.

Later, Jamal and I take a ride to the park in my car, where we throw frisbees and talk things over. He tells me he doesn't want to see his mom get hurt again; that she'd gone through a lot with his biological father during their separation and divorce. For a moment, that messes me up, because it reminds me of my personal sadness as a kid, even though my parents were together until death. Kids know when something is not right. Jamal says he hasn't seen his mom this happy in five years, since he was seven or eight.

"Tony," he says, very seriously, "I hope you're for real, because it's too late for her. She loves you man; I'm her son, and I would know."

Wow! I'm not sure how to respond or what is appropriate to say, but I tell him that my intentions are honorable, and I will NEVER intentionally hurt his mother physically, mentally, or emotionally.

He looks me in the eye and says, "That's good enough for now."

We do one of the cool dap handshakes that kids were doing back then. This becomes the beginning of a close and trusting bond between two men, and even though Cynthia and I will go through our share of trials and tribulations over the next four years, Jamal and I will remain connected for many years, including through his college years.

Later that evening, the three of us go out for dinner and a movie, and for that entire day, we are a big, happy family. But back home, Cynthia can clearly overhear me in the guest bathroom mumbling to myself. It must sound to her like confused jibberish profanity. Thankfully, Jamal is asleep, and she's too tired to even deal with me until tomorrow.

Dimly, I realize that somehow, I had managed to turn lemons into lemonade and make today a special day to remember, even though the Kim and David demon is still very much present. I'm not sure why this has been so hard and time-consuming to sort out and shake off. It almost seems like the professional athlete experiences when he or she gets distracted and plays badly because of an inability to shrug off a minor incident. I'm now well-aware that my personal distraction has mostly to do with a bruised ego and my complete misjudgment of how Kim felt about me. Nevertheless, I'm determined to move past this defining moment. I'm glad it happened. And now, 40 years later, my mess is a part of my story and my message.

There's an old saying, "The wind helps the sailor who has set his sails." After this big emotional upset about Kim and David, I begin to replay the events quietly and secretly – and ask myself very seriously, "Tony, what is your real purpose? And what direction do you have your sails pointing?"

It's not the first time I've had to acknowledge a "defining moment". I love those moments, and I embrace them. I refer to them as my "Stirring Up the Spirit Moments". It's as if you know or feel that you've shifted the

Universe ever so slightly. Moments like these stand out, resonate, and usually represent real change, even if the message arrives in a package of experiences wrapped in horror, shame, embarrassment – or even pain. In this particular one, I just hadn't seen the blind spot in time. For me, this moment is a Victor Frankl "Man's Search for Meaning Moment" that wouldn't end in my extermination, but it certainly did sting like the bee that would ultimately represent real growth and change.

For some time after this incident, I kept asking myself, "Tony, are you simply waiting for the wind to take you wherever it wants to, hoping for some type of Las Vegas luck and good fortune? This isn't the philosophy you've been living by up to now, and it's certainly not the type of courage you've demonstrated in the past. You've always been an independent thinker, and last week riding with those sales guys did not change who you are on the inside. *Whatever you do Tony, don't forget who you are and why you are here.*

Remember when you signed a full-ride scholarship to run track at Texas Tech University, instead of going to Oklahoma University? Many followers and fans in your home state of Oklahoma were expecting you to sign with OU, but you changed your mind and didn't. Remember, August 1980, when you chose to quit your teaching job one month before school started to move to Southern California? You and the other coaches were already prepping for the upcoming football season and at the last minute, you asked the athletic director if you could be released from your contract, said that you had to move to California to pursue your dreams, and couldn't wait another day. You must have sounded as silly as a teenage boy. But you did it anyway. You moved straight away from South Texas to Southern California without any prospects of a new job? Just you with your master's degree in tow, courageously pointing your sails toward Los Angeles in all its glory and opportunity, and the rest is history. You didn't wait on luck or the wind to blow or something or someone to help you. In fact, Uncle GQ, who lived in Los Angeles for more than twenty years, told you it was the worst time in history to move to L.A. He almost scared you out of your dream and made you wait. You might still be waiting. But you made it happen, despite his warnings and without his assistance. You made it happen. You hardly knew anyone in Los Angeles, yet you believed in yourself, and you took 100 percent responsibility for your life and whatever was about to happen. You believed that you were divinely protected and pushed forward believing that the Universe conspires to assist those who take action.

So, Tony. Let me say it one more time, "GET YOUR SHIT TOGETHER, TONY! YOU WERE BUILT FOR THIS."

The truth is that what I didn't know and couldn't predict was the length of time this so-called "sacrifice and paying your dues" of working the nighttime Operations shift would last. I knew Dan had told me it would take at least two years in Operations before I could go into sales, but I also knew that it could take much longer. It could take five or ten years. Many guys love Operations, but I am not one of them. I was not built for this. Many women and men don't think they're cut out for selling, but the truth is, we're all in sales and have been our entire lives.

Here I was, about to embark upon a minimum of a two-year stretch of hard knocks, with no guarantee that I'd ever get out. Working a minimum of ten hours, five days a week as a Supervisor in Operations for Roadway Express, but that time need not be in vain. Instead, it can become invaluable cornerstones for building character and determination to succeed. As much as I was already hating the nighttime hours, weather conditions, and the hostile attitudes of some of the Teamsters, I was beginning to realize that I would need every experience in order to build my survival muscle for growth and excellence in the industry.

Most importantly, I would be unconsciously creating my own Mental Training Success Program which today (40 years later) has evolved into "The 5 Pillars for Success," also known as "The DARE to DO YOU Success Formula". Read on my friend, I promise to tell you more about "my process" and my game-changing life story.

Here's what was so meaningful and invaluable about that week's experience in sales: No one can ever take away what I saw and felt observing those Roadway sales guys in action. I would never quite be the same again, and nothing would ever erase from my mind what I had felt, seen, and heard. I had been shown "the life of a salesman," the land of milk and honey. I loved it and wanted a piece of that land, lifestyle, and honey. In fact, after riding with the various sales guys all week and being exposed to Casino Night and hearing about the fun outings with customers at the Lakers, Rams, and Dodger ball games, the dinners in Beverly Hills, happy hour in Marina Del Rey, horseback rides in the Hollywood Hills, the striptease clubs, Transportation Night at Disneyland, and much more, I realized and declared that I wanted that lifestyle more than I could ever want Kim. Indeed, she was really like a prop used in advertising, at least in my mind. You know, the ad with the pretty girl next to the red Corvette? You want the pretty girl and so you end up buying the red Corvette, hoping and wishing that the pretty girl standing beside the car will magically show up in your life. So, I envisioned a lifestyle that included the red Corvette and the girl.

What a subliminal message I had attached to Kim without even realizing it! She was by far the prettiest and most exotic looking woman that I had met in transportation-logistics so far, and somehow, I had unconsciously attached her beauty to symbolize the lifestyle of a transportation salesperson. "What a crock of bullshit!" I laughed to myself.

It reminds me of the subliminal messages used in beer and smoking ads. You see the pretty woman on the beach in a skimpy bikini smoking a Newport or Kool cigarette or perhaps drinking a cold bottle of Budweiser beer. She turns and looks your way and smiles as she offers you a cigarette and a bottle of beer, and as you light up and exhale, the camera pans out, encapsulating the sunset and beautiful ocean and the two of you, laughing, smoking, drinking, and holding hands. Wow! What a picture... what an image!

Twenty years later as a non-smoker, I can still smell the smoke in my mind just thinking about this image. That's how powerful and permanent advertising can be.

Back to my story. I vowed right then and there that I would never look at Kim in the same way again. She and David were an item, and I would respect the "man code" and keep their secret. I would take back my power in the process and keep my eye on the prize. As a result of this hard-won conclusion, my overall mood for 85 percent of the weekend at Cynthia was decisive. I dedicated the weekend to accomplish four goals, and I did it. As you are realizing, I'm a big fan of goal-setting – especially written goals – as keys to one's personal success. So, here are my short-term accomplished goals from that weekend:

1. Make peace and heal my bruised ego regarding Kim and David.

2. Bond with Jamal and have fun.

3. Make amends, have fun, and create beautiful memories with Cynthia.

4. Get my mindset, (mentally, emotionally, and physically) ready for next week as an Outbound Operations Supervisor at Roadway Express.

I'm also a big fan of affirmations, and I use them a lot. So, much as I was affirming aloud and repeating over and over, "I am not a victim," there were also moments of sarcasm and comedic humor where I would pretend to channel Richard Nixon and his famous iconic 1970s quote, "I am not a crook." Yeah, I attempted to channel the ghost of President

Richard Nixon, aka: old "Tricky Dick" to help me find ways to have fun and accept my reality. One thing I knew for sure: I refused to be a victim, because that was not behavior I would accept for me or anyone else.

So, here's how I did it to make it fun, and to fire off those positive endorphins inside me: I would hold up both hands in the mirror and give the peace sign (coincidentally, V is for Victim), just like old Tricky Dick would do back during his presidency, and then, I would say, "I am not a victim." I would try and sound just like ole Tricky Dick as I spoke it out loud, and then I would shake my head back and forth and say it again, "I am not a victim." This brought a little bit of humor to a very gloomy subject for me.

I would laugh and without any prodding, Jamal started imitating me and doing it without a clue as to why. He knew who President Richard Nixon was in theory, but probably didn't know or care why he was impeached in 1974 and had to leave office. I think now that Jamal had started to like me and trust me a little bit, I wasn't such a strange bird after all, and he, too, was now acting just as strange. Here we are both walking around saying "I am not a victim," but for totally different reasons. "I am not a victim," and we would both laugh like it was top secret as to what we meant. Cynthia was still not amused.

Yet, other times I would take this verbal ritual quite seriously and take advantage of a moment all to myself to yell out loud to the heavens, with all the courage and boldness of a warrior, "I am not a victim… I am not a victim," while using my James Earl Jones deep bass voice. Bottom line, I realize it was only a fantasy of Kim that I allowed to become more believable than my reality. See it and believe it may work great for material things, regarding how to manifest your dream house, car, or boat, but when it comes to people, well, that's a different story—when it comes to people, we all have free will, and I cannot project my will upon another person's will without their consent. That's reality.

Looking back, I have no idea why God or those sales guys trusted me enough to allow me to observe the secret life of a transportation salesmen, but I'm grateful they did, because it stimulated and sparked my imagination, and made me a truth seeker for life. Since then, I've always sought the naked truth in others, and I work to understand the why.

In retrospect, I see that these transportation salesmen, plus a few elite women, were forerunners to the television series, *Mad Men*, on HBO, although it would not emerge for another 30 years. When it did, it won multiple awards for honestly revealing the luxurious, opulent lifestyle of the 1960s New York ad men. It could just as easily have been the transportation salesmen of California in the 1970s and 80s. There is no doubt in my mind that the 1960s New York City lifestyle was real. Men and women, all boozing and sexing it up with random partners in restaurants, late night meetings, and love affairs with employees and customers. All the well-dressed men and women in their nice suits and ties, having the time of their lives in the New York 1960s, were also alive and well in Southern California's transportation industry in the 1980s.

This was intoxicating stuff for a young African American man experiencing Southern California for the very first time. Remember, I was 27, single, and I desperately wanted to mingle. I wanted sales now more than the air I was breathing. My inner child, Little Tony, a.k.a. LT, the cute little curly-headed three-year-old blackish-brown boy from Hugo, Oklahoma, could not BELIEVE what was going on in Southern California. I was still adjusting to just LIVING in Southern California, but that last week, riding around with those salesmen, took the cake for me. I had never seen, or imagined, anything like what they exposed me to. Further, I had no idea that this lifestyle was even possible for me, and to get paid to live and breathe it. If I'd returned to teaching school for the rest of my working life, I might still have no idea this type of lifestyle was possible for me or whether what I'd seen that week was even real. So, let's take a look at some of the perks:

First, a brand-new company car every two years with free gas and ongoing car-repair maintenance, a credit card with an infinite credit line, an unspecified spending budget. A wardrobe of three-piece suits and power ties every day. Parties…more parties, like it's 1999.

You literally had access to every type of entertainment event in Southern California, provided you can get your good customers to tag along.

So, if you're me and 27 years old and single, tell me what part of this job you don't like so far? Oh, did I mention that women, song, booze, and dance are always welcome? You may think I'm making this up – but I can't even begin to tell you the whole story. What I'm talking about is common knowledge to most in our industry, but not usually shared with the outside world. All I know is that after that last introductory week, I was absolutely ready to sign on the dotted line and drink the Kool-Aid. What those salesmen had shown me that last week was unforgettable, and I wanted it in my life every day. So, I started preparing for the opportunity.

Bottomline, my clear takeaway was that in the career of selling, in the 1980s, the industry was run by the hearts and souls of the "good ole' boys", and it had everything to do with customer relationships. The customer wanted to know, like, and trust you. Every competitor out there was competing for that customer's relationship and time. Every trucking company had a sales budget to support that effort and achievement. Building personal relationships were king and queen over any mandatory sales negotiations.

Deregulation had just become law, but the old rules of customer relationships were still alive and well in 1981. And even though the rules would eventually change, customer relationships still remain king and queen over any typical sales negotiations. What I know for sure is that people don't buy products and services. People buy people. There's a reason why I will drive 20 miles across town, passing up 15 barber shops to get to my personal barber. I know, like, and trust my barber, and that's why we do it.

Next week begins my indefinite assignment to the dock. My 12-week training program is coming to an end a little sooner than expected. Dan needs me to get started helping out and learning how to run the Outbound operation, alone. I guess you could say it's time for me to earn my keep. I'll start out on the Outbound dock and eventually move to the Inbound side. Dan says Outbound is easier than Inbound, mainly because Outbound is primarily "blow and go", which is a term that means all freight picked up on the street that day, with an out-of-town destination will be loaded and shipped to Adelanto, the new breakbulk for Southern California. That means there's less coordinating and thinking required, unlike the Inbound, where you have to know all the surrounding cities and zip codes and how to load accurately, so as to not mess up the driver's route. Now, I understand why Bill comes in early to help out. He does not like the Inbound supervisors messing up his loads and causing his drivers unnecessary delays. Now, I get it.

After that beautiful week in sales, little did I realize I was about to embark on a three-and-a-half-year journey in Operations, nothing like I'd ever imagined and certainly nothing like the week I'd just experienced. Dan had already warned me that I had to pay my dues first; pay the ultimate sacrifice by working the nighttime operation shift(s) for a minimum of two or three years before I could be promoted into sales. Dan says it will take a couple of years of sacrifice, so in the famous words of the late, great Marvin Gaye, "let's get it on."

CHAPTER SEVEN

GRATITUDE AND REFLECTION

"If the only prayer you said in your whole life was,
"THANK YOU," that would suffice."
–Meister Eckhart

Monday morning, 8:15 a.m., and here I am still at Cynthia's house – but finally, all alone! It was a very nice night and weekend, to say the least, but I'm having trouble figuring out how to feel about the level of trust and freedom this interesting and surprising woman has suddenly given me. I mean, after all, this is *not* my home, but Cynthia sure as hell has treated me all weekend like it could be. Mi casa es su casa? Hmm…

On one level, I feel like a king. She has spoiled me all weekend with food, drink, fun, and laughter. Now, to top things off, she's given me a set of spare keys to her home, told me to stay as long as I want, and be sure to lock both doors when I leave. Oh, and to remember to unhinge the back porch doggy door, so that "Magic", her blackish German Shepherd, can roam in and out of the house. And off she's gone to her job!

Thank God I'm good with dogs, especially German Shepherds, which are my favorites. Magic has liked me from the time I got here, choosing to sit beside me whenever he's allowed inside, perhaps recognizing an Alpha male. I'm not sure how friendly he'll be this morning without Cynthia and Jamal here, but I think it'll be okay.

This woman has literally trusted me with her entire estate. What kind of woman shows such trust and confidence so early in a relationship? As that old song says, "we've only just begun!" Don't get me wrong, I feel honored, but also a certain responsibility I hadn't felt until now. I also know I can't give her the keys to my humble little apartment. First of all, my roommate, Zach, would oppose it. I think I need to get up and go home. It's getting close to time to start preparing for my new life at Roadway Express. Still, the bed is really comfortable... maybe in a little while. I truly feel safe and secure here, like I'm back at home in Oklahoma at my parents' home, but this is Los Angeles. And, *what if someone comes by???*

Now that I'm finally alone with absolute freedom to scream and shout, "I am not a victim!" at the top of my lungs, I realize I don't have to. What I feel, instead, is summed up in one word: GRATITUDE! If I were to shout right now, it would be, "Thank you, Father!"   Thanks to the Universe and this amazing woman, my need to affirm my Personal Power at the top of my voice has passed, and been replaced with a quiet, peaceful sense of gratitude. If this was another one of Cynthia's tests, I think I've passed with flying colors. That means she probably likes me even more than she did last Friday, when this adventure began, and I was struggling with that damned pool party fiasco.

I mean, after all, what's not to like? I'm a good person. Her son has picked up on that instinctively. In my years of teaching, one thing I learned is that kids are great at seeing through bullshit. So, if her son likes me, she probably loves me, even though the "L" word hasn't been used yet. As for me, I know I'm definitely not yet ready to say that word, but I *am* grateful.

As I look around this big, beautiful home, I can't help thinking this is insane. How in the world did I get here? It's starting to sink in how different my life is about to become, and it's way too soon to tell how these nighttime hours are going to affect me, not to mention this new relationship. But today, I have this big ass house all to myself! I said goodbye to Cynthia and Jamal an hour ago and was awarded the keys to her castle. With my new crazy work schedule, I may not see either of them until next Saturday!

My workday doesn't start for another eight hours, and I'm not excited about it. Tonight is my first official night as an Outbound Supervisor for Roadway. I'm no longer a "management trainee". I've earned two small raises in three months, and I'm already making three times the money I was earning in Texas as a full-time teacher and athletic coach.

Teaching school was so natural for me it never felt like work. Growing up with a teacher mom and lots of aunts and uncles as educators made the profession second nature for me. Still, I once read a quote that said, "Just because it's second nature, doesn't mean it's second class." Teaching and helping others has been my calling. It's not necessary to explain, it just is. And only time will tell what may – or may not – be my calling in this new job in an industry I barely knew existed.

Damn…I really do need to get up and get moving. Honestly, part of me feels like an unauthorized intruder, enjoying this big, comfortable bed. What if someone knocks on the door? Am I supposed to open it like I'm the man of the house? What if it's Cynthia's old boyfriend? Now that *would* be awkward – and furthermore, he may still have keys to the house and walk right in. *Come on, Tony,* I chide myself, *get out of your head! Yeah, but maybe I should get out of here instead, and go back to my own home and start preparing for tonight.* I glance at the bedside clock…. well, maybe just a half hour more….

They say it's a thin line between love and hate. I'd witnessed both of those emotions from Cynthia over the weekend, but best I can tell, love prevailed, because I'm still here! I smile as I realize how silly the whole thing with David and Kim looks on this new day. I can't believe I'd let my emotions take over my common sense, but today, I'm so over that moment of jealousy and rage, I can hardly believe it was there. In hindsight, Kim represents misplaced sexual tension—the one who got away. It's amazing how the mind plays games if you let it. I have so much more here with Cynthia, and I'm going to try hard not to mess it up.

Wow, these Monday morning work jitters are real. I don't actually report until 1600 hours, eight hours away. My men report and start their shift later, at 1730 hours. I plan to go in early and talk it over with Bill and David, so I'll understand exactly what freight is coming in off the street, and what will be the easiest and quickest loads to top off with freight and close, in time for the early bird runs that start at 1900. This will be my first night on the Outbound shift in an official supervisory capacity. I'm working with Richard, the lead supervisor, but I still want to get the information directly from Bill, in case Richard is a no-show. In that case, I'd be on my own, so I need to be professional and ready. I remind myself that Richard is not training me tonight. I'm now his equal, so I need to be ready at any time to take over.

I decide to get up and go out to Redondo Beach and ride my bicycle up and down the strand for an hour or so, and then go back to my apartment and start preparing mentally for my shift. The beach and the ocean are two of my favorite California experiences, and it's obvious that sleeping will be out of the question until this shift is over, so I might as well do something I enjoy. I know my body, and I'm way too wound up to sleep, so I might as well enjoy the day. I hope, in time, that my body will adjust, and I can sleep doing daytime hours.

By the time I get home and start on my ride, I'm able to leave the job worries alone, more or less, and return to the fascinating subject of this new "thing" with Cynthia. The main thing that baffles me about this new experience is how much of my mother I see in this lady. I can even hear echoes of my mother's voice when Cynthia speaks. She's managed, in a very short period of time, to command my total attention and respect. In her garage the other day, how did she so effortlessly force me to "snap out of it"? Or did I do that to myself? I'd like to think I did it, but hell, she's a lot like that E.F. Hutton banker advertisement with the pitch that went, "When she spoke, I listened."

I've read that many men look for a wife who reminds him of his mother. Wait a damn minute! Who said anything about looking for your mother to marry? I'm not looking for a wife, nor am I remotely ready to settle down into family life! Honestly, I can easily see myself as a bachelor for at least another ten years, not that I'd mention that to Cynthia at this point. Admittedly, I'm new to the Los Angeles scene, with a lot to learn, but I must say that Cynthia is adept enough at spoiling the hell out of me to cause me to shrink my ten-year plan to a three-year plan.

My gosh, before heading off to work this morning, she even cooked me a T-bone steak with eggs, hash browns, and toast. Man, I must be doing something really special for her – but I'm not quite sure what that something is. But, for the record, I *do* care a lot for her and her son already, even if I seem confused. I have a soft spot in my heart for Jamal, just as I did for many of my former athletes back in Texas.

I guess I should mention that, although she doesn't look it, Cynthia is eight years older than I am. In fact, most of the time, she looks younger than me, but her maturity as a responsible adult is way ahead of me. It was obvious from the day we met that I'd be playing catch up for a long time in a relationship with her. Her whole attitude has been one of keeping flirtatious young men in their place. Everything she projected warned me that she wasn't an "easy lady". And, before the relationship had progressed very far, she'd also repeated that warning frequently before she ever agreed to go out with me.

Hell, six months ago, she wouldn't have remotely considered inviting me to her home. No way. Nor was she willing to introduce me to Jamal! Getting her to go out with me was like pulling a steel bar out of solid concrete. Then, suddenly, one day, everything changed, and everything became simple and easy. Even now, I'm not sure that I'm in control of anything except my own thoughts and imagination. And there are obviously times when I'm not sure of that either!

We'd met six months ago at one of the downtown public parking lots. She'd parked right beside me that day. As she was getting out of the car, she lightly bumped her car door into my passenger door. It was definitely fate, or perhaps interfering angels, because I took a good look, did a double take, looked again – and wow! She looked *good!*

I quickly pulled myself together, took several deep breaths and considered how to quickly handle our unexpected "collision". The bump was hard enough to require a response, and frankly, I didn't want to let it go by without comment.

So, I mustered up my courage, pretended to be slightly perturbed about my passenger door, and blurted, "Hey, if you wanted to get my attention so you could introduce yourself, I can think of better ways to do it than banging up my new car!" I was careful to make sure my smile was friendly.

"I'm so sorry," she replied. "It was just a little love tap. I'm sure your brand-new car didn't mind. And, after all, you *were* a little too close to the line, even if you were here first." But she was smiling.

We began to walk and although it was my first time in that neighborhood, I noticed we were headed in the same direction. As she walked in front of me, I noticed her backside – a seriously beautiful apple bottom!

"Are you stalking me?" I asked.

"What do you mean, stalking you? I've been working downtown for the last 15 years; how could I be stalking you? Where are you going, sir?" she asked. "You look lost."

"Hell, no, I'm not lost, not really! I'm headed to the One Wilshire Building. What about you?"

No answer to that question, so I asked again. This time, she replied. "Let's just say I work around the corner from your building. I should be asking you if you're stalking me."

I smiled. "Hi! I'm Tony L. Harris, and no, I promise you, Miss, I'm not stalking you. You're completely safe with me."

"So where are you really headed, Tony L. Harris?" she asked.

I pointed. "Believe it or not," I replied, "I really am headed to that big white building over there. One Wilshire. I kid you not!"

"Okay, so what do you do, Mr. Tony L.?"

I'd had enough of her dissembling. "Really? So, you're going to skip past telling me your name while you're the one asking all the questions?"

She sighed. "If you must know, I'm Cynthia."

"Hi, Cynthia. It's a pleasure meeting you."

"Same here," she said. "So, what do you do at One Wilshire?" she persisted.

"I'm trying to learn about the insurance business, so I took a temporary job with California Life. I'm not sure it's what I want to do, but it works for now—at least it's paying the bills. I moved here a few months ago from South Texas, where I was a schoolteacher and athletics coach."

There was a brief pause while she considered that piece of information. "Oh, well good luck with that," she finally said.

I took another deep breath.

"Thanks. What are the chances I'll see you again if I arrive tomorrow morning at the same time, same parking place?"

"Well, I'd say your chances would be about 50 percent."

"Really? That's all?"

"Yes, really. Why do you ask?"

"Because I really want to see you again," I persisted. "I'll be coming here for my training each morning, and I just hope we get to see each other again."

"Well, Mister Tony, don't hold your breath. We'll just have to see what happens."

So, we said our goodbyes, but something told me It wasn't the last time we'd see each other. She was delightful, and I couldn't wait to see what tomorrow would bring.

That's how it all started. For the next three months, we found ourselves walking together almost every morning, having upbeat, friendly banter. It was so much fun! We always had something to talk about, usually lighthearted, but as the days went on, it became more serious. I started routinely asking her out, and for her home phone number – and she, routinely, wouldn't give up any information.

I enjoyed complimenting her, but no matter what I said, she rejected my advances. No phone number. No dates.

"No way," she would say, "My old man would whup your butt and mine, plus, no disrespect, but you're a little too young for me."

Seriously? True, I was 27 to her 35, but she didn't seem that much older – certainly didn't look older, although she was definitely more mature than I was. She insisted that (a) I was too young for her, and (b) she already had a man. She refused her last name, too. In fact, I wasn't even sure if Cynthia was her real first name.

After all, it WAS Southern California, new territory for me, and I'd been warned about the "pretenders".

So, for a while, it was definitely flirtation at its best – the age-old jockeying for position that determines whether a relationship is possible, or whether it's all just a game. And for several months, it remained a game. For example, one time when I asked her out, she laughed and said she wanted to introduce me to her 24-year-old sister.

I responded, laughing. "A 24-year-old woman can't do nothin' for me but show me where the 30-something woman is."

Lying my ass off, obviously. First, her sister was in Cleveland, Ohio, safely out of my reach. And second, the snapshots of said sister showed a woman just as fine and pretty as she was – and with the advantage of zero children. Cynthia offered the "pretty sister" gambit several times, and I worked out my classic bullshitting response: "Nah, I really prefer and want a mature woman like you." And the game continued.

Her chosen soundbite became laughter, followed by redirecting my attention to the fact of her two sons; the oldest age 17, somewhere in the Midwest on a baseball scholarship.

"He's practically the same age as you, Mr. Tony, and besides, I've already got a man – remember?" She would finish that gambit off by flashing her ever-handy photos of her sons.

"Age is just a number, and you've got some great-looking sons," I would respond. Eventually, I tumbled to the fact that she was testing me to see at what point I'd get scared and run away. Once she showed me a photo of her mystery man, which I found interesting, but definitely not off-putting.

Then, one day, she moved on to something way more telling.

"So, what do you really want from me, Mr. Tony? Because you're really too young for me. And I can't have any more kids. So, let's just take all that off the table."

I was floored. How on earth did we get to that topic? I must have looked puzzled, because she segued from that into another attempt to matchmake me to her sister, Janelle. She reminded me that 24 was the ideal age of a woman for me; that she was coming in November for Thanksgiving and would be available for two weeks; that if I came for Thanksgiving dinner, I could look her over. Out came the photo of the sister in her sexy red bikini at the beach, followed by a discussion of her physical attributes, leaving little to the imagination. All of which Cynthia carefully and graphically pointed out.

The approach was starting to get to me: first, because Janelle was a fine specimen of womanhood, with all of the attributes a man enjoys viewing, but also because in spite of my inexperience, I dimly sensed that somewhere under her obvious effort to tempt and strike a light, flirtatious note was a serious attempt to hide her own pain. In an effort to keep it light, I seized control and struck back.

"Hell yes, Janelle looks good. She's pretty and fine as hell, just like you, and she lives in Ohio and I live here in L.A., and one more thing, lady: I want YOU, Cynthia, okay? Stop all this bullshit. What part of 'I want you' do you not understand? And, for the record, I'd leap ten feet in the air and up over 20 women who looked just like Janelle to be with you. I wouldn't care if they came in all different colors: black, brown, white, bright, light bright, yellow, red, green, and everything in between. So put your pictures away, because I want YOU, Ms. Cynthia." I said it and shut up.

Dead silence.

Quietly, Cynthia put the pictures back in her purse and we started walking. I reached out for her hand and this time, she put her hand in mine. I'd definitely given her something to think about.

I'd won that round, but it definitely wasn't over yet. The next installment came quickly enough.

"What do you want, Mr. Tony? Are you looking for your mommy?"

I took a deep breath. "Stop with the bullshit, Cynthia," I said firmly.

She took a deep breath, and then in her purry baby voice she whispered, laughed, and tried to pull her hand back. I smiled and hung on.

"First of all," I went on, pursuing my lead, "I want you to stop calling me Mr. Tony, okay?"

We stopped walking and she turned and looked deep into my eye. "Seriously, Tony, what if I did get rid of my old man, and let's say we were together as a couple. Eventually, you'd look at me and want kids, wouldn't you? And that's when I'd have to say what I already told you. That I can't have any more kids, dammit. Read my lips, okay? The kitchen is permanently closed. And then what would you say?" She was sort of smiling, but in her eyes, she wasn't smiling at all.

In that moment, I knew all the cards were on the table. I decided to play the Einstein card.

"Well, we could pay someone to be a surrogate – maybe your fine-ass baby sister Janelle would help us out. Also, we could adopt," I said.

In retrospect, I can't believe how full of bullshit I was. I was on a roll, because, for the first time, I knew I had her on the ropes, and it was only an instant before "game over". Or, more likely, I was the one on the ropes and just hadn't realized it yet.

Something tangible had changed. I was holding her hand, and she was holding mine – tightly. However, we still had a long way to go.

Over the next weeks, I realized I was practically in a serious relationship, and we hadn't even kissed. Evidently my budding salesmanship persuasion style was working, but I hadn't yet learned when to turn it off. The courtship – if that's what it was, continued with mixed results.

One day, in the parking lot, after she'd pulled back a bit, I yelled loudly, deliberately creating a scene, and ignoring passersby who were pretending not to notice.

"Cynthia, just give me a chance, sweetheart! I'm new in town, fresh off the boat, harmless as a little kitten. I know I'm a bad man, but you can't really be that scared of me. What on earth do you have against GOOD-LOOKING YOUNGER MEN, like me?"

And back came the defense. "You're the one scared, honey. You can't handle this. I'll have you crying for your mama like you used to when you were two years old."

Each time I saw her, I made her day with a combination of laughing, talking, smiling, and then pulling back when it threatened to get too serious. It became like having mini dates every day as we started to trust and like each other. Technically speaking, we had over 90 of those little mini dates in three months, without anyone getting kissed, let alone get pregnant.

I still didn't know her last name. Eventually, she did give me a work phone number, but not her home phone. Remember, there were no cell phones in 1981.

I finally became convinced she was truly single, and it was just her, her pain, and her beloved son, Jamal. Nothing about her sounded as if she was involved with a man in a live-in relationship. It sounded lots more about the self-protection of a woman who'd been hurt and didn't intend to get hurt again.

We came to count on those morning walks. If we missed a day, I'd be so disappointed, but I never stopped to consider the level of commitment I was about to take on. She was so pretty, fine – and vulnerable – that most of the time I felt I was the older one, and just as mature – but underneath, I could sense that very soon, I was going to have to back up my "grown man" talk with some real manly action – whatever that meant. I had no idea what that would look like, long term, at this stage of my life.

As things evolved, we did a lot of pretending – "what-ifs"—without realizing we were actually making plans and strategizing about a future together. It became increasingly obvious that her inability to have more children was a huge block for her – and lack of agreement and understanding on the topic was not a game she was willing to play. One day, I bought her a cute soft, fluffy stuffed animal and asked her if she would hold onto him while we continued working out the details of our relationship. I asked her to give the little guy a name, and she said, "How about Brutus?"

"Brutus is good," I replied.

She loved the little creature and the creative gesture – and Brutus became my little spy inside her bedroom, keeping her company at night and in the mornings, while he kept the bed warm for several more months before I was invited into her home.

Over the next days that we shared, we returned frequently to our ideas of family. It is a measure of my immaturity at that point that I shared with her the fact that I was my father's only son and my Harris grandfather's only grandson, which meant that my family's name technically could die with me. My cousins were all female. I should have realized the implication of continuing that discussion, but at some level, I was still enjoying the game too much to worry about whether my words would affect us later.

I did often wonder if she was the one for me; I knew that I was stimulated on every level by her beauty and her mind. I think her skill at playing hard-to-get was working. I was certainly impressed with how much she had accomplished in the last 18 years, but I also felt a comfort when I was with her, and I also could feel that she was genuinely becoming interested in me. I could see it in the way her eyes would light up, glow, and soften every time we would meet.

Then, judgment day happened.

It was 5:15 p.m., and I was late getting to the parking lot. Cynthia was about to drive off when I arrived. So, I yelled and flagged her down just before she was about to pull into traffic. I stood in front of her car and held up my hand like a traffic cop, stopping traffic, and then I yelled:

"STOP, IN THE NAME OF LOVE!"

People all around could see and hear me. Some laughed at my temporary insanity. I walked casually over to the car and noted that her window was already open, which meant she'd heard me yell.

I looked into her beautiful hazel eyes and said, "I'm so glad I got to see you again, because I found out just 20 minutes ago that tomorrow is my last day working downtown. I'm being reassigned to the Torrance office. I just wanted you to know I'm really going to miss walking and talking with you every day. And then, I went on in detail about all the things I'd enjoyed about our friendship and how phenomenal I thought she was.

I finished by telling her I thought this was our judgment day, and it was time to stop playing around and have our first official date. I asked her to go home and sleep on it and tell me tomorrow morning. Then I turned away and she drove off without saying a word, but squealing her car wheels as she jumped into the downtown traffic.

I could see the sadness in her eyes the moment I started talking, and I remember thinking as she drove away that maybe she was, for the first time, really feeling me and would truly miss me.

I had officially "closed the sale" and given her an easy, simple "call to action" – just like the salesmen's books advised. I had been completely serious, cool, and matter of fact. This was no game, no joke.

The next morning, I arrived at my usual time, and she was waiting for me in her car. *Interesting*, I thought, *she beat me here*. I got out of my car and started to walk toward her, noticing that she seemed nervous. And then she opened her car door and got out, dressed to kill. She was looking so damned fine I could scarcely breathe. Like a million dollars in her tight-fitting casual Friday Jordache Jeans and red high heels. *Tony,* I thought, *you are definitely out of your league. What are you going to do with all this woman?*

She walked toward me, all seriousness, like a woman on a mission. When she was about 16 inches from my personal space, I could see her hands shaking nervously. She stared deeply into my eyes and whispered so softly I could hardly hear her.

"Okay, you win."

And then she sighed with relief as if she had just set down a ton of bricks that had been balanced on her head.

"Really? What did I win?" I asked, somewhat stupidly.

"ME!" she responded.

"Oh, shit…oh my goodness," was all I could think. My heart was racing as it dropped like the Freefall ride at Six Flags Magic Mountain. Time stood still. My emotions were so jumbled, I could hardly think anything except, *Oh shit, what am I going to do with all this woman?*

Somehow, I quelled the panic attack. Feeling clumsier and more off-center than at any time in our relationship, as I realized game over, I sprang into action, seized her in my arms and hugged her so tightly right there in the parking lot in front of all those passersby…and I didn't even care who saw us. Apparently, neither did she. We just stood there, locked in a full, tight embrace…and there is where the scene, Hollywood-style, must fade to black, leaving you to imagine the rest.

But on that day, for the first time in my life, the world stopped briefly to celebrate "judgment day". It was just the two of us, and time had stopped. In that final moment, in that parking lot, I experienced a surprising flood of emotions that touched me like a tsunami, and I realized for the first time that I was no longer pretending. What had been a game, a passing of time in a fun flirtation, had suddenly ended. This was real life. It took a while before I realized that this woman on this day wasn't smiling or playing around.

In fact, she never had been – and if I'd been a bit more mature, and a bit more sensitive, I'd have known it from the git-go. She was saying, "I'm yours, and you're mine."

This wasn't about a damn date. Single moms don't date if they've had their hearts broken often enough. Nope. This woman was surrendering and agreeing to give her complete self to me, working 110 percent on a future together. She was all in. All that I could think about at that moment was, *I have a girlfriend, I think, and I'm happy about it!*

And here I am on this damn bicycle today, trying to sort out my head and realizing that I am now in the middle of an exclusive journey – one that I'd never really thought through. Uncharted territory for me. I'd never been with an older woman eight years my senior, and it felt quite different and more mature than previous relationships. But I was excited —and I remain excited to take on the challenge. And on this morning, I am still way too immature to realize what a treasure I had been handed by this good and beautiful woman. She is one of the many angels God has sent me to guide, protect, and care for me along the way.

They say that we encounter three types of relationships on our lifetime journey: A relationship for a reason. A relationship for a season. A relationship for a lifetime.

On that bicycle ride this morning, it is clear that Cynthia was checking two out of three of those boxes. And I am eternally grateful that she showed up when she did and had the grace, skill, and presence of mind to share herself on her terms with a boy working hard at becoming a man.

Thank you, Cynthia, and thank you, Jamal, for enriching my life. And thank you, God, for guiding me through the deep waters toward a measure of maturity and sensitivity.

The next four years with Cynthia would prove to be a significant bookend, marking the beginning of my journey into the logistics business. It chronicles much of my spiritual growth and maturity, as well as the challenges and struggles I encountered, personally and professionally. I grew up and matured a great deal in those four years as I approached my thirties. I would not have survived Roadway without her encouragement, love, and support, and for that, I'm profoundly grateful to her and Jamal. I hope they can say that we all benefited from our journey together.

Okay, that's enough reflection. It's time for me to go home – to my little two-bedroom humble abode of an apartment and start preparing for tonight's supervisory debut.

Okay, Roadway, you win. For now. I yelled out loud as I looked at myself in the bathroom mirror. Then, I started reciting the scroll marked 2 from *The Greatest Salesman in The World*.

"I will greet this day with love in my heart. For this is the greatest secret of success in all ventures. Muscle can split a shield and even destroy life, but only the unseen power of love can open the hearts of men..."

CHAPTER EIGHT

CHANGING THE GAME

"CHANGE THE GAME.
Don't let the game change you."
– Macklemore

Over a lifetime, there have been many special moments when I clearly remember making a decision that would shift my life's course for good or bad. Truly, choosing to go to work for Roadway Express has been one of those moments. This one decision, which was supposed to have been a four-month summer job, would begin a 40-year spiritual journey. From the first day on the job, it's been a life-changing experience of learning about myself and my level of patience, understanding, and awareness when working with adults. It's been as life-changing as going back to college and obtaining an advanced degree in human behavior.

I have now expanded my private reading and study program and am currently reading six key books: *How to Have Confidence and Power in Dealing with People*, by Les Giblin, *The Game of Life and How to Play It*, by Florence Scovel Shinn, *The Greatest Salesman in the World*, by Og Mandino, *The Dynamic Laws of Prosperity*, by Catherine Ponder, and *Think and Grow Rich*, by Napoleon Hill. And last, but by no means least, the Bible. I have come to understand and believe that leaders are readers.

Each day, as part of getting ready for work, I am now reciting Scroll #1 and #2 from The Greatest Salesman, three times a day, plus I'm meditating. This is all part of a conscious effort to create my own fool-proof system for success. So far, the only part of this incipient system that isn't working is my apparent inability to get eight hours of sleep in the daytime.

Despite my previous jitters, the first three weeks as the new Outbound Supervisor have gone well. I still dislike the hours, but I'm starting to get the hang of things. Apparently, Dan is satisfied, because he's giving Richard, the lead Outbound Supervisor, two additional days of vacation, so I can run the Outbound shift alone. Truthfully, I think I'd prefer that Richard be gone permanently, because, to be honest, this job is easy and at times, boring, and sometimes, he's actually in my way. I feel restricted being under him. It's hard for me to be me with him around. In fact, if I could get the Teamsters to cooperate a bit better, this wouldn't be a bad job.

For the most part, most of the Teamster Brotherhood are good guys, but there are a couple of really bad apples that truly test my patience. They're on Roadway management's "hit list", and everyone knows who they are. The management team would like to get them fired, and whichever manager is successful getting that done could have a long and prosperous future at "The Big R". It's a matter of catching them in the act of wrongdoing and taking the necessary steps to get them fired. As I suspected when I was being trained, it seems that getting a bad employee terminated, and making it stick through the grievance process, is celebrated at the highest level of Roadway. I've been told that, if you're the manager who gets the job done, the top executive brass will fly down from Akron just to shake your hand and tell you that you have a job for life at Roadway.

Right now, however, my biggest challenge is about to come this Friday, without Richard there to help or interfere. Dan wants me to do what Richard has not done the last two Fridays. He wants me to close the entire operation down by 0200, without any overtime from the men. That's almost impossible to accomplish, especially on a Friday night when you have so many unpredictable circumstances. No overtime. Are you kidding me? I haven't seen anyone accomplish that feat yet since I started here, but maybe I will be the first.

I have the rest of tonight to work out the kinks before I'm thrown into a Friday night baptism by fire. What I know for sure is that Friday is our biggest pickup day, where we normally pick up between 400 and 500 Outbound bills. Richard, a five-year seasoned veteran, hasn't shown me how to do that yet. But they want me, a rookie, to do it. I'm not even sure Dan could do it, no matter how much he cracks the whip. I've carefully observed the last two Friday closeouts, and Richard always went over the limit by an hour or more. That may not sound like much, but overtime at double pay adds up quickly if you've got ten guys working. Dan's asking me to do something his long-time, loyal supervisor hasn't done, which means I haven't even seen a model for success. As casually as he'd ask me to pass him a Coke, he's asking me to do this. I may well have the same problem on Friday that Richard has, which means I'll spend the following Monday explaining to Dan why I wasn't successful. Unless he decides to call me over the weekend and pretend that the world is coming to an end. I've heard about him pulling that, just to get into someone's head. The man thrives on chaos and starting trouble. He's a hard taskmaster, but in many ways, I still respect him. I don't necessarily like him, nor do I trust him, but he's damned good at getting the most out of people. And he certainly knows how to challenge each person, which makes the job and the shift go quickly.

This afternoon, right before the shift begins, I get my full dose of Dan at his most typical.

"Guess what, Tony," he says with a big smile. "I told Richard not to come in today, because I want you to get your sea legs tonight, so you'll be ready for Friday."

"What's happening on Friday?" I asked.

"It's business as usual, but you'll be by yourself. I've got you all set up with a security clearance and your code to turn on the alarm once you close down."

"What? I thought Richard's vacation started next Monday," I reply, surprised.

"Yeah, but I want to reward him for taking on those double duties and helping out these last weeks after we lost Earl," he said.

Immediately realizing that there was no point in arguing, I just nod. He isn't asking permission; he's just informing me of his decision. I figure I can and will do it, and immediately start thinking about the positives. Like having total autonomy each night for the rest of this week and all next week. The challenge excites me.

Dan isn't through, though. "By the way," he says, "Richard tells me you're more than ready to take on the shift by yourself."

"How will we handle the Outbound shift when he comes back from vacation? We don't need both of us," I reply, puzzled.

"Glad you asked. He's going to be my new office manager/driver/inspector when he gets back," Dan says. (Which is a nice way to say he's going to manage the office staff while doing some private investigations on some of our drivers, those with poor performances.)

"Also," he continues, "I'm moving David to sales, and we're planning to increase our coverage, which means we may need to hire additional sales personnel next year."

For just a moment, I get excited, wondering if just maybe he is thinking about me for one of the new sales positions. It makes me happy just to consider it, and also makes me resolve to increase my production on the dock and hit new record highs – because I might really end up in sales in less than a year. However, my immediate second thought is, *Well, yeah, but if I become too good at my job, they might consider me indispensable and therefore the least likely to be promoted.* Now that's crazy. One can get too good at doing one's job.

So, that's how my management career in logistics kicked off. For the next several months, I'd be working the dock as the Outbound Supervisor, and later on, I switched with Jim and moved to Inbound. In some ways, I preferred Outbound, mostly because it was much easier to get the equivalent of a night's sleep if I got to sleep at 0300 or 0400 while it was still dark. However, Inbound was more challenging, and because of that, I enjoyed it more, although it was nearly impossible for me to start my sleep at 0900 and 1000 in the morning and expect to stay asleep. When I was working Inbound, I was a walking zombie, but all the while, I had the one person, the one constant I could rely on: Cynthia. Her love, support, and encouragement were absolutely critical to my survival, growth, and development in the early years of my new career.

It's funny how, after that first weekend together, Kim and David were so far in the past I could scarcely remember how stupid the whole thing was. And I never, ever needed to recite "I am not a victim" again. Along with that lovey-dovey office-romance couple, the surreal week in sales was quickly becoming a fading dream. At times, I questioned if it had even happened or if I had simply imagined it.

Over the years, reflecting on that garage scene at Cynthia's, I've realized that it was, and clearly remains a definite "deal breaker." Cynthia was all business that day. She definitely changed the game for me. They say that a lion doesn't have to roar for you to know it's a lion. That was

Cynthia, that morning, holding me hostage to my immaturity, as she stood firmly planted, almost pinning me to the wall. I've never forgotten that moment. She was so beautiful, but trust me, at that moment, I didn't see anything beautiful about her. She had stepped into her power. Her little 5'3" frame was standing in my direct path to freedom, blocking my escape while my heart skipped a beat, and my breathing became irregular. She wanted answers then and there.

That day, one of my lessons was that you never, ever mess with a mama lion's cubs. She'll hurt you and be prepared to die to protect them. Here I was, meeting her "pride and joy", and I needed to step up or get out. She had seemed possessed. Seething with fury, her eyes piercing through me, she was ready to spring into action and devour me if I didn't immediately say the right words in the right voice and with sincere humility.

Sitting here at work in the quiet hours of the night, I am finding myself returning to that pivotal moment, remembering it, but also feeling yet again the terror I'd felt just three weeks ago. That feeling of being lonely, trapped, perhaps a bit depressed, and wondering again what I've gotten myself into, personally and professionally.

Not the job. The job's okay. It's Cynthia, and that's a whole other kettle of fish. I can't wait to see her again. Among other things, I miss her good cooking. I'm excited to have been invited to be an assistant coach on Jamal's soccer team. They have a big game Saturday morning, and I'll be one of the assistants, mainly on the sidelines, offering encouragement and passing out water or Gatorade, since I certainly don't have time to attend weekday practices or be the head coach. As happy as Cynthia makes me, I only get to see her on weekends. We talk a lot while I'm at work, but we live for those weekends.

Nighttime can be lonely if your job includes the dark hours, which, if you let them, will play head games with your mind. Yet, when I experience a moment of clarity, it's obvious that Cynthia is falling in love with me. I can't forget what Jamal said about not seeing her this happy in the five years since the divorce. Now that I've met Jamal, I'm scared I'll ultimately hurt her, and in the process, let him down. The last thing I want to do is mess up this young Black boy's life. I want to be there for him, no matter what happens to me and Cynthia.

Working these night hours has unexpectedly revealed to me also that I have serious jealousy issues, something I'm definitely not proud of. They're worse during those dead hours of the shift, and if I seclude myself in the office, away from the action too long, I think all kinds of crazy thoughts – the ones that kick in about 2300 hours, heading into midnight. Is Cynthia really asleep? Or is she home in bed with another man—maybe the old boyfriend I've never met? It's way too easy to let my mind run down the rabbit hole. Ever been there? It's worse when you're at work – basically a prisoner for those hours with too much time to think.

"Hey, Tony, can you come outside? We've got a serious Hazmat problem," Michael interrupts my thoughts, through the driver dispatch window. I like Michael. He's one of the best dock workers, and already, I feel as if he can be trusted.

"Sure, Mike. Be right there," It takes me a minute to pull my mind back to business, but I handle Mike's problem and return to the office where I try – but not very hard – to master my mind. I *hate* these crazy hours. Maybe I should try to meet a female doctor or nurse who works nights, so we could have fun in the sun and play in the day.

I could almost appreciate the job and its challenge if it were in the daytime, but that's not only not the case, but I can expect that the next two years will be years of crazy nighttime hours with too much time to think. The more I want out of this night life, the deeper it seems to be pulling me in. Dan's promise of promotion to sales in two years is already starting to fade in only three weeks – and it no longer seems valid or important. What is important, I know, is doing this job every night with all my energy and attention. It's not the time for dreaming or obsessing about a love affair. *Please, God,* I pray, *don't let me die with my music still inside me.*

As I brace to prepare for the next tidal wave of drivers who will arrive in the next hour, my men must be ready with the next set of loaded trailers headed outbound to Adelanto, since we receive linehaul drivers constantly through the evening. Each linehaul driver brings in our inbound loads for the following business day, which we will start breaking around midnight. This inbound/outbound process is a precise, predictable, and well-oiled machine. I must admit that this company is efficient and damn good at our system. This part I do like and appreciate about Roadway. Later, as I start to move around from job to job in the industry, I'll discover just how advanced, predictable, and efficient Roadway's cookie-cutter supply chain system is, compared to the other companies, especially other union trucking companies.

The goal is to not allow the linehaul drivers to sit and wait, because they're being paid while waiting, and if they run out of hours, we'll have to bed them down for the evening, which is another expense. So, the intent is to have them in and out in 30 minutes, or we'll definitely hear about it in the morning from Dan and his new Assistant Manager, Todd.

I don't like the new guy, Todd. He's a stone prick. Someone like that shouldn't be given any power over people, because he'll misuse it. He's not a good leader. He's an enforcer of Roadway Policy. Roadway has a well-oiled machine, and in many ways, things work smoothly on their own. The employees generally are professional and know what they're doing. They don't need micro-management, because they'll work faster if I don't stand over their shoulders. I continue to believe, as I did the first time I walked onto the property, that as management, we need to learn how to be more respectful to one another and not micro-manage the workers. And that's one of my quiet personal goals. I want to change the game.

It was over this particular issue that I made a typical rookie mistake and experienced Dan at his most fierce. I've never liked the way Dan describes "Teamsters" and "Casual workers" as if they're sub-human and expects us to treat them both the same, except you can treat the Casual even worse. He has made it very clear that he expects me to treat them both very harshly. I can't do that, and I can't believe this man, a Terminal Manager, is talking about treating human beings more cruelly than you treat animals. Now, I see how Ronnie Luster got so brainwashed and misguided. Dan believes my men already like me too much and has "counseled me". He told me that during the week I was absent, due to my assignment to work and observe sales, five or six Teamsters had asked about me and said they were hoping I wouldn't quit. Two of the Teamsters, he said, had referred to me as a "good find". It took a moment to realize that in Dan's mind, that was not a compliment, and he was just warming up.

"Let me tell you right now, Mister, that it's not a good thing around here if Teamsters like you. You'd better watch yourself, and I mean it." Obviously, he wasn't joking, and he was just warming up. "Furthermore," he continued, "you haven't been here three months and already you've created a new practice where they can play music on the dock when they're working."

"What's wrong with that, Dan?" I made the mistake of asking. "I like listening to music when I work."

He was so mad, that he slammed his notepad down on his desk. "You just don't get it, do you? We're not running a nursery for Teamsters. Next thing I know, you'll be giving them 30-minute sleep breaks. We pay these guys good money to work hard and not pass the damn time away. Now, because you did this, for the rest of eternity, they can play the damn music on the dock, instead of focusing on doing their jobs."

"I'm sorry, Dan, but I like music, too. It makes the shift go faster."

"For your information, we're not trying to make the shift go faster. We want the MEN to go faster. It's not designed to be fun and easy. You need to get this through your head. These are Teamsters, and I've already told you how you're supposed to treat them. I like making Teamsters suffer, and believe me, they like making us suffer. Damn, this feels like a Jimmy Hoffa standoff. Now I gotta listen to all this damn heavy metal crap and rap music on the radio when I get to work in the morning, and it's all because of you."

Oh. Suddenly, I realized what I'd done. My "friends", the Teamsters, had tricked me. They got me good on this one. Hell, I didn't know playing music wasn't acceptable according to management rules. But because I'd said "yes", they can now play music. It's going to become a new ruling based on "past practice", where music is allowed now at LBC, and it's all my fault. The truth is, I hope they win this one, because I like music, too, and I'm starting to not like Dan as much. He's becoming a thorn in my side. Further, I'm not sure everything he told me when we had lunch is true, especially the part about me getting the chance to go into sales in two years. I knew I'd definitely have to think about the implications of this inadvertent misadventure. For the moment, I put Dan and the music out of my mind and concentrate on getting the job in front of me done.

I'm learning so much being here, and yes, working nights has its pros and cons. I'm learning more about myself, how to challenge myself and push past adversity and self-doubt, even while being deprived of sleep. I've thought a lot about that chewing out, though, and wondered how I could turn it to my advantage. The more I think about it, the more

I realize there are possibilities for quiet, more humane treatment of my subordinates.

One really big kudo I give myself is that I've begun learning to play union politics to get ahead. There's this one big guy, a Teamster representative named Dewey, also known as Big Dewey or Big D, who's the leader of the Teamster dock workers at LBC. He oversees the local union and every one of his teamster brothers is terrified of him. Nothing happens on the dock without his approval. If he tells one of his guys to "slow down, you're working too fast", you'd better slow your ass down or get ready to rumble. If he tells one of them to pick up the pace, they'd better start running.

Big Dewey is The Man. He's about 6'6" and he wears his hair in a ponytail with a blue bandana tied around his forehead. He's so big, and reminds me of that big, tall Native American guy who played the character in the movie, *One Flew Over the Cuckoo's Nest*, opposite Jack Nicholson. What Big D says, goes? If I want these men to work faster and smarter for me, I've got to get Big D on board. I need his buy-in and belief that I'm going to play fair and do right by them. I'm positive that's one of the things they really want; to be treated fairly as human beings with courtesy and respect. But they also want to earn a certain level of extra money, which is why sometimes they will slow the work pace to make overtime, even if it costs us money on the back end, with driver delays and inbound loads not worked on time.

My only tool, as Ronnie Luster so elegantly put it, is the "power of the pen", which is to give warning letters often to bad actors, in order to send a message. I don't like it, but that's my recourse for a slowdown. I wait and find errors, and when someone makes a mistake, I give them a warning letter. Two warnings equals a suspension without pay, which causes all kinds of personal disruption. Personally, I hate the game, but it's my only weapon to change the behavior. They know just as I do, that there are rules you can't break and certain consequences if you break them. I, too, must adhere to the rules, or they'll file a grievance on my violation, so it goes both ways.

For example, I can't do union work. I can't drive the truck. I can't operate the forklift. I can't lift the boxes or sort the (I/B and O/B) bills. If I violate those and other rules, I'm stealing union wages and denying a Teamster employee a job. So, they'll file a grievance on my actions and probably win. That's how the game is played.

At Dan's level, he's always trying to stack the deck in hopes of making a termination stick. So, as an example, on any given night, he may call (or leave a note) and tell me to get him three warning letters: one each on Marques, Brown, and Garcia. "Have them on my desk first thing in the morning."

Now it happens that these particular men are my three best and fastest workers. It doesn't matter. There's a reason why he wants it, and I'd better deliver it without fail. There's a method to his madness. We're not really going after our good workers, but we have to balance the files for the many warning letters we're giving annually to bad performers.

Bottom line – I don't question his direct order. I just need to do it. I need to find three mistakes they made and give them warning letters for those actions. So, in a system like this, in the course of a year, even the best workers may have three or four warning letters in their file, because the bad actors will have enough to plaster their bathroom walls. And I'd better find and produce those three warning letters and have them signed and delivered on Dan's desk in the morning, or I am fired. End of story. No questions asked. Once I argued with Dan, pointing out that those were my three best workers.

"Are you saying they're perfect?" Dan asked. "Get me my damn warning letters and have them on my desk at 0700 hours, or don't bother coming in to work tomorrow."

Some of the managers love this bullshit. They eat it up. They love playing God with the Teamsters and making them do stuff. In the early 80s, a lot of freight came in as loose boxes and bundles. One of the toughest loads to give to a man to unload was a 48-foot or 53-foot trailer full of Huffy Bicycle Tires, loose in bundles. That was cruel and unusual punishment. It was a back breaker, and you usually saved it for your bad actors, or a Casual who was hungry to work. I wanted desperately to change some of that; try to hit the restart button for fairness for all, but I didn't know how to create that trust so quickly. This was systemic punishment and unfair treatment, entrenched in the DNA of these men and women and the companies that they worked for, and it's part of the history going back to 1903, the inception of The International Brotherhood of Teamsters, when men made deliveries driving with horse and carriage. (Note: FYI... Today, the entire Huffy load would be double stacked on several pallets and would easily take one man and a forklift less than an hour to unload)

Well, I had made up my mind I was going to somehow find a way to be different. I just wished that Dan and some of those other managers would stop acting like General Patton. Some reminded me so much of Ronnie Luster it was ridiculous. I decided that my first approach to a change should start quietly with Big D. I truly didn't believe anything could change without his buy-in.

I take a walk on the dock purposely to talk with him. I feel my answer to get more production can only be resolved somehow through him. He's working in Door 42, very busy stacking huge boxes. I can't help noticing that this man is all man, strong as an ox. The kind of guy you do not want to get into a bar fight with. I offer him one of my cigarettes and ask him to take a cigarette break and come into the office with me, so we can talk.

He seems surprised, then he says with a smile, "I'll come in 20 or 30 minutes after I finish closing out this trailer. You're going to need it ready when the drivers get here, so I don't want to mess you up."

"Well, okay," I reply. "High and tight, baby. I'll be in the office when you're done." I'm not sure what I'll say to him, but I know we need the conversation and my respect for who he was to the men, if I want to win." He comes in, happy and pleasantly upbeat. This big, tall guy seems honored to be asked to take a break and join me in the office to talk. This moment comes to symbolize the beginning of both a friendship and a bond.

In a symbolic gesture of equality, I take off my tie in front of him. I only realize later that dock workers and drivers are rarely invited to come inside the main office to sit and talk. Most never see past the drivers' break room. Occasionally, it might happen at night, but not so much in the day, that a dock worker might need to make an emergency phone call and the pay phone is already in use by someone else. If they asked specially, and say it was an emergency, I'd already made a practice of allowing it, because I had understood intuitively that it's not easy working these hours and trying to be head of a family. A person's whole life on the night shift is being on the other side of the clock from one's spouse and children.

I offer Big D a cigarette again and get him some coffee, and we both light up our cigarettes. "I already know what you're going to say," he says.

"You do?" I asked.

"Hell yes, man I've seen this thing for the last ten years, and do you know how many guys like you have tried to do this job and crashed and burned? Many don't last a month."

"No. Honestly, I don't know."

"In the last five years, I've probably seen at least 20 of you guys come through here," he said.

"Damn! So, y'all already figure I'm not gonna make it, right?"

Big D laughs. "Yeah, well we think you'll make it for about three more months before you find something else and call it quits."

"Big D, I don't want that story, man, but you're probably right. I might not make it. This is insanity, some of the stuff they have us doing; and then you guys, when you start slowing down on me, I can't explain that shit, man, not to Dan. You KNOW how anal Dan is," I sighed.

"Hey, I wanna whup Dan's ass so bad I can taste it," says Big D.

"Listen, I know y'all want some overtime, but I can't get the shift done and get drivers out on time when y'all start laying down on me. Dan's on my ass first thing every damn day, whenever I see him about getting rid of all the overtime. Honestly, I already feel like quitting, because the way it looks, it's a lose-lose proposition. I wish I could be the best to ever do this job, man, but I can't do it without your help," I said.

"Why should I help you?" he asks, mildly.

"Because I'm for real, man, I really do care about you and the guys, but we got a fucking job to do, and some of those guys are screwing me, and you know it. They aren't working, and you know who they are better than I do. You know all their little tricks and secrets, but you're their leader. They'll change for you and do whatever you say. I can't change shit, especially these work conditions, Big D, but I care and I'm respectful, and I don't want to quit. If I quit, you're just gonna get somebody new that will make your life just as miserable as the other 20. At least with me, it's not my intent to make you miserable. But you and I both know that Dan and Todd can come in here tomorrow and make all our lives miserable. I guess we'll just have to live with those isolated moments of misery, 'cause it ain't gonna change no matter how mad you or I get. This is just a damn game, man, and we all got to eat. I want you to know I respect you and I just want us to develop a mutual working understanding and open communication with each other when it's just us here at night. When it's just us, this is our world, baby, and we can do what we want to do. We can get the work done and have fun, too. That's all I got – my word that I'll do right by you guys whenever I can, and when I can't, then you know the deal and you know the drill, and it is what it is."

Big D stares at me, takes another drag off his cigarette and a sip of coffee, and then he says, "You stay in the office about ten minutes and then put your tie back on and come out on the dock. I'm gonna have a meeting with the guys. You come out in ten minutes and interrupt our meeting, like you're just curious about why we're having a meeting during crunch time. Okay? You leave the rest to Big Dewey."

So, I wait, and look out the window and all I can see is Big D pointing fingers, cussing, and eyeballing guys as he gets in people's chests. Man, he's looking scary as hell, and threatening like he's gonna whip somebody's ass. I watch the clock closely, and then, its's time. I walk out, but before I could speak, I hear, "Tony, can you come here for a moment?"

"Yeah, what's going on?" I ask.

"I just want to make sure everyone's officially met you, and that they know you're our new Outbound Supervisor. So, guys, like I was saying, this is Tony Harris, our new supervisor, and we're going to do whatever it takes to make this dock one of the best in the company. Anything you want to say, Tony?" Big D turned to me.

"Ah, yes! Thanks, Big D. Hey guys, I just want y'all to know I'm honored to be working with you guys. Richard is going to be moving inside the office as Office Manager, and I'm going to be solely in charge of Outbound for now. It's gonna be just us at night on the Outbound shift, and Jim, my partner in crime will be handling Inbound, so crank up the music, Mike, and let's have some fun, and let's load these trailers high and tight."

That's all I say, and they start clapping like we we're getting ready to play a football game. It isn't my best speech, but it seems to work.

"We're all gonna be here," I say, as they continue clapping, "so we might as well try and enjoy it. Y'all know I've got to get six loads ready in the next two hours, right? So, help me out, guys. Let's close them out high and tight, and let's go home, so this Inbound shift can get going."

Everyone laughs and claps, and we are off to a new beginning. It's like day and night how much faster everyone's working, even the bad actors. I instantly start to see faster movement and a sense of urgency in each man as they proceed in their respective jobs. This is incredible and unprecedented.

I come back around, close to the end of the shift and do a quick "huddle up" to tell them, "I know y'all like drinking a cold one in the parking lot on Fridays after we shut down, so tomorrow, I'm gonna chip in and bring a case of beer, too."

Man, they really start cheering and clapping then.

"Also, y'all be sure and save me a couple. I'll join you as soon as I closeout my paperwork and set the alarm. And one last thing: I sure would appreciate it if we could do one more thing tomorrow night." I pause and take a deep breath. "No overtime on Friday! Can we do something that would be historic and unprecedented? Can we close out on time without any overtime?"

The applause is silent on that statement, but I had said it boldly, anyway. I'll be curious what happens with this one at our Friday closeout. This is a special moment for all of us. So, I close it out by restating that the beer was on me, which gets me another burst of applause. Dang, I'd better stop while I'm ahead, I realize.

As I walk away, I started thinking about my days as an athletic coach and how I could get players inspired to exceed their limitations. Then, I thought about my mother and how proud she'd be of me right now. She and my dad raised me to treat people right, and this truly is a moment when I was saying to a group of men that I would do my best to do right by them, at least within the limits of the game we play as Managers and Teamsters.

At the end of the shift, Big Dewey circled back and came into the office as we were winding down. "Que paso, amigo," he says.

"Big D, my man, gracias," I reply.

"Looks like you hit a home run, Tony T. Now don't blow it," he says.

"I promise I'll try like hell not to," I reply.

Looking back today, I realize what a special moment that was in my professional life. I learned the real value and power of identifying critical circles of influence, and then influencing key players (with integrity) inside that circle.

Oh, in case you were wondering, I didn't quite close down at 0200 on early Saturday morning, but we did close at 0215, which was pretty damn good production for a rookie.

CHAPTER NINE

BURN THE BOATS

"Success is no accident. It is hard work, perseverance,
learning, studying, sacrifice, and MOST of all,
love of what you are doing."
– Pele

Then Big Dewey and I raised our Bud Light beer cans to the heavens, along with the other men, and we all shouted repeatedly, *"To the best damn Outbound Team in Southern California! To the best damn Outbound team in Southern California!"*

Then, Big Dewey raised his Bud Light once more. "To our new leader! Our New Boss! Tony T., may you survive and thrive, my man. We got your back!"

And all the fellows started yelling back in enthusiastic approval. Then, a familiar chant rose from the group. The kind of chant you hear in war movies, sounding like something the Marines would yell:

"Hoorah! Hoorah!"

My throat closed with emotion as I realized the honor they had just shown me. In that moment, I knew they had unconditionally accepted me and my leadership style. They were ALL IN, and so was I. There was no turning back. "HOORAH!"

And we all realized, at 3:00 a.m., in the Roadway's parking lot, that we'd just established a sacred code of conduct, unique only to us. We'd confirmed our secret bond, not with a handshake, and not with a signature on the dotted line. Just each man simply raising his beer can and pointing upwards toward the stars. The covenant was officially signed, sealed, and delivered.

But it wasn't over yet. As we continued to huddle around, laughing, talking, drinking, and listening to music, we began considering the night's assorted challenges and the sweet victories of success. I will never forget the pride in the voice of Mike, a quiet accountant type, and my Number One Guy as he spoke up to remind us in detail of the significant goal we'd achieved by nearly eliminating overtime costs on a busy Friday night shift. Collectively, we realized that by our joint cooperation, we'd achieved a small, but astonishing miracle.

Wow!

As a practical matter, these men had just, hypothetically, taken money from their own pockets and food off their tables, and worked harder and faster to make us all look good as a team. And here we were, with dawn on the way, in that huge parking lot, where it didn't seem like such a preposterous stretch to simply say to each other, "I'm going to start treating you better, respecting you and your opinions more; and in turn, you're going to start demonstrating a more reliable and predictable sense of urgency and priority in your work." As for me, it wasn't a real stretch either, to promise I'd treat my fellow human beings with basic human kindness and fairness. This moment in time was symbolic and represented UNITY for ALL, the moment we ALL became ONE!

It should have been part of our birthright, but somehow in the chaos of the 1980s, our world of transportation logistics remained locked in the mentality of "Them vs. Us." I wasn't at all sure we could pull this off permanently, but we sure as hell felt confident that morning, especially after two or three beers, that we intended to re-establish the fundamental code of conduct which honored and respected everyone, at least at the LBC/820 Outbound dock.

For now, in this moment, the world was just fine; and we knew that, for this moment at least, all was okay. Even though we all knew that Dan and Todd could throw a monkey wrench into the machinery any time and destroy everything we'd just built.

I looked around at them, really seeing them for the very first time. I realized that several had served in Viet Nam and were still recovering, struggling with the very personal challenges that war causes. It was a sobering thought for me. I hadn't had to serve in that war, missing it by only a fraction of a year, but I had many friends who did serve, and some who gave the ultimate sacrifice. The 1960s and 1970s had been a terrible time: Vietnam, the Civil Rights Movement, the Watts riots, the horrific deaths of President Kennedy, Medgar Evers, Malcom X, Martin Luther King, Jr., and later on in the same year, Bobby Kennedy, were just a few of the difficult and disappointing battles that had dominated our minds and shaped our country, for good or bad, into what now, in the 1980s, was our America.

More and more, I was finding how applicable the materials I'd been studying so carefully were to this new life I was experiencing. Like one of Napoleon Hill's examples in his book, *Think and Grow Rich*: the tale of a great warrior who was faced with a terrible, decisive battlefield decision on which success would depend. He was about to send his armies against a much larger, more powerful foe, so he loaded his soldiers into boats and sailed to the enemy's country. He unloaded soldiers and equipment. Then, he gave the order: BURN THE BOATS! – the ones that had carried them to the battle. Addressing his troops before the battle, he said, "You see the boats going up in smoke. That means we cannot leave these shores alive unless we win! We now have no choice – we win, or we perish." They won.

Hill continues, making the point that every person who wins in an undertaking must be willing to burn his boats and cut all sources of retreat. Only by doing so can he be sure to maintain the _burning desire to win_ that is essential to success. I knew a bit about "burning desire to win". All my life, beginning back in high school, I'd been reading on the fly, learning and receiving confirmation at each turn about what I'd been doing to achieve success. I had long had that instinctive burning desire Hill was writing about, and he presented many stories illustrating the need to possess this relentless mindset. It is the winner's attitude that one must adopt. That Saturday morning, as I raised my Bud Light to the heavens one last time, I knew I'd personally received the message loud and clear: "You, yourself, must burn your boats, Tony, you must. Or you will surely perish."

As I pondered that idea, I realized I'd already done that. I was way too far into this new discipline to turn around. I'd already committed my life to this idea, just as Bill had warned me that very first day. Truthfully, though, I'd been doing it unconsciously for years. My abrupt resignation from the teaching job in South Texas and my decisive move to Southern California last year was only the latest of my many boat burnings.

I raised my Bud Light one more time, in total ecstasy, as if I'd discovered a secret success formula, which I now silently declared:

"I am all in. No fear. No retreat. No plan B."

It was getting close to 3:30 a.m., and even before I popped my third and final cold one, I knew, with the certainty of the most proven psychic, that I could, in fact, do this job, and I could lead these men and women to a new level of success and victory over the next couple of years. I also realized that morning that I was willing to commit two years; but once they ended, I'd be ready to move onward and upward. I knew in my soul that it would then be time for me to go into sales.

I looked at my watch. It was getting toward 3:45 a.m. on Saturday, and we all needed to get home to our families and our other lives. There would be lots for me to ponder on the long drive to Cynthia's, where I hoped she would be wide awake and ready to share my new discoveries. In any case, the drive would give me time to process the amazing lesson I'd just seen demonstrated. And so, after saying my goodbyes to Big Dewey and the guys, I drove slowly away. Carefully, as I was realizing I'd drunk my fair share of Bud Light – but also, metaphorically, I'd also chugalugged down a fifth of "Roadway's Kool-Aid". I was technically, but not officially, ALL IN. I didn't scream it from the mountain top of Yosemite, and so far, I didn't have my Big R tattoo branded on my left butt cheek, but I was definitely ALL IN. Lots to ponder. *What a difference 48 hours can make*, I thought, in wonder. My meeting with Big Dewey two days ago had become a game-changer that made all the difference and might well prove to be one of the smartest career moves I'd ever made, considering the hand of cards I'd been dealt. I knew in my soul that if I could successfully change the game, it would pay big-time dividends for both Big D and me.

Now, from my vantage point 40 years later, I remain eternally grateful to Big Dewey, to whom I owe a huge eternal thank you! In the 1980s, in our industry, the prevailing truth was that it was not easy and certainly not popular to make friends with a Teamster, nor could you be both buddy and boss. I didn't believe it at the time, and I don't believe it now. We were all once just kids. Then, one day, we grew up and adopted labels and titles and life assignments. Big Dewey could have easily been one of my best junior high or high school friends, before labels and titles were placed on our foreheads. He could have been a right tackle or defensive end at my high school; my protector in football, my post man on the basketball team. He could have thrown the discus and shot put in track and field, and he could have come to the house for Sunday dinners with my family. We could have ridden around town, checking out the young ladies in the area, maybe even have attended church together and gone to summer Baptist Bible Conventions.

Bottom line, during that short couple of days, I saw who he really was: a man with a big heart, if he was approached with respect. And if you didn't, you might get your ass handed to you on a platter. So, I must respectfully disagree with those who think that you can't be both buddy and boss. There's a way to walk that line, and that day, I'd just found it. Over the years, I've continued to believe that people are just people. If we are to survive, we must get past the fears and stereotypes that divide us. I have personal experience with that "divide", for I have been affected by it my whole life, in terms of my treatment by the majority because of the color of my skin. It's natural to fear that which is different and unfamiliar.

Skin color can be a real challenge initially for many of my fellow citizens. For me, however, I always recognize this challenge as an inconvenience, a worthy test I can nearly always overcome. Once they get to know me, we can begin to build a bridge. "To know me is to love me" is how I continue to live my life. My motto throughout my sales career and well before has always been, "I love all people and all people love me." I'm used to the apparent and initial resistance. It doesn't bother me, and I will persist until I succeed, because NOTHING can stop my progress. What I learned from that experience on that long ago night has never left me. There is an old saying that the two most important dates in a person's life are the day you are born, and the day you discover why you were born. And this day was the latter, because it revealed and confirmed the path I must follow in preparation and alignment to meet my "why", that which I was born to do.

Obviously, there were dynamics that were basic "givens" in the industry that were not going to change easily and had to be accepted – just like the Serenity prayer. For right now, the established lines were clear: one side for management, one side for the union, something determined well before I showed up, way back to 1903, even before Jimmy Hoffa. And those lines were formidable. Change would be slow and hard, but I believed at some level, I could be part of turning the ship around, like turning cold water hot.

What I'd just demonstrated was that, in only two nights, Big D and I were starting to establish our own subset of rules about how we'd get along at night on the dock, and what we might be able to accomplish in two months or two years. We weren't looking for short cuts or putting something over on the establishment. We were simply trying to get along and create a civilized work environment. That was it. Just basic things: respect, cordiality, cooperation, collaboration, dedication to a job well done – basic, fundamental things that would make for a better day, a better attitude, and overall, better persons, performances, and outcomes.

Before that Friday night shift began, Dan had left me a note earlier on his way out the door. I had read it right before I started the shift. Basically, it said, "Good job, Tony. Your bill count per man hours were up last night. Keep doing whatever you're doing, and you'll be blazing a new path for yourself and LBC. Don't start celebrating and writing your book yet, but whatever you're doing seems to be working. Glad to have you on the team. Dan"

I doubt Dan would have written that note if he could have seen all of us drinking beer together in the parking lot. I can't even imagine what he'd say if he knew about Big Dewey's and my collaboration. This new agreement didn't denote a "sell out" or a "treat a Teamster to lunch" campaign. My intent was simply to be consistently respectful, honest, fair, and friendly toward my staff. We all understood that if they mess up, the same rules may well apply, but everything is subject to negotiation. On the other hand, warning letters which are like parking citations, aren't negotiable and we all know it. Nothing has changed about the harsh warning letter rules, but at least we can do it civilly. Right is right and wrong is wrong.

Paying "overtime" in our industry has often been seen by the Union as an 'entitlement', one of the perks of the job for Teamsters. What I was requesting from these men was a paradigm shift – forfeit the overtime, move faster, work harder, and get finished by 2 a.m., and they did it. They did it for me, with Big Dewey's support and approval, and no one else. I still have unanswered questions about working in this type of environment, especially in a company which has such a strong union organization as its sole workforce provider. I'm learning on the job about what's possible, what's definitely not possible, and what might work later. Truthfully, I'm just holding on for dear life and trying to win. I will say, though, that after this weekend, there's a lot to celebrate. I see the men walking a little taller and faster, with a new sense of urgency and a pride I'd not witnessed in my first three months on the Outbound shift. We did that together.

Finally, my personal question that I had feared the most could now be answered. *Yes, I can manage adults, grown men and women, and get the most out of them! I CAN DO IT! HOORAH!* In my mind, I hear the last two lines of William Ernest Henley's famous poem, *Invictus*: "I am the master of my fate – I am the captain of my soul."

Look at me! I'm becoming a man – and it feels good.

Later that weekend, writing in my journal, I note: "I'm discovering my personal formula on 'how to lead and influence adults with integrity'. If, at the ripe old age of 27, I were to describe what I've learned, it would be this: "Be Authentic. Be Genuine. Be Confident. Be Sincere. Be Clear.

Be Honest. Be Vulnerable. Be Committed. Be Fair. Be You!" I'll let you know in 40 years if my initial assessment in leadership is correct." (*From a journal entry written August 1981.*)

As I pull into Cynthia's driveway, I'm still over the moon with my spectacular professional success and newly emerging maturity. Little do I realize I'm about to learn that my love life, wonderful as it has been in every way, isn't quite ready to match that new level of maturity.

I'm completely pumped as I enter Cynthia's spotless house. I wonder if I can wind down, and I know I'm definitely not sleepy. I wonder what her mood will be. After all, it's now after 4 a.m., and she'll probably be tired, but I can't wait to see her and tell her my good news.   T o my surprise, she's up and cooking my favorite new breakfast sandwich: hot links with jalapenos and onions (onions optional). That's a great sandwich. I never knew how much I liked this spicy-hot combination until Cynthia surprised me with it one day. And no one makes it like Cynthia. So, we sit at the kitchen table and talk and talk. I share with her how my leadership skills are winning, and even though it definitely is not the way my bosses lead, I've discovered it works for me.

Cynthia is attentive and excited when I tell her about Big Dewey and what a powerful influence he is on that dock.   And I can't help but notice how cute and sexy she is, in her oversized white t-shirt with little or nothing underneath. With food and relaxation, I'm surprised to find myself so incredibly sleepy I can hardly hold my eyes open. So, I sleepwalk to the bedroom, fall into bed, and sleep like a baby. She might be sexy as hell, but I'm pooped. Thank God she still has Brutus to hold.

I wake up, sort of, about three hours later from a deep sleep, when I hear the doorbell. I can't open my eyes or get up. I'm not even sure what day or time it is, or even where I'm sleeping. As I gradually regain consciousness, I can hear what sounds like two people whispering in the front room, followed by a light scuffle from the front door area in the living room.

Huh. I force my eyes open, realizing it's a man's voice I hear, louder and closer – and then Cynthia's voice raised in distress. "No, don't go in there, Ray," Cynthia yells.

From my place in the bedroom, it sounds like he's pushing his way past her. Before I can begin to react, I hear a man's voice yelling, "Where's that motherfucker?" And I realize he's already standing at the bedroom door, staring down at me.

"So, you're the motherfucker," he announces, loudly. "The new man of the house! Well, I got just one thing to say to your ass. You're layin' around and eating up all the food. Why don't you fix some shit around here?"

What the hell….am I dreaming? I'm still so tired and half-asleep that I have no energy to fight, which, in retrospect, probably saved my life.

"You layin' around enjoying yourself," he glares at me.

I don't say a word; just stare at him and keep my eyes locked on his concealed right hand.

"Why don't you FIX SOME SHIT around here?" he asks, loudly.

"Fix some shit" seems to be what he's fixating on as he moves closer, blocking my exit; and now he's standing directly over me as I lie there in bed in my underwear. As delusional as it seems, this feels like some surreal dream. I'm not feeling afraid. I feel somehow divinely protected, senseless as that sounds. It just doesn't feel as if it's my time to die. It feels more like God, or maybe my guardian angel, has my back 100 percent.

As things began to slow down, I remember that Cynthia used to joke about her "old man" who'd whip my butt and hers. And I wonder if today is the real moment of truth. What is he prepared to do? Shoot me? Cut me? Kill me? I have no idea what's concealed inside his warmup jacket, and he isn't about to take that damn right hand out of his pocket, nor shut up, for that matter. He just keeps shouting over and over, "When are you going to start fixing some shit around here?"

Finally, I gather myself up and begin to speak softly, very careful to keep any tension out of my voice. "What are you talking about?" I ask, mildly.

"You heard me! I said fix some shit!" he replies.

"Like what? What do you want me to fix, man?" Now, I allow my voice to sound a trifle agitated.

"Hell, man, I'm here to fix the damned kitchen cabinet right now. You should be doing that shit! Two weeks ago, I fixed the damn leak in the bathroom. You should have been doing that shit, too. You here enjoying yourself, but who does she call when she needs something fixed? Me. Mister Fix-It Man! I'm Mister Fix-It Man around this motherfucker, while you're lying around enjoying yourself with my ex-old lady."

Oh.

"Hey, man, I don't know you. This is the first time I've ever seen you, and I'm sorry if I'm causing you a problem by being here," I say carefully, keeping my voice mild.

"Nah, you ain't causing me any problems, but I'm about to cause your ass some if you don't come at me correct."

From outside the door, Cynthia is standing and pleading. "Come on, Ray.... Ray, you know that's not true. I never asked you to do any of that. You volunteered to fix everything you fixed. You volunteered, Ray. You *wanted* to do it, so don't act like you did me a favor. *You know* I would have taken care of that."

"Well, I'm just saying I did the shit. I volunteered, and I did the shit. Why didn't this motherfucker volunteer to do the shit?"

In my defense, at this point, I have no idea there had been a leaky pipe in the bathroom, nor do I know about the kitchen cabinets needing attention. Obviously, our relationship is still at the honeymoon level.

Needless to say, I am rapidly realizing that this is one of those times when "silence is golden." I am a man of very few words on this day, realizing that words won't help repair this situation. It's tense enough so that a tragic and permanent ending is a real possibility, and for the first time, I understand what a "crime of passion" could mean and look like.

This man is hurting and angry and feeling violated by me for being his chosen replacement. He is feeling a lot of conflicting emotions and just wants the pain to stop. It's pretty obvious that, in his mind, I'm the catalyst for the pain, and "dealing with me" will make the pain stop. Thankfully, the tension is beginning to lessen, and I can see him regain a measure of control and allow his "right mind" to emerge and prevail. As I lie there trying to pull my own right mind together, I wish briefly that Big Dewey were with me. Second thought, probably good he isn't.

Ray is still muttering like a broken record: "Why don't you fix some shit....fix some shit around here....damn leaking pipes in the bathroom.... damn cabinets need fixing....you need to fix some shit around here.... if you're going to be here....then you need to fix some shit....fix some shit....fix some shit, motherfucker...."

Finally, Cynthia walks timidly through the open door. "Ray, please, please come out of here." She gently touches him on his left shoulder, attempting to caress and guide him away. "Please. I need to talk to you."

Slowly, he begins to move away and back out the door, never taking his eyes off me. I assume she is convincing him to come back another time to "fix some shit", but the whole time, I can hear them talking in the living room.

Quietly and quickly, I dress and sit on the edge of the bed from the farthest side of the room, smoking a cigarette and listening to their verbal exchanges. I'm aware of one thing – an asterisk has been placed beside this relationship that might never recover. I wonder why she didn't ask Ray to go to the garage and help her find a hammer and some nails.... And then there was a 10-second relapse as I wonder briefly if I should have waited for her baby sister, Janelle, still expected in November. Presumably, Janelle wouldn't have this kind of drama in her life—yet.

Well, this dude, Ray Duncan, has certainly crashed my big parade that morning. It apparently wasn't a planned visit. Yes, he had volunteered to fix the cabinets, but Cynthia had not told him when to stop by. I know nothing about this man. I don't know if he's dangerous; a businessman, a criminal, a Christian, a preacher, a pimp, a drug dealer, or a gangbanger, and have no idea what he's capable of doing. I do know one thing, though, he doesn't have his own key to Cynthia's house, and I do.

If she weren't the object of both of our desires, we probably could have had a drink together and at least been civil. Friends – well, that might be a stretch. I figure he'd come with bad intentions, and all it would have taken to indulge them would have been in my voice level, my tonality, temperament, and physicality. Thank God, I'd learned how to stay cool. I was as cool as if I'd been stopped by the LAPD. I continue to stay cool, and my body has stayed still. I hadn't had much clothing on under those sheets, and if that had registered on him, it might have started a riot all by itself.

Magic, the dog, out in the backyard, is barking up a storm, wanting in the house like it's on fire, aggressively bumping the doggy door over and over. I'm not sure whether he's coming in to protect my ass or attack me on Ray's behalf, but it feels as if he doesn't much like Ray's presence. It's logical that his concern is more about protecting Cynthia and Jamal than concern about me.

Surprisingly, Jamal never comes out of his room, but I doubt if he's asleep. Sitting there smoking, I'm wondering what to do next. Go into the living room and confront Ray? Or let Cynthia handle him? Eventually, I hear the front door open, and slam shut, and just like that, the house becomes quiet.

Cynthia reappears in the bedroom looking scared and upset. "Tony, I'm so sorry this happened, but he's gone."

"I'm sorry it happened, too."

"May I have one of your cigarettes?" she asks. I hand her the pack.

"Hey, I think your ex-boyfriend is still in love with you." I try to keep the emotion out of my voice. "Don't you think it's about time you tell me a bit more about the two of you?"

"Not right now," she replies. "I'm not in the mood to discuss Ray and me." The silence lengthens.

I try again, gently. "Until today, I hadn't given much thought to your ex," I say, "but after today, I'll never take him for granted, and I'll never trust him. This dude is a dangerous loose cannon. I think he's got some serious anger issues and can't be trusted. He stood over me in his maroon warmups and white Adidas, and kept his right hand concealed like he was gripping a weapon in his pocket. Just tell me, Cynthia, what's going on? What did he have in his pocket, and why did this happen?"

"We got our wires crossed," she replies. "I asked him if he would fix the hinges on two of my kitchen cabinets next week, but for some reason, he decided to come this morning. He said he wouldn't have time to do it next week. I know that's a lie, but that's what happened. I'm sure he's been wanting to check you out and meet you, so now you've officially met," she smiles.

"Meet me? I think you meant confront me. Well, I hope to hell he's not coming to the Thanksgiving dinner when Janelle gets here."

"No, he's not invited to Thanksgiving dinner," she smiles. "Please don't leave, Tony. He won't be back. I know him."

Well, I figure that all this excitement will put a damper on soccer plans for today, but it doesn't seem to affect them. The moment we get to the soccer field and start the first game, Jamal gets lucky and scores the third time down the field, giving us something to celebrate! Wow!

I'm on the sidelines acting as an assistant coach, and Cynthia is across on the parents' side. I give Jamal our secret handshake at our first break. Jamal played quite well, scored points in each game, and his team won both of them. We celebrate at Chuck E. Cheese and eat pizza with the soccer team, and then we come home.

It had turned out to be a nice day after all, but I know now that I seriously need some time and space alone to process all this nonstop activity. I excuse myself, saying I need to stop at my apartment and will be back later. I end up visiting my friend, the ocean, at Redondo Beach, and wondering.

"What are you doing, Tony?" I ask myself. "This could get really dangerous. You need to decide if you're 'all in' with Cynthia, or you need to get out now." And if the answer is "all in," I'd better be damn sure I know what I'm doing. Suddenly, the fairy tale is over, and this shit just got real.

I end up at Cynthia's sometime after nine that evening and ask her if she and Jamal want to go with me in the morning to visit a new church I'd heard about. Her response was my second let-down of this decidedly odd weekend. Cynthia didn't want to go to church and didn't want me attending that specific church, ever. She said it would eventually break us up, because going there would cause me to change drastically. I tried to assure her that it wasn't a cult, nor was it Jim Jones heading off to Guyana; just a progressive non-denominational church that teaches spiritual principles and effective meditation practices.

So, Sunday morning, I went alone and enjoyed it very much. The minister talked about the power of intuition, and I couldn't help but notice the many beautiful L.A. women that were in attendance. I wondered if I'd be happier with a more spiritual woman who meditated every day and seemed graceful and peaceful. I figured they were less likely to have some ex-boyfriend breaking down their front door and threatening their household.

I was becoming a regular meditator, and I envied those people and their meditation skills. I'd already learned that Cynthia didn't believe in meditation – at least not yet. Jamal told me he'd tried it once but decided he wasn't ready for it.

Anyway, after church, I went back to Cynthia's, and I'm glad I did. I took a good look at her; decided I continued to find her beautiful, even though she didn't meditate, and I remembered how fortunate I was to have her. She was still upset about that church, though, and refused to discuss it, except to say that it would be the Achilles heel in our relationship.

Could be. I knew I was growing spiritually in ways I couldn't have imagined, and I knew I couldn't, nor shouldn't, stop that growth. I knew even early on that I would absolutely have to follow my intuition. I cautioned her to slow down, and I reminded her also that right now, Ray Duncan was the real Achilles heel. She smiled and agreed, but she also indicated that she did not intend to stop objecting to my involvement with what she saw as a dangerously non-traditional church. I invited her to attend with me next week, telling her the music was wonderful, and reminding her that this was a predominantly Black church and

Black people are known for getting down and serious with their music. I assured her that she would love the music, and it would help her to feel totally at home.

And that pretty much ended our problematic weekend. Back home, and thinking about work, I noticed that the Sunday evening jitters were no longer a problem. In fact, I was pretty excited about it and eager to hear what Dan would say about my Friday night no-overtime production. I concluded the weekend in meditation and prayer and accepted whatever challenges would come my way. I resolved to take time to list and give thanks for all the things for which I was grateful, including my life being spared.

Nevertheless, as the hours went by, I continued to try to make sense of the unanticipated realities of my fairytale romance. I eventually came to terms with the fact that the drama between me and Ray Duncan would continue for who knew how long, and undoubtedly would affect my relationship with Cynthia. To the best of my knowledge, she never cheated on me with him, but I was not yet mature enough to accept this kind of possessive interference from a former boyfriend. I believed his level of participation in her life had been over-the-top – and I realized also that his connection with Jamal was also solid and uncomfortable for me to accept.

I guessed the bottom line was that the way we started out had put us on an awkward footing forever. Too many moving parts for me to feel good about my place in this woman's life when compared to him. They were older than me, and at a level of growth, maturity, and approach to life I had not yet achieved. Looking back from the vantage of my full maturity, I have realized that they were great role models – a team that made investments together, including personal and commercial real estate, business investments, and companionship – but we just weren't on the same page, and certainly Ray Duncan and I weren't friends. Ever.

I was beginning to understand that my entire life would be a learning process in multiple categories, personally and professionally. I guess without drama, life wouldn't have a way to measure good vs. evil; happiness vs. sadness; hot vs. cold; and the ebb and flow of life, all wrapped up in drama.

So, what was my final takeaway from this astonishing weekend? It was the knowledge that I had burned my boats. I am all in. Spiritually, mentally, emotionally, physically, and professionally, I AM ALL IN.

CHAPTER TEN

THE BLIND SIDE

"Everyone has a plan until they get
PUNCHED in the mouth."
– Mike Tyson

It's Monday afternoon, too early to head out to work, but perfect for journaling, and I've had a lot to journal about. I'm pumped, self-motivated, and ready to go.

I am ALL IN!

As I stand in front of the bathroom mirror preparing for work, I yell, "All IN, baby!" while demonstrating my "stare-down pose". My voice echoes from the other room. I listen attentively as I continue by proclaiming the "Scroll Marked II" from *The Greatest Salesman in the World.*

This exercise is my latest creation: turbocharging each of the Ten Scrolls, by reciting them at every opportunity; many more times than the basic prescribed three times a day. The extra effort is for serious students only – like me, the ones who seek permanent personal power and success in life. I've taken on a serious challenge toward this goal. My hypothesis is this: if a student is as serious as I am, committing to read each scroll a minimum of three times a day for thirty days, and then moving on to the next Scroll, positive personal change is inevitable. And I intend to prove it.

When I began my self-education in personal power and success a few months ago, I was naïve enough to believe in the science behind the principle. All my research endorsed the idea that "repetition, repetition, repetition is the mother of skill, and rehearsal is the father of learning." So, I'm "all in." Basically, this is a ten-month study commitment, as well as a lifetime spiritual journey to build a foundation in my chosen field of sales. I intend to live and breathe these ten scrolls for the next ten months. Period.

Now that I've created my own mixed tape containing my own voice blended perfectly with popular-choice music, I'm able to easily enjoy listening several more times a day as I hear my own voice reciting each scroll word for word. I can listen to it while driving, when I'm at home, and when I'm falling off to sleep after a long hard night at work. The possibilities are endless as I continue to discover new creative ways to saturate my mind with these repetitive positive words via this tape recording. Right now, I'm working on Scroll II: "*I will greet this day with love in my heart.*"

Today, I'm saying the words, but honestly, I'm not connecting with the feeling of love. How can I feel and express love in my heart of hearts when just 48 hours ago, Cynthia's ex-boyfriend stood over me in her bedroom and practically threatened my life? Reciting these positive words after my weekend experience with Ray Duncan is a definite stretch and feels quite non-productive. However, I'll keep doing the process to see if I really do start to change from the inside out. Theoretically, this repetitive process is supposed to encourage and nurture my greatest and highest good to start manifesting. Some say it takes 21 to 30 days to change a habit permanently. We'll see about that.

Bottom line: regardless of obstacles, I remain determined to become the best version of me. I understand this means that I must do the hard work to create the solid foundation first. Then I can build my dream mansion for success. It must be a foundation that will withstand and endure any kind of attack, no matter what type of spears and arrows are flung at me. My motto since leaving South Texas has become: *"Before I become a teacher of men and women, let me first teach myself, and become the change I want to see in others."*

And, in spite of the weekend's life-threatening drama, courtesy of the infamous Ray Duncan, I'm in a good place today. I actually meditated for over an hour and feel very much at peace. It's either denial, or I've simply suppressed the emotional impact of the situation, but however I've accomplished it, I've not allowed myself to dwell on that frightening near-death experience. I refuse to allow that isolated moment to ruin today's joy and excitement. I've still got my swagger, and I'm highly excited about going to work today. In fact, I can't wait to get there. That's right, I'm ALL IN, BABY! And I've made a solemn vow to myself and my crew, that for the next two years, we're going to make history at LBC and build something great on the Outbound and Inbound dock.

Well, so much for that. My exhilaration lasts just long enough to walk through the office door, when I am immediately blindsided by a blow I never even saw coming. I had decided to come in a bit earlier in case Dan was planning to throw a surprise victory party in honor of our Best Ever Overall Performance on a Friday Night. Probably that was asking a bit much, and possibly I'd overstated my expectations, but I had at least expected some public praise, especially after that complimentary note he'd left for me last Friday afternoon. And while I'm aware that I'm new to the business with a lot to learn, I was utterly convinced that compared to the night before, that Friday night's dock production was so over the moon, that even Stevie Wonder could see it. I mean, "practically no overtime, Dan, I think you should give me a raise. Now what new mountain can I scale today?"

So much for that dream! Dan's opening words in his damned loud, condescending voice was like throwing ice water in my face:

"We need to talk! Stop whatever you were about to do and come into my office right now!"

Seriously? Why is he so upset? No love, and certainly not a single compliment. Just curt, angry, and belittling. I take a deep breath, walk into the office, and stand tall in front of him, eyeballing him as if he'd just stolen my favorite lucky baseball cap. I try not to wonder how this moment is going to play out. Sometimes, when I look at that man, I shake my head and wonder if he actually has a soul.

Still, this is my boss, my mentor, who has made it his mission in life to forever challenge me to stretch, stretch, and stretch, all the while making my life miserable. Just now, he's staring at me, disgust written all over his face—and he's still standing, so I keep standing, too. Clearly, I am somehow in his personal doghouse.

He's much more upset than usual, and when he finally begins his rant, the only thing he wants to talk about is that I had failed to "pre-set" the Inbound Dock for Sunday night. I have no idea what he was even talking about, let alone why he's so angry. Finally, with a frustrated sigh at my apparent stupidity, he elaborates.

"You didn't bring any of the empty trailers that were available in the yard up to the dock to help jumpstart Inbound for Sunday night. You didn't put any of the Inbound loads in their designated assigned dock doors for easy breakouts. We have multiple systems in play for each and every department here at Roadway Express. Tony, didn't you read the damned manual three months ago, like I told you to? I told you then you'd be held responsible for everything in that manual, didn't I? You didn't even use common sense, man, and at least leave me an empty trailers list, so we could easily and quickly locate all the empties and get them repositioned."

I notice that his uncontrolled rant didn't mention our no overtime, nor our tremendous bill count per man hour production. I take a deep breath and decide silence is not the answer.

"Are you serious, Dan?" I ask, not bothering to hide my bewildered anger. "How can you look at me with a straight face and act as if setting up Sunday night's Inbound Dock should have been one of my priorities on a Friday night, my heaviest night of the week? Hell, man, we moved over 500 Outbound bills last Friday night." I realize I'm yelling, but I don't care.

Dan's barely listening anyway. He just keeps getting louder and louder, for a solid five minutes more about how much I had delayed the Inbound shift from getting off to a good start Sunday night, and how Bill's P&D operation was suffering greatly all day long out on the streets – "never mind the heavy costs and delays we would incur, all because of YOU, because YOU didn't set up the empties and Inbound loads currently on the dock. I strongly suggest," he finishes, "that you review that manual, starting on page 94, where the proper way to set up an Inbound Preset is clearly explained. Obviously, you haven't been paying attention."

I simply cannot believe what I'm hearing. No one before me has ever mentioned an Inbound Preset, much less been held accountable for performing it. And here's Richard, with his promotion to Office Manager, sloppy habits and all, and me getting yelled at once again. I am getting hot under the collar again and decide to try one more time.

"Dan, I never once saw Earl or Richard do a 'Friday Night Inbound Preset' whenever I shadowed them. Not once. Plus, just two weeks ago, Richard was averaging two hours of overtime per man on most Friday nights."

"I expect you to be better than Richard. This is not a damned debate, Tony. We're not having an election here. This is strictly about what I expect from you as my Lead Outbound Supervisor, moving forward. This is not about Richard and what he was or was not doing. Hell, I'm the first to admit that Richard has a couple of bad habits he needs to correct, but I'm not training you to be Richard. Hell, I need you to be better than Richard. The best there is. The way we want our managers to be in the future. Hell, Tony, I don't want the status quo from you. I don't want the norm from you, not ever. I want you to AMAZE ME every time you come to work! Every single time you show up! Your training is much more elaborate and detailed than what Richard got five years ago." He stops to take a breath.

"Well," I reply, still furious, "you'd think after five years on the job, Richard would have got up to speed by now and got rid of some of those bad habits you mentioned. But instead, it looks like he's being rewarded with a promotion and a raise, despite his damned bad habits." I realize I am yelling again.

Then, I do something really stupid that should have cost me my job. I turn and walk out of Dan's office, without any further comment. I don't have shit else to say to him, and I don't give him a chance to respond to my last Richard comment. I walk back toward the parking lot, wondering what I'd just done. But I just keep walking, one foot in front of the other. I no longer care. I just keep walking. Not sure if I'm quitting and going back home, or if I'm just acting like a spoiled brat. I just keep walking.

What the fuck is wrong with me? I wonder. *What just happened here? Roadway doesn't tolerate this type of behavior. I'm probably so fired by now, and I can't even try to justify it.* I'd heard stories of guys getting fired for much less, and I wonder why I've allowed myself to get so angry about Dan's feedback critique. That's all it was – critique and feedback. I'm still learning, and as my boss, he has the right to critique me. But

I hate his tone, and the more I think about it, the more I hate it. It was demeaning and insulting, especially when placed beside the adult civil way we'd handled matters on Friday night.

Well, I tell myself, *Tony, you'd better grow up, get a tougher skin, and get past this, because he's still your damned boss.* Yeah, but today of all days? My special day, and all he wants to do is criticize me. No one has trained me on this Inbound Preset procedure, and to my knowledge, nobody else has been doing it. Richard sure as hell hadn't, and neither had Earl, when he was working here. This was some bullshit. I can't even imagine how I am going to sell this new wrinkle to Big Dewey and the Outbound crew:

"Hey, guys, don't forget – no overtime on Friday night, okay – and oh, by the way, we need to start doing something a little differently…yeah, from now on we're going to start setting up the Inbound Dock before we shut down on Friday night. Which basically means, guys, that we'll start repositioning all the available empties and Inbound loads into their designated assigned dock doors during our Friday night shift – and all of it must be completed before we go home and before 2 a.m., because as you know, there will be no overtime, regardless. Now, if I need to bring in an extra casual (one or two, for four hours only) then I'll do just that, but only if we really must. Mike, Big D, would you guys take turns rotating the hostler duties throughout the shift tonight? But please remember – no overtime – we gotta make this work!"

Yeah, right. I'd have to practice saying this one because it sounds weak just thinking about it. I decide not to discuss this with Big D. Instead, I'll just man up and be the leader I was hired to be and get the damn thing done, provided I still have a job here, of course. Suddenly, I realize that my maturity has kicked back in! Thank you, God!

The hell with this victim mentality bullshit. I know I'm better than that. I hope cooler heads will prevail between Dan and me, so I'll have the week to figure out the best way to sell this to the crew. Thank God I'm meditating, and saying my affirmations and scrolls religiously, because today, Dan really got to me. I was ready to implode. The man is never satisfied. So, Dan, let me recap what you want me to do, besides review the damned manual:

*Friday night Inbound Preset

*With no overtime

*With mandatory 2 a.m. cut off, without fail

*On Friday, my busiest night of the week.

DAMN YOU, DAN! Damn, damn, damn!

With that, I take one more trip back into victimhood. Here, I'd just accomplished something last Friday on Outbound I hadn't seen done since I've been here, but instead of congratulations, here's my boss complaining that I didn't preset the Inbound Dock with all available empty trailers. This guy's just unreal. I haven't been here 30 minutes, and I'm ready to beat his face in before I quit and go home. Just when I made a vow to start loving this job, even accepting the nighttime crazy hours I hate, and here's Dan with some new work assignments to make the job even more impossible to do.

And then just in time, I catch myself. I realize I've let all my pre-spiritual work, meditation, prayers, and affirmations fly out the window during that 15-minute encounter. Obviously, I've got a LOT more work to do. A lot more spiritual practicing and preparation to do before this can truly become a way of life for me and my new path towards spiritual enlightenment.

Well, sitting in my car to take a breath, regroup, and try to figure out why this moment of truth had rattled my chain so badly, I finally pull myself together. But as I sit there thinking, smoking a cigarette to calm my nerves, I begin to realize and consider that in the last 48 hours, I've experienced two explosive man-to-man confrontations, each of which could have ended in disaster. First, the very personal confrontation with Ray Duncan; and this one, today, professional, but equally explosive in nature. And, I realize I had responded to them very differently, realizing the incredible value of personal choice in responding to every situation without pre-meditation. In each case, the responses I'd chosen contributed significantly to the ultimate outcomes – both very different, but yet very similar. My ability to remain cool and show a lack of response in one situation very likely saved my life Saturday morning. The outcome of the scene with Dan remains to be seen. So, what's the operative formula?

"E+R=O"

(Event + Response = Outcome)

Wow, that's powerful! Maybe the real question I should ask is, "Why did I attract these two vastly different confrontations?" I can just hear the minister at church asking me, "What did you do to attract this controversy into your life, son?" Very good question. Maybe I'm not ready for all this spiritual enlightenment stuff. Maybe Cynthia is right. This church and their way of perceiving an event or situation is going to be problematic for me – and for us. Hell, I don't think I did anything to attract conflict in either situation, and right now, I don't feel like trying to be spiritual and psychoanalyze this "law of attraction" mumbo jumbo. Right now, it just feels like so much bullshit.

Bottom line, I'm still mad as hell, and I really want to just say, "I quit," and walk out the door. It's simply not possible to be spiritual and work in this business environment. I think I need to choose.

Then, that small voice inside me whispers ever-so-softly. "You'll never leave this industry, Tony, until you figure out how to be both man and spiritual."

I stopped dead in my tracks. Huh? Taking several deep breaths, I reflect on each event. In the first confrontation, somehow, I had remained passive, cool, calm, and levelheaded when Ray stood there challenging and threatening me. But today, why did the second confrontation with Dan upset me so much more, that I turned and walked out of his office? I had actually verbally lashed out at my boss and spoken my mind without hesitation or concern for the consequences.

Maybe I didn't think Dan was going to shoot me or stab me to death, but he certainly could have fired me on the spot. Maybe I didn't care about being fired. With Ray, not only did I not know what he was capable of doing, I strongly felt I should try to protect him from having to see my half-naked body under those sheets. Instinctively, I knew he would never be able to erase that picture from his psyche, and his reaction could well have been fatal to me, since he had already demonstrated uncontrollable jealousy and rage.

Here's what I know today, 40 years later: If I'd shown the same level of emotional upset with Ray Duncan as I had with Dan, I believe that a fight would have occurred that could have cost me my life. I have always believed I could have easily been killed that day, but I had felt under control despite the danger all around me. Call me naïve, but I just didn't feel that it was my day to die at the hands of a man supercharged by a high voltage of negative energy, bad intentions, and perhaps several early morning cocktails or drugs. I had seen – and would never forget – what a "crime of passion" was and how easily it could emerge without pre-meditation. I wonder how many people are in prison for life because they didn't know how to breathe just five seconds longer before reacting? (You should try the "Five Second Countdown Rule" by Mel Robbins: Example: Inhale and hold it….5,4,3,2,1 Exhale. A powerful exercise to use prior to taking appropriate action. I highly recommend that you try this exercise.

It could save the lives of thousands of people around the world – Five Second Rule – Just. Like. That.)

Until that day, I had never in my life been as close to a confrontation that could have so easily erupted into a homicide, an ugly and permanently disastrous situation for all parties involved. To this day, that situation clearly remains in my personal history book as my "moment of judgment day". Although we all emerged safely, I still acknowledge that the years reflected on my tombstone could have been much fewer than I've been blessed to live. And I feel a monumental twinge of sadness at all I would have missed: my beautiful and loving future wife, Lora, and my very smart, talented, and handsome twin sons, Jacob and Josh; also, my spiritual calling and professional mission with its opportunity to assist tens of thousands of people who were scheduled to arrive exactly when they were supposed to for my personal guidance and coaching. Following that train of thought with my emerging new maturity, I was struck by the sadness, lifetime grief, and suffering that my death during such a bizarre encounter would have brought to my parents and only sister. And then, it hit me, full force, that my untimely death without leaving at least one son would have been the death of my Harris grandfather's line. Seventy plus years of regret if that bedroom moment had turned into my final day on earth. I continue to thank my God for always being my source and protection for my every need.

Now, the Dan confrontation was an entirely different matter, and the difference in the way I handled it makes me suspect I was two different people. I was much more aggressive and outspoken with Dan. I didn't care who, outside those walls, heard me yell at him. I was just plain pissed, and I let Dan know it. However, I had let Dan get under my skin. Dan had stepped on my ego, and all I wanted was to retaliate and hit back. Les Giblin in his book, *How to Have Confidence and Power in Dealing with People,* writes that the unforgiveable sin in human relationships is when you crush another person's ego. Well, by God, I'm a living witness to the truth of that, because my little ego was crushed, and it immediately reacted negatively to Dan. I had pictured and planned for a completely different movie than the one that was playing when I got to work, and I couldn't recover quickly enough to be aware of the actual movie Dan was watching.

However, with Ray, I'd felt sorry for him, despite his threats and fury. He clearly had the upper hand, but I could also see that he was a wounded man, and as dangerous as a large, wounded animal if you came too close. Being somewhat passive was a better, gentler path, for it was Ray's anger, not mine, that was challenging the situation.

$$E+R=O$$

A valuable lesson here in this hot car while I sort myself out before checking to see if I still have a job. I can't control the Event, but I can control my Response. "The Response in every Event is on me." I'll cherish that lesson forever and remember the circumstances that created this learning opportunity.

But, I wonder, what happened to my Scroll Marked II? My actions were completely opposite and contradictory to everything I was learning in my self-help books. Hell, Scroll #2 is all about LOVE. It says, "I will greet this day with love in my heart," and I'm still about two steps from bashing Dan's face in. Where's the love there? I feel more like, "I will greet this day with bitterness and resentment in my heart." Suddenly, the humor in all this mess strikes me square in the face, and I burst out laughing uncontrollably. When I can think again, I realize that from now on, I must rise above this insanity and be the bigger man. I can't allow Little Tony to control Big Tony. I can't allow Dan to get under my skin again with his negative critiques, criticism, and condescending manner.

I put out my cigarette, get out of my car, and go back inside to prepare for an exciting night of work with my guys on the dock, provided of course, that Dan hasn't terminated me in the last ten minutes. I can't wait to see my team again and thank them one more time for their great effort and performance last week. Our celebration and salute to the stars in the parking lot remains a real moment for each of us, as we made that serious confirmation and joint commitment.

And I'm going to tell them we're having a 15-minute Pizza Party Strategy Session Meeting on Wednesday night, 15 minutes before their lunch break. I'm ordering pizzas to be delivered for lunch on Wednesday to all the Outbound Dock guys while we plan the rest of the week. No, I'm not trying to buy them. I'm modeling what I saw the sales guys do with some of their customers. If it worked for them, it would work for my dock guys. Together, we are smart enough to figure this out and have fun in the process.

Note to self: Two things I must not fail to do: #1 – Get each man to promise me they will not write me up for Past Practice and start demanding Pizza Party Strategy Sessions every Wednesday night. That will not fly. Deal Breaker.

And #2 – Discuss the idea with Dan first and get his approval and buy in. After all, he did tell me to keep doing whatever I'm doing to get the job done. I think I can sell him on the pizza. I'm the one buying -and it's my money. I hope he says yes.

A few minutes before the start of my shift, I go back into Dan's office and apologize for my outburst. I assure him that moving forward, we will start setting up the Inbound dock on Friday nights, according to the Inbound Dock Pre-Set Load Plan on page 94.

He thanks me for my apology, and then, he apologizes, too, both for his tone and his over-the-top display of authority. Lastly, he FINALLY says it: "Good job Friday night! Keep it up! I've been racking my brain all day trying to figure out how you managed to streamline that OT, and you're right. Richard never could, but whatever you did, keep it up." We smile and shake hands, and I am off to the races to check in with my main man, Bill, in dispatch.

I still have my job and learned a valuable lesson. Now, it's time to get ready for my shift.

And just like that, one of the many arguments and verbal fights with Dan was over. The moment had come and gone. It was becoming obvious that Dan and I might always have some level of a toxic love/hate relationship, but at the end of the day, we also have a mutual respect that's awkward in nature but seems to work. We've found some ways to co-exist and compartmentalize our weak and strong emotions to get the job done. I must say, though, Dan's better at it than me, and he's certainly one of the best in the business at getting the most out of his people. Even though I hate it and it makes me crazy when he squeezes me and challenges me to stretch, but I'm sure it's good for me. Maybe this is one more thing that becoming a man is all about. I must remember I'm only 27, and I don't have all the answers. I know I've got a lot of growing up to do, but I'm working hard to figure out "This Thing Called Life".

I wonder if all this is a rite of passage into manhood? Dan has always said I haven't paid the price of real sacrifice. He told me once he's been married and divorced two times and working on a third marriage, and I haven't even gotten married once. Some battles aren't worth trying to win, so I didn't respond to his comment. As they say in the transportation world, "It is what it is."

As I walk out on the dock, I remind myself the only thing I can control is me. I must assume – act as if – the other person is going to behave properly and do the right thing, until they show me otherwise. I guess this is why the Serenity Prayer was inspired and created: "God grant me the courage to accept the things I cannot change and the wisdom to know the difference...."

Dr. Wayne Dyer, one of my favorite spiritual teachers, once offered the powerful metaphor of an orange, from which, when you squeeze it, you get orange juice. Not lemon juice or pineapple juice or some carcinogenic poison juice. You only get orange juice. Because, he said, that's what's inside the orange. Orange juice. He went on to ask "What do we experience from you when someone squeezes you? Do we get to experience your anger, hostility, resentment, fear, retaliation – or do we experience your love, peace, joy, and kindness? Because if there's only love inside you, the only thing that can come out of you when squeezed is love." Guess I've got a lot of work to do before you can squeeze me and get only love to come out. I may have to think on this one a while.

Finally, I get it. I understand the importance of the scrolls, and the necessity of a 30-day, three-times-a-day, repetitive program. "Repetition, repetition, repetition is the mother of skill, and rehearsal is the father of learning." What I also have learned about myself, and Ray, is that even though we each "displayed" our emotions differently on that day, the bottom line at the very core of our hearts and souls, we were both afraid, even though we didn't show it.

What I don't know is how to anticipate the unknown on the horizon. All the mini-battles between Dan and me may well just be "a practice rehearsal" for the ultimate knockdown, drag out break up, that's likely destined for later, but not now. Not today. Today, all is good with the world, and all is good with Dan and me. Perhaps the secret to working successfully with Dan is to learn to anticipate what he wants and will ask for next, which will allow me to go beyond what he expects. When I was a child, I remember having to learn how to take out the trash and make my bed and do other chores before being asked by my parents. My willingness to do them without being asked is what made the difference. I need to outguess and outsmart Dan in that same spirit, if possible. He keeps surprising me and catching me off guard. Over the next three years of my "Transportation-Logistics Journey", this will become my obsession. But, ultimately, all my efforts must lead to my promotion into the field of sales, or, as far as I'm concerned, my hard work and commitment will be for naught.

It's been said that people don't quit companies. They quit bosses. If Dan doesn't deliver on his promise of a promotion to sales in the next two years, I will not stay here. That's my truth, and I take 100 percent responsibility for this reality and the actions I will need to take that will support my position. In two years as a Lead Supervisor at Roadway Express, I'll be a very desirable candidate for hire in the Transportation Logistics Industry, and the possibility of being promoted into sales by one of our competitors will be extremely good. I will do everything necessary for Dan and Roadway toward that ultimate payoff, but I refuse to allow anyone to tell me, as Dan once did, that I'm not sales material. Or try to groom me to stop thinking about sales, as I've already seen them try to do. Unconscious bias was very real then and is still real today, but in 1981, it was truly a stretch for many companies to fairly implement and embrace diversity and inclusion for all employees.

Working with Teamsters can be tough, but truthfully, it's been my experience that people react to you based on how you treat them. Like that old cliché: "People really don't care how much you know until they know how much you care." Today marks the beginning of my two-year commitment to Lead Operations Supervisor. I refuse to allow Dan to upset me, and I will not worry about sales for the next two years. I am going to become as cool as he appears to be. I am going to commit myself to the work in front of me, while building a solid foundation (mentally, physically, emotionally, and spiritually) for success. Self-motivation is my personal responsibility – all the time, not just in my spare time. It must become a way of life for me.

Dan's last comment today was, "Hey, I need a couple of warning letters this week. Just leave them on the desk. Doesn't have to be today or tomorrow; just make sure you have a couple of them on my desk by end of shift Thursday."

"Okay. Got it, will do!" I replied. "Anyone in particular you want me to go after?"

"Nope, just surprise me. You know who's been naughty and who's been nice." Then, he picked up his phone to place a call.

There's no point in arguing about warning letters – this craziness goes with the job and is a way of life here at LBC. The game we play. I will play it to perfection, without fail.

Interesting that just when I was building trust with my Outbound team, Dan threw his monkey wrench into the machinery just as I predicted. Yet, he also said, "Keep doing whatever you're doing, because it's working." Do I dare tell him he's making my success twice as difficult to achieve? Hell no. I say nothing. Today, I was caught off guard and didn't see it coming. Well, that one's on me. I probably should have anticipated the warning letters last week, since I knew it was about time for him to want them. Not sure it would have made a difference, but it is worth considering.

So, for the rest of this week and this year and next year, this is the game we play. One day at a time, filled with surprise, disappointment, anticipation, and excitement. The job has moments of good times, and it's definitely already in my blood. No matter what, we survive and thrive.

The curtain is up. It's showtime, baby. Time to go to Work! Let's get ready to rumble!

CHAPTER ELEVEN

THE WINDS OF CHANGE ARE BLOWING

"You can't go back and change the beginning,
but you can start where you are and change the ending."
--C.S. Lewis

Well, Dan disallowed the pizza party, but was totally in favor of me having a strategy meeting, and to my surprise, he offered a compromise, suggesting that I could bring in a couple of dozen donuts once or twice a month – but nothing else. He even went so far as to give me money from petty cash to pay for it. I was impressed, because Dan's normal answer to ANYTHING that rewards a Teamster is usually "NO!" and that's that.

And, since my guys never knew about my original pizza plans, the donuts were a big hit, and the strategy meeting that followed was very productive. I had made some fresh, hot coffee, nice and strong, the way we all like it, and I made it a point to congratulate each individual for his contributions and the way it made all of us shine like new money.

"Game changers!" I yelled. "Difference makers! Success creators!"

Then I shared with them how complimentary Dan had been regarding our Super Friday Night Performance, and his request for me to extend his compliments to the entire team.

Now, I admit that was a small white lie, but not really. I didn't dare mention anything about the knock-down-drag-out verbal fight that had occurred about 20 minutes before his compliments and both of our apologies. Hey, I was on a roll! What can I say? I had a commitment to the truth, but only to the extent it inspired better performance and a better work environment. They all clapped, smiled, and some even laughed – yet there was a new sense of pride visible in each man. And then, it was time to discuss page 94 of Roadway's Policy Manual. I took a deep breath.

"Gentlemen," I began, "this is a direct order from The Top. Starting this Friday night, we will now be 100 percent responsible for setting up the Inbound Dock for Sunday night, without fail. Believe me, I KNOW how challenging Friday nights are already, especially with the mandatory no overtime, but I'm looking for ideas from each of you on how we might attack this assignment and make it work." *Damn*, I thought, *that sounded good*, even to me.

My words were met with dead silence for about 15 seconds. I took another deep breath. "Guys, this is real. I *need* your ideas about how to make this work. Because it has to work simultaneously with everything else we've got going on. In other words, we must find a way to integrate this one procedure into our regular Friday night workload and still complete our shift on time. Come on, guys – I need *your* feedback. I'm looking for solutions. We only need one good idea to make this work. Who's got something to share?"

Then, Big Dewey spoke up, his voice calm and relaxed.

"Hey, Tony, no big deal. Just bring in an extra casual at the beginning of the shift, and it's a done deal. Okay? No big deal, my man. We got this!"

Whew! I knew I'd been right to build a relationship with this good man.

"Well, alright!" I yelled. "I'll bring in one of our favorite Casual superstars – one that we *all* love – you know who I mean! I'll try my best to get Mr. J.C. Carlos!"

"Hell yes, that'll work!" cried Mike, enthusiastically.

I knew all the men respected and admired J.C. Carlos, a 25-year-old five-foot-seven-inch Casual from the Union Hall. He would literally beg me for the hardest and toughest loads to work each night. His work ethic was off the charts. He was half man, half robot – like the Six Million Dollar Bionic Man – this guy could flat out work his ass off without taking a break. You'd have to MAKE him take a break with the other guys, or he'd just keep working. He just wouldn't stop. We called him Mister J.C. Carlos out of respect, putting him on a pedestal right next to Jesus Christ.

I was told that the first night he worked for us, the Brotherhood of Teamsters reps pulled him aside and told him if he wanted to work full-time and join the Brotherhood, he'd better slow his ass down, because he was making everyone look bad. He told them not to worry. He said, "I only have two speeds: fast and faster."

What manner of man is this, they all wondered? The man can't slow it down.

Earlier in this book, I talked about Huffy Tires as one of the most difficult loads to work – considered "cruel and unusual punishment" at LBC/820. They would arrive in 48-foot or 53-foot trailers filled with hundreds of loose bundles of bicycle tires, from floor to ceiling, all the way to the nose of a 53-foot trailer. Backbreaking hard labor – like the kind you'd give a prison inmate for punishment. Most Teamsters, with any seniority at all, would get unbelievably angry if they were assigned a Huffy load without a helper. So, Huffy loads usually are assigned to people the company feels need a little punishment or correction. And then there's Mr. J.C. Carlos, who demands the right of first refusal of the

Huffy loads. He'll beg for those loads and destroy them in less than three hours; whereas, most men working alone will need eight or nine hours to unload.

"Okay! So be it!" In my excitement, my voice raised an entire octave—and to my astonishment, the men started clapping again with echoes and yells of approval, similar to last Friday night.

"Hoorah!"

It was a powerful revelation for me to observe myself staying calm and allowing the process to unfold, and then to watch them slowly start to participate and take ownership of the solution, instead of waiting for me to shove the orders down their throats. The thing is, everyone knew the solution, but what needed to happen was for them to collectively buy in. I realized that Big Dewey is so in tune with me now that we didn't even have to discuss this privately ahead of time. He knew what I was up against, and my desperate need for cooperation. *Wow*, I thought, *that's leadership*— his – and mine! I loved watching it all come together. One voice. One sound. One team.

"All In, baby!" I yelled. And as I started to walk away, I was so excited that I added, loudly, without thinking, "Pizza and beer on me in two weeks – Friday night in the parking lot. Be there or be square!"

WTF! What had I just done? Still, it was such a good meeting, and I was so overcome with joy and empowerment that I knew sponsoring a pizza party on my own dime, despite what Dan had said, was the right thing, albeit in the parking lot after hours. Nobody would know, and I wouldn't have to deal with Dan. So, in two weeks, they've got something to look forward to, and they'll have delivered on their word come this Friday night. I was a little nervous at the commitment – but—well, it is what it is. And I wouldn't take it back.

Also, this time, I'd started this process through the proper chain of command and protocol, thus helping me avoid creating another Past Practice, which would have been career-limiting, and costly!

From the book, *The Power of Nice: How to Negotiate So Everyone Wins, Especially You,* by Ron Shapiro, I've learned quite a lot about the law of reciprocity, during which a simple act (donuts, pizza, and beer) begets another act of kindness from the recipient. One of his examples describes how a university professor sent Christmas cards to 1,000 random strangers, using the phone book yellow pages, and 600 of the recipients responded back with cards addressed to him. This law works every time, which is why giving begets receiving, especially when it's genuine giving.

Here's what I know for sure: these men are starving to be treated with respect, as men, and as equals. We're building a bond of trust here that is becoming the true spirit and essence of cooperation and collaboration that strengthens our foundation for success. This approach is quite different than what they were used to from past experiences. I'm starting to believe that my sincere attempt to be fair and transparent is more important to these men than even overtime.

For the most part, things settled down for a while after the big blow up between Dan and me. I think we both understood, after that heated exchange, that we might not want to push it further. He had seen that even though I was a rookie, I didn't take any shit. I said what was on my mind, and now, we both knew that we could easily go too far and say the wrong things. Also, it certainly wasn't an example of professional behavior in the workplace, and no doubt, some of the staff had noticed. We were both treading in quicksand if we didn't find better ways to show restraint, and we both knew it. So, the next few months of silent lull became the calm before the storm. We closed out the year with extraordinary success leading into the Christmas holidays. We were already pumped for our celebration, because we were so confident of the outcome for the year and the close of the fourth quarter of 1981. A remarkably successful year, and the terminal growth had been tremendous.

We were all smiling on the inside, because we knew our bonus checks would be nice and fat whenever we received them. I say "whenever" because there is always a slight delay as to when we receive quarterly bonus checks after the quarter closes out. I think it's one of Roadway's tactics to keep you from quitting, no matter how mad you are, or how bad things get, because you would not get your final bonus check for the previous quarter if you quit prior to receiving it. You move, you lose. You quit, that's it. Those are the rules. So, we'll probably not see the checks until February 1982—and that means one might as well sit back and relax, because no one's going anywhere any time soon. We want our money, first.

As you've no doubt noticed, juxtaposing what I'm learning in my new profession beside what I'm learning about romantic relationships, has turned into my personal demonstration that we all grow up and mature "in pieces", instead of all at once. Work was going great. Relationships— well, that's a whole 'nother thing.   That fall, Cynthia and I are still in the honeymoon phase. She is a very nurturing, caring, and loving lady, and I'm doing my best to try not to let my eyes nor my attention wander. Serious relationships can be terrifying to young men of a certain age – and this is definitely an occasionally scary serious relationship. There are days when I wonder if I'm up to the challenge of a real commitment.

And the interference of Ray Duncan remains real. This dude will not go away. He isn't in my face anymore, yelling obscenities and demanding that I become a carpenter and plumber. Instead, he's behind the scenes, working hard to destroy our relationship, using the mechanism of the many business deals he and Cynthia had developed together before I entered the picture. He is forever trying to force her to stay attentive and in the investment game with him. Every other day, he's phoning, wanting to communicate about a business meeting or a stock or a new investment. At times, it feels more like he's her ex-husband and they have joint custody of the children.

I find these apparently permanent shared business interests extremely intimidating. They not only remind me of a husband-wife relationship, but also keep me focused on how much more growth I need in my personal life, especially when it comes to business and financial literacy. I'm no Bill Gates, Steve Jobs, or Warren Buffett, but I'm hanging in, and doing some things right.

We certainly got through Thanksgiving without any major problems from Ray. Jamal and I are still growing and talking often, while playing basketball in the backyard, another one of his big interests. We play and compete, while Magic, the dog, tries his best to officiate and play along with us. Oh, yeah, I still got some moves on the basketball court, and I can still teach Jamal a thing or two as a former athlete and coach. It's been "good times" getting to bond with Jamal.

Also, Jalen, the older son, came home for Thanksgiving, so I finally got the chance to meet him. We were civil and respectful with each other, and we talked a lot about his college baseball team, and his aspirations to go pro next year, but I can tell he's not one of my raving fans yet. He was intrigued to hear about my full ride track scholarship to Texas Tech, and qualifying for the Olympic Trials in 1976, as well as my brief stint as an athletics coach in Texas. Also, he loved discussing the power and possibilities of meditation, and how that could improve his overall performance in baseball. All in all, what more can I really expect from an 18-year-old man-child, who's seen his mother suffer at the hands of his father? He's going to wait and reserve judgment to see who I become in his mother's life. Until then, that's all I can ask for.

Then, there's the beautiful Janelle, a petite 5'4" slender-tender young lady who showed up for Thanksgiving, as promised. Yes, I finally met Cynthia's younger sister, and she is, indeed, stunning – a spitting image of Cynthia, equally as beautiful and fine as hell. A bit on the quiet side, somewhat shy, which I didn't see coming. You don't typically see beautiful women in Southern California openly having shyness issues. Her shyness is the type that only makes her sexier and more desirable – the kind most men will want to try to rescue and lavish with the finest of everything. The two sisters look very much alike, except Cynthia is bold, superfine, redbone (like my mother), with dark, shoulder-length hair. Janelle is quiet, shy but sexy, with skin tones a shade darker (paper sack brown), with longer dark hair extending halfway down her back. Both have hazel greenish-brown eyes, and both are sexy and exotic.

Thinking back on this introduction, I realize that I haven't quite gotten myself past the "appreciation stage", and into the "commitment stage", in my relationship with Cynthia, because this visit raised a few complications I couldn't possibly have anticipated.

First, it was obvious that Cynthia had wanted me to eyeball Janelle's pictures from the git-go and was clearly wanting to see my reaction and restraint towards her little sister, before she got too involved with me. Obviously, she was wondering if I could be trusted around this beautiful young creature. Second, I should point out that those pictures and the red bikini she was wearing in them did not do her justice. The young woman is drop-dead gorgeous, intoxicating to look at and be around, and it's a good thing I dismissed the photos from consideration after about two seconds, because if I hadn't passed the picture test, I am sure Cynthia and I wouldn't be together right now. I guess it was my litmus test, and my passing it when I did was probably a fluke.

In retrospect, I'm not even sure why I dismissed it; except originally, I thought Cynthia was not telling the truth about Janelle actually showing up for Thanksgiving – but here she is, in the flesh – and for one brief second (or maybe two), I consider whether she would have been the better choice. In the flesh, Janelle is overwhelming. But, once I get a firm hold on my hormones, we all get along like family. She actually likes me, too, with no pretense – just a down-to-earth young lady. Unfortunately, I do not realize that having such a beautiful little sister is Cynthia's secret nightmare, or I would have told her that she has absolutely nothing to worry about. I always knew that no matter what, I would never, ever cross that line with her sister. As it turns out, though, I am about to get another lesson…

Later on that evening, Jalen and Jamal went outside to play basketball, and the three of us drank wine, watched television, and discussed the idea of Janelle being a surrogate for us someday, and to my surprise, she agreed. Not immediately, but an hour and three glasses of wine later, after she relaxed and got to know me a little better, she then told us yes, but under one condition. If Cynthia and I continue to grow as a couple towards marriage, then yes, she will commit to having a child for us, but only under those conditions. There has to be a wedding.

I was impressed with her maturity and the thought of her carrying our child excited me more than the wedding. I was also impressed with the idea that she was willing to go through all the unpleasant aspects of pregnancy, putting her life on hold, just so her big sister could have my child. I didn't even focus on the marriage. Of COURSE there'd be a wedding. After all, I was my proper mother's son. This young lady was offering a hell of a sacrifice. I started thinking about what Dan once said about "sacrifice" and paying the price and his going through his two divorces, but to me, what Janelle was willing to do for Cynthia and me was real sacrifice. I was truly honored that she had said she would have our baby if we wanted her to.

Well, we made it through the remainder of the evening with just small talk, wine, and watching mindless television. Yet, to my surprise, there were no more discussions about babies and Janelle being a surrogate during the next two weeks of her visit – and then, just like that, Janelle and Jalen were gone. And Ray Duncan was also gone. In fact, I hadn't seen him and hoped I wouldn't see him again for a very long time.

I wondered if there were issues between Cynthia and Janelle that I wasn't aware of, because I truly found it strange that we didn't have any more surrogate discussions before she left. I also wondered if Janelle was a silent problem for Cynthia, like Ray Duncan remained a silent problem for me. Still the invisible thorn in my side, and Cynthia remained deeply involved financially with him, which meant he wasn't going anywhere.

I was beginning to realize that I was as jealous of Ray as perhaps Cynthia was of her sister, but Janelle was long gone, and here I was working nights. No way to know what was or was not going on in my absence. I keep wondering why she quit him. What did he do to lose her? Did he make a pass at Janelle? Cynthia won't dignify the topic with a discussion. And my jealousy remains a problem.

Meantime, though, I've learned a lot from Cynthia, particularly about the type, attitude, and belief system required to prosper in Southern California. I must admit, she's been surprisingly very generous with what she and her friends have shared with me. Like for example, short cuts in the investment game and multiple ways to navigate the real estate world, besides having lots of money or being rich. As much as Cynthia would like to marry me someday, she says, "being married should be my last option to consider, not my first, when it comes to real estate investments." WOW, what a woman!

Property prices in the area in the 1980s were very high, and the conventional wisdom in my circle of friends was that you can't purchase a home in Los Angeles County without two incomes – and besides, you must be married to qualify for a loan. During my first four years in Los Angeles, when I was living in my small, two-bedroom apartment, I would often ask friends, or even strangers, what if I choose to remain single and just have a dog – you mean I can't have a home in California unless I'm married? What about my dog, who needs a backyard? Cynthia was finally the one who set me straight and helped me squash all that nonsense from my brain, once and for all.

"Hell no, Tony," she would say. "Look at me. Look at my friends: Carol, Brandi, and even Ray – we all own property, and we're all single. If you want to buy a home, Tony, I can hook you up with my real estate broker today, and she can help you. If she can't, nobody can." Cynthia was so resourceful; she knew someone who specialized in almost everything. You name it, Cynthia knew how to network and unselfishly introduced me to all the right people. People who could get things done – the tax consultant, the realtor, the car repair guy, and others in her network. In that respect, she was the most selfless person I'd ever known, and I really didn't know how to appreciate it or process it until much later.

I felt encouraged by her confidence in her realtor and her offer of help, and I knew when I was ready to buy a home, I'd be able to do it. This knowledge was the beginning of building my confidence one brick at a time and starting to save my money for the down payment. I was learning that I could make that prosperity jump and achieve a life of abundance, just like many of my peers were doing. This was a wise, experienced woman whose practical side kept me balanced. She provided me with a visual I could touch, feel, and believe in, and as time went on, I knew I needed to cancel out some of the people in my circle whose "stinking thinking" was draining my growing spiritual consciousness and confidence.

But no matter how hard I tried, I just couldn't move past Ray Duncan, his ongoing association with Cynthia, and the horror of our bedroom confrontation. And the nighttime work schedule just gave me too many hours to let my jealousy fester. I resolved to get serious about working on it from a positive perspective.

So, today is a new day, and I can see real progress with my scrolls. I've been consistent and am into my fifth month of commitment. Today, I recite from Scroll Marked 5, which states, "I will live this day as if it is my last." Thank you, God. And so be it.

During the homestretch for the year, things in the trucking business have been slowing down, and I am finding myself often on automatic pilot – reflecting often in the quiet hours of the night about my accomplishments for the year: my new job, Cynthia, increased income with bonuses, new car, new clothes, spiritual growth, health, wellness, and so much more. I have been in the process of creating my goals list for 1982, including a gratitude journal for all the good I received in 1981.

However, as if 1981 hadn't brought enough new experiences, changes, and excitement into my life, one more remains: job-related and mighty unpleasant. One night, in that quiet moment of solitude, I am interrupted from these pleasant thoughts by a group of hostile visitors from the home office in Akron, Ohio.

Just what we need. Top brass intruders from the home office. If there were a poster out there that said TOP BRASS BULLIES, it would have all three of those guys' faces plastered on it. They definitely need to get a life. I mean, they sneak into our Long Beach yard in the early morning, about 06:55 (riding three deep, all three Men in Black).

I'm working the Inbound shift for the next two weeks to close out the year, at Dan's request, to help Todd and Jim, who are both on vacation. Richard is also helping by taking on my Outbound shift. So, lucky me, I get to see all the fun this morning.

I'm told that this is how they normally do it: come to your terminals unannounced in groups of three and four, always without warning, to achieve maximum surprise. They sneak inside the gates, driving recklessly, instead of simply parking outside the gates in the designated visitors' parking area. No, these dudes circle around, taking a couple of laps in the car, driving fast, around and around the yard, looking for anything that would be considered a violation of Roadway's rules.

They look to see if any trailers are not choked properly, and they look to see how orderly the trailers are lined up and positioned in the yard and at the dock. They also check to see if we have the proper allotment of "red lined" trailers sectioned off in the yard. (Note: redline trailers are those labeled out-of-service, but in reality, there's nothing wrong with them except that you aren't allowed to use them. It's a game the company likes to play. Basically, redline trailers have an out-of-service status for no good reason other than to force you to operate your facility lean and mean, with a certain restricted allotment of trailers. The procedure is supposed to enhance your load average by forcing each manager to load higher and tighter and be more efficient, thus increasing the load averages and cube per each trailer. It's important to note that redlining is such a serious strategy that each terminal is forced to Play. If you didn't comply, you could be fired for using "redline trailers without permission from the proper authority.")

Once the Top Brass Bullies complete their drive by, instead of parking back outside the gate in the designated visitors' parking area, they park somewhere right there in the yard, in some restricted area, where cars shouldn't park. Then, they walk up on the dock like they're the landlords. They don't speak to anyone, and they don't ask for directions to Dan's office, nor do they crack a smile. They look mean and disgruntled, as if they are on a mission to hurt someone. They walk straight into the main building, sporting their three-piece black suits and red power ties.

As they do, I make it a point to follow them a few paces behind. I want to see what's happening, and I don't want to miss anything, so I pretend I have to communicate about a P&D load with Bill. The truth, though, is that I am just being nosey as hell. I want to know who the hell these men are and what the hell is about to go down.

Once inside, they immediately take over Dan's office. I mean, they claim ownership over the entire office like a hostile takeover, and they start by treating poor Dan like a homeless squatter. They literally order him to get out of his own office immediately. I am in total disbelief as I see and hear the whole thing. I wonder if they're getting ready to fire him— and if so, what has he done? Their tone of voice is two times louder and more hostile than Dan's tone on his most agitated day. Their demeanor is that of an NFL linebacker who wants nothing more than to kick your ass. Their sole purpose seems to be intimidation and to find a reason to curse somebody out before firing them. I have never seen anything like this. Dan seems to be caught totally by surprise. He hasn't even had a chance to drink his morning coffee and do his traditional "daily walkabout" – the one where you get to tell him, as the Inbound Lead, what every trailer at the dock and in the yard represents, and how you plan to utilize it today in P&D.

For the first time in our acquaintance, he looks like a helpless little child. The Bullies tell him to stand outside his office door and not to wander out. That message is delivered by the Godfather, also known as Nick Popoff. The other two are carefully anonymous. "You stand there, right outside your door, until I tell you to come inside. If I have a question, I don't have time to look for you, so don't wander off," he yelled.

No one seems to know who they are, but they have come with authority and power, and the shock is palpable. The entire office is in terrified disarray. No one can focus on answering the phones, which are ringing off the hook. It seems like the worst is about to happen. The thing about these men is that they look very familiar. In fact, I start remembering where I'd met them. It was an all-day conference I'd attended early in my orientation training in Los Angeles. Nick Popoff, the Vice President of Operations over the region, was yelling, cussing, and threatening everyone in that conference room that day. I remember him saying to all of us that we should knock hell out of anyone who was falling asleep during the meeting. And if we didn't, he was going to knock hell out of us. I cannot make this stuff up. This actually happened.

I remember asking myself then and there, *What kind of world is this and what have I gotten myself into?* Some of those poor managers had been up all night working 10–12-hour seven-day shifts and were about to begin their seven days off. And just when it was time to end their shift and start their seven-day vacation, they were told in the final hour before closing out that they had to attend an all-day mandatory meeting. Talk about cruel and unusual punishment – but they all did it and tried their best to stay awake. I never will forget that experience, because at the time, I was brand new and felt like I'd landed in a war zone.

According to Bill, when the top brass comes to town, one of two things is sure to happen. You're either going to get a harsh reprimand resulting in probation; or termination, resulting in being escorted off the premises; or congratulations, resulting in a promotion, special favors, and/or raises.

However, regardless of your fate, the ritual of intimidation and hostile takeover remains a tradition, and so does the "office coop." However, by the end of the day, after getting beaten down to nothing but your underwear, your dignity and ego just might be restored and made whole again.

What a difference twelve hours can make! When I left at the end of my shift, I couldn't stop worrying and wondering if Dan was going to get fired and if they would be escorting him out of the building today. I thought about his promise to put me in sales in two years. If he got fired, he obviously wouldn't be able to deliver on that.

That was the first time – but certainly not the last, that I witnessed such bullying and abuse at the top management level. I had thought that with Dan's clout, he was insulated, but boy, was I wrong. I actually felt sorry for him. Dan was a legend and exceptionally good at his job, and to see him treated this way by these goons, I couldn't believe how helpless and weak he appeared. That morning, I clearly understood what Ronnie Luster meant on my initiation night at LAX/821 when he remarked that "Shit rolls downhill."

So, while Dan was standing outside his office for hours, humiliated and embarrassed in front of his staff, the Professional Goons were sitting around, hanging out in Dan's office, feet on his desk, smoking cigarettes and having a good ole' time, using his personal office phone to conduct business. I wondered what it would all mean by the time I came back to work that night. Meantime, my heart went out to him.

Well, when I got back to work that evening around 2200, I was told that Dan received his restoration about lunch time, apparently through offering him a raise and a transfer to a brand-new facility in Gardena. He could bring any of the managers with him that he chose. The whole thing reminded me a lot of the way college fraternities treat their pledges.

So now the chief topic of conversation was who would be staying in Long Beach and who would get the chance to go to the new Gardena terminal. I won't know for a few days where I'll end up. My fate, just like everyone else's, hangs in the balance and prompts a question. Do I want to stay with Dan, or would I rather stay in Long Beach and start over with someone new? That's the $64,000 question, and it's not my decision.

In my mind's eye, as I recalled the last six months and all my spiritual growth, development, and commitment, a thought came over me in that special, still, small voice: *Peace, be Still. None of this is an accident, Tony. God is not playing a joke on you. Choose to trust and believe in God, not man. How you got here is bigger than you and Dan.*

So, today, I am living and breathing 100 percent the Scroll Marked 5 which states, "I will live this day as if it is my last. Today, this moment is all I have. Thank you, God."

And so it is.

CHAPTER TWELVE

FOLLOW YOUR PATH

"God prepared a path for everyone to follow;
you just have to read and follow the Omens."
– The Alchemist

It's been over two weeks since we first heard the news about Gardena. So far, Dan has officially invited only Todd and Bill to join him, while all the other managers are still waiting, whispering, and desperately wanting to know their fate. This new Gardena initiative is a big deal for a lot of people, especially the top brass, because there are going to be a lot of potential opportunities, so there is considerable uncertainty about its actual rollout.

The new facility is destined to become a beacon of success in the Roadway hierarchy. That means anyone associated with it from ground zero has the potential to become a major rock star of the future. There's simply no way to predict how one's future could be impacted just by being in the right place at the right time. Nor can one ever be certain which is the better choice, but I'm beginning to feel strongly in my heart of hearts that all roads lead to Gardena. However, I'm totally declaring peace regarding the entire situation. I refuse to allow this profound interruption to steal my joy.

People are becoming upset, agitated, and pointing fingers – and in many ways, it reminds me of the Adelanto situation just a few months ago. That was when so many managers' lives were disrupted. Some even left the company, rather than be forced to move one hundred miles away to the hot desert. This is by no means that kind of a big deal in terms of basic commute, because nobody would have to uproot their family and relocate just to work in Gardena, but nevertheless, change is always disruptive. Like everyone else, I've looked at the pros and cons of the situation. Yes, Gardena would be a shorter commute for me, but who I would be working with and what I'd be doing are much more important questions for me. At this stage of my career, the key for me is to continue to create work/life balance while keeping my eyes on the prize. How appropriate it is that I am officially beginning the next Scroll Marked 6: "I will be master of my emotions."

In fact, my daily meditation prayer is simply this: *"Each day, as I relax my mind and body, I am being shown what to do. For today, I will be master of my emotions. God is revealing the truth about this situation as I utter, 'Peace, be still.' Make it so plain and clear for me that I cannot mistake it. I am at peace. God is in charge."*

From my point of view, there's no way to predict if Dan chooses me to go to Gardena would be cause for celebration, or concern. So, why sweat it? I truly want to just be open and receptive to my highest good for my life. Which means I've decided that I'm okay with whichever way the wind blows. I'll make my life a success, no matter where I end up, and others who will join me will be blessed by my presence, whether I stay, or whether I go.

That being said, I have suggested to a few of the Teamsters who are presently working for me, particularly Mike and Big D, that they consider going to Gardena if their union seniority and status prevails. That's because, for the next three years or so, that location will grow by quantum leaps, since it is starting out with a clean slate, with no past history or performance comparisons. In other words, the new Gardena staff (the pilot group) will get to set the standard for the terminal: bill count, revenue, load average, operating ratio (O.R.), etcetera. The sky will be the limit, and there will be lots of opportunity to set the bar, achieve bonuses, and participate in profit sharing. It also means more people will be needed for every type of job: more drivers, more dock workers, and more office personnel. Rumor has it that Gardena is the happening place where you'd want to be, so it would be smart to try and get on board if you can.

Initially, I've been more concerned about those two excellent performers than I am myself. I've already put in a good word for Big D with Bill and suggested he should try to transition Big D from dock to driver when the time is right. Big D's a very good man and will do a lot to help us achieve our mission if he has the chance, in addition to serving as an inspiration to the others. And now that we're splitting off into two terminals, going to Gardena could mean it will happen a lot quicker than if Big D decides to stand down and remain in Long Beach. I guess you could say, this is my clumsy attempt to play the politics game on Big D's behalf. I owe him an incredible favor, and I will always be grateful for the credibility, inspiration, and assistance he provided me in the early stages of my tenure as an Ops Supervisor. The turnaround in our Outbound operation performance was short of a miracle, and no one has been able to explain how we became such a well-oiled machine so quickly and easily under my leadership. My success has been amazing, and it is directly connected to the voluntary participation and cooperation of Mike, the crew, and especially Big Dewey.

Bill, who talks to all the right people "in the know", says that the growth in Gardena will be incredible – tenfold by 1983. We're going to pick up several cities once covered by the Los Angeles terminal, and our bill count is going to go through the roof from increased sales with our new sales staff, both Inbound and Outbound. Obviously, all this will dictate the number of drivers we'll need, as well as office and dock personnel. If Big D opts out and comes to Gardena, I doubt he'll work the dock very long, based on his present seniority. So, I told him that much as I want to keep things the way they are, things have already changed, and he's sure to end up driving and working the day shift. "Hell, look at me," I said, "I'm working Inbound now instead of Outbound, so everything is changing right now before our eyes. Who knows what I'll be doing in a month or so – perhaps dispatching?"

Well, the new Gardena terminal is scheduled to be up and running by March 1, 1982, so Dan and his people had better get a move on, whoever he's inviting to the party.

I also ask Mike if he is considering going to Gardena, and he says he is. I agree with him that I think it's a good move for him as well, and he's sure to ultimately end up driving. To my surprise, however, Mike says he likes the nighttime shift, because he has special daytime things he does related to his personal businesses and caring for his three young daughters while his wife, a schoolteacher, is at work.

Bottom line: I really do care about my men, and I only want to see the best happen for them. They've performed so well for me both Outbound and Inbound over the last few months that I hate we'll have to break up the team, but it is what it is. Maybe this whole experience was intended to be short-term, to show me the depth of my leadership capabilities and how effective I can be on my own. I will always be grateful to Big Dewey and Mike and the rest of the crew for their patience and assistance in helping me jumpstart my career in logistics. Now, though, it's time to put my Big Boy Pants On and go for it, whether I stay in Long Beach or move to Gardena.

Well, today is Friday, TGIF (Thank God It's Friday), and as I am preparing to close out my shift and get ready for a fun-filled weekend, Dan calls me into his office for his weekly Inbound re-cap meeting. So, I walk into his office, and before I can even close the door for privacy and take a seat, he ambushes me with a simple heads-up question. "So, Tony, what do you think about staying here in Long Beach?" he asks.

"Well, if that's where you want me, Dan, I'm all in. Long Beach is where I cut my teeth in this business, and it's really all I know, so I can just as easily keep doing what I'm already doing here. It's not a problem." I am careful to keep my voice warm, friendly, and cheerful.

"Okay, I see," Dan replies, noncommittally.

"Yeah, but I should tell you one thing, Dan," I continue.

"What's that Tony?" he asks.

"You're really gonna miss me, man! And you can take that to the bank!" I laugh.

"Now hold on, Tony, I was just checking your pulse to see how badly you'd like to stay here, or how badly you'd prefer to go with me to Gardena."

"So, are you saying I have a choice?"

"YES! I'm giving you a choice! Where do you want to be—honestly now? Long Beach or Gardena. It's your call. Speak now, or forever after hold your peace."

I pause for a long ten seconds, then, taking a deep breath, I reply, "Dan, I would LOVE to go with you to Gardena!"

Dan grins. "Well, that makes two of us! That makes two of us!" We shake hands.

And I yell, "ALRIGHT!"

I can't believe it! But I am so excited – like I'd just won the lottery or something, when the next words out of his mouth are, "I want you to go with me to Gardena, Tony. You're doing a good job out there, and we're going to keep this team as strong as we can!"

I actually yell again. "ALRIGHT! YEAH! Let's DO IT!"

The fact that Dan *wants* me and has chosen me to come with him to Gardena is music to my ears, even though I'd just said in all seriousness that it didn't matter. I guess I lied. It did matter, much more than I realized. But Dan wasn't done yet.

"Yeah," he says, "I do want you to come, but I have to tell you that I'm not the only one. So does Bill! Bill wants you to join our new team in Gardena, too."

"Really," I am surprised and dumbfounded.

"Hell, yes! Bill loves you, are you kidding me?"

I am momentarily speechless. I can't think of an appropriate comment to acknowledge that moment of joy.

So, Dan at least likes the quality of my work, even though he is forever trying to find something to criticize about it. Evidently, I'm doing some things right.

That morning, I also learn that Richard and Jim didn't make the cut and will both remain in Long Beach. Jim will continue to work the Inbound shift, and Richard will be demoted and reassigned back to the dock as Lead Outbound Supervisor. Surprisingly, David, who is now in sales, won't be coming either. I think his new sales territory is more in the Huntington Beach and Long Beach areas, so he'll have to stay in Long Beach. I'm not sure what is going to happen with Eric, the sales manager, but there's talk that he is considering a transfer to Northern California. However, Kim will be coming to Gardena. It no longer matters to me, but I just thought I'd mention it.

Dan also tells me he'll need to hire new salespeople, and he is getting a new sales manager transfer in from Philadelphia. I'm still optimistic that I'll be called up for sales duty in the next year or so, but I'm not holding my breath. Larry, Greg, and Huckabee are the main three sales guys that I know for sure made the cut and will be transferring to Gardena. Greg and Huckabee are very different than Larry but equally good in sales, and I'm glad that all three of them are coming with us to Gardena, now that I know my fate.

Our sales staff is being totally formed based on the new alignment of territories, cities, and zip codes. And there's this big seniority bulletin board in the drivers' room for all the union personnel to sign, if they are interested in coming to Gardena. However, in the end, it will all be based on their seniority as to who will make the cut.

Dan was right when he told me earlier that to be successful, you must learn to embrace change. "It's inevitable," he had said, "the one thing you can count on in this business. So, learn now to embrace change, Tony, and go with the flow." I'm glad I listened.

As the meeting is winding down, Dan lowers his voice to a whisper, and just as I was about to leave his office, he says that Bill had suggested on several occasions that he would prefer that I'd be permanently assigned to the Inbound shift as Lead Supervisor. "Bill likes how you get your men to move their asses, and he definitely likes how you're building his P&D runs each morning. What do you think about that suggestion?"

I take a minute to frame my answer carefully. "Well, I guess the cross training has paid off and shown I can do both Inbound and Outbound equally well on my own, and I do find Inbound more stimulating and challenging, although I dislike the hours. I'm not going to lie. I know I sleep better working Outbound because it's still night out when I get home. But I'm willing to try, because it's Bill that's asking. Okay, I'll give it a serious try!"

"That's great! This will go a long way toward your career development as a future manager. In fact, Bill says you have a memory like an elephant and everything he taught you, he sees you do it each and every time almost to perfection."

Wow! Bill said that? That's really special. He was my first great mentor, and I made a mental snapshot of his decisions each morning, and to this day, I try to replicate everything he did, except his chain smoking, of course. But his work ethic and efficiency are beyond reproach.

"He's the best," I reply.

"Once we get to Gardena, can I get your commitment that you'll be ready to take the Inbound shift as Lead?" Dan asks. "Bill says that you are not only ready, but you're the only one he trusts to run Inbound. In fact, he says that if I assign you to it, he's ready to trust you to do something he's not trusted others ever to do. He's going to trust you to close out his P&D loads each morning while he gets a couple more hours sleep before coming to the office."

"WHAT?"

"You heard me. No more 4:00 a.m. starts for Bill once we get to Gardena. I've been telling him the last five years to trust the system, but until you came along, he never did. So, you should feel honored."

Well, I definitely do feel honored, and it is a testament to the good job my men and I were doing, but I'm not sure how honored I was going to feel working those hours each night. Yet the thought that it would help Bill preserve his health and get more rest is a great compliment and the greatest gift I can give my mentor. I often worry about Bill, because he doesn't look healthy most of the time, and he works too many hours, not to mention his chain smoking. He's skinny as a rail.

"This is really good news, Dan – I mean really good news! However, I'm worried that I might do too good a job in Operations and may never get the nod from you to go into sales. I surely hope this change will not negate my chances to go into sales in the future."

"Don't you worry about that right now, Tony. We've got a lot to do this year to make this work. I need you to focus on the job at hand. Everything else will take care of itself," Dan assures me.

That pretty much ended our meeting. So, I've been considering the positives, and there are quite a few. Now that I've been chosen to move to Gardena, I'll be closer to my Los Angeles home and Cynthia's home as well. The more I think about it, I'm glad I'm going with Dan. The truth is, I really wanted to go with Dan to Gardena. Why? Because he's a tested and proven commodity. You know what you're getting. He's a sour pill to swallow sometimes, but at other times, he's like a good friend I can laugh with. In the sports world, he'd be like a Bill Belichick or a Nick Saban. He knows how to win, and he's damn good at running a tight ship and operating his terminal efficiently. His terminal's O.R. is always well in the mid-80s… always yielding large profit margins and bonuses every quarter. Also, he did promise me a job promotion in sales eventually, in the next two years or so. If I chose to remain in Long Beach, who knows what the new Terminal Manager would be like. Plus, that person has made me no promises. So, bottom line, I know Dan is a hard taskmaster, but he's good at what he does, and we will make money. In the next two months, all of this will get sorted out, and we'll be on our way to Gardena, ready to write a new chapter in the game of life. However, I continue to learn that the more things change, the more they remain the same.

As I recall the last six months of my spiritual growth and journey, I breathe a heartfelt "Thank you, God." It is a moment of pure gratitude as I walk outside to my car in the parking lot, preparing to leave work, yet finding myself still reflecting on the events of the last few days. I must admit that I'm walking about two feet taller this morning, for I am one of the chosen ones.

As I drive through the chain link security gate, I can't resist the temptation to blast my master cassette as loud as I possibly can with the Scroll Marked 6:

"TODAY, I WILL BE THE MASTER OF MY EMOTIONS."

Our grand opening, on March 1, 1982, was so uneventful it felt just like another day at the office. It was almost boring it was so routine.

The best thing so far about moving to Gardena was when I saw, with my own eyes, for the first time, that our next-door neighbors, McClean Trucking Company, with whom we share the same building, had a Black Sales Manager!!!   OH WOW!!! This is a big deal to me. It may not be a big deal to you, but it was – and is, even after all these years, for that matter—a very big deal for me to see someone who looks like me doing the job I aspire to. Who is this Black man in this $1,500 suit working for McClean Trucking Company, a relatively small niche family-owned trucking company, compared to Roadway? But – the fact that they have already embraced Diversity and Inclusion in their sales ranks gave me so much hope! Each morning, I would see this cool, good-looking Black brother stroll across the parking lot in his finest three-piece threads with such swagger and confidence that I could not wait to join this elite fraternity of men and women in sales.

I asked around until I found out his name: Mr. Hal Armstrong. He's been in the freight business, (operations and sales) for about 15 years and has been Sales Manager for McClean Trucking for the last five or six. Wow! I remember thinking that Roadway needs an Affirmative Action/ Title VII Diversity and Inclusion Intervention. Yet, finally, I had an image of someone who looked like me doing the job that I so desperately wanted to do someday. I was, however, forbidden to talk with him or anyone else working at McClean, under any circumstances, except one. It was totally against the rules, even though we shared a terminal. The only thing that separated us was a chain link fence that divided our docks halfway dead center of the building. We each had separate entrances to our quarters. It was like a shared warehouse/duplex building for two trucking companies under the same roof.

Unfortunately, the only way I could legally speak with anyone at McClean was on Fridays, and only to coordinate the approximate closing and opening time schedules for Friday and Sunday nights and the responsibility for setting the alarm for the building. Roadway was so conscious and paranoid of the anti-trust laws of the 1980s that you could be fired on the spot for talking to anyone who worked for the competition. That meant I had to admire this Black man from a distance, without communicating. Nevertheless, I was so grateful to have this constant visual reminder every day of what I aspired to become. The truth is that for me, it was worth it to come to Gardena just to see this confident Black man strolling across the parking lot in his three-piece suit every morning, carrying his briefcase. I saw what I could become each time I had that vision, and my consciousness was expanded forever more.

The second thing I loved about Gardena was meeting my new "partner in crime", Tom Donovan. A California transfer from back east by way of Ohio and Adelanto, he knows his stuff and is a smart, confident man with air freight experience, Irish red hair, and about my age. We immediately hit it off. I knew after the first night we worked together that we would be friends. There was just nothing awkward about being around him. For the first time, I felt as if I had a real comrade in this crazy business – someone I could trust. We both agreed that some of the rules Todd and Dan enforced were excessive and unnecessary, yet neither of us tried to fight Dan or City Hall. We looked so different, and we sounded differently, but we had such a common bond that he was like my "brother from another mother".

Tom told me many years later that the greatest compliment I'd ever paid him (and I don't even remember it) was when I said to him, "Tom, you are the first white man I ever met that makes me totally forget that he's white." We had each other's back on everything, no matter what. We hung out on weekends, sometimes at his house or mine. He introduced me to his entire family: dad, mother, brother, sister, and best friends from back east, and they were all cool people. I invited him to our annual backyard summer parties and introduced him to all my friends, including Cynthia, my California Play Mom, Mabel, and my roommate/brother, Zach. I loved celebrating some of his incredibly special Irish celebrations, especially his birthday and St. Patrick's Day events. The latter was quite a party, and I loved it. Tom wasn't one of those 1980s white guys that was trying to be a cool vanilla-ice-type. Tom was just Tom; intelligent, sophisticated, authentic, genuine, and cool – and we trusted each other.

What I liked most about our relationship and our family connections was that neither one of us had to rehearse and practice how to act or be around each other. It was just natural for us – no pretense, no difference, and I loved it. So often in those days, Black and white interactions were awkward and uncomfortable for both sides – but never with Tom and me. We partied together like it was 1999, and we sacrificed blood, sweat, and tears on that dock together.

I still wanted to go into sales, but now, because of my newly formed friendship with Tom, I was more tempered and content to wait my turn. I even stopped counting how many times Dan hired someone new into the sales department without making them pay any dues on the dock in Operations, dues that he had once said were a requirement before going into sales.

Tom was the first real friend and "partner in crime" I connected with in the workplace since moving to Los Angeles, and it was a game-changer for me. I always knew that one day, the hardest part about leaving

Roadway would be parting with my friend Tom. He is truly a genuine, good dude.

What stood out the most about 1982 was our Christmas holiday celebration at Dan's house. Yeah, Dan decided that he wanted to have the Christmas party at his home in Signal Hill and invite all the managers and sales staff. There was only one problem. Dan lives in Signal Hill, and I didn't want to be within 30 miles of Signal Hill because of the recent scandalous Ron Settles incident. Most of you would not know anything about Ron Settles and what happened to him, but I sure as hell remember. It was a dreadful event that happened to this young Black man in Signal Hill, and I told Dan I wouldn't be attending this year's Christmas party. Dan told me it was mandatory, and we all had to attend – no exceptions. I didn't see how I could possibly comply with the command performance.

In June 1981, Ron Settles, a 21-year-old African American college stand-out football player from Long Beach State, was mysteriously found dead in his jail cell while in custody of the Signal Hill police. This was before iPhones and mobile cameras, but it hit hard for many Black people around Los Angeles and the surrounding areas. It would have almost been the equivalent forty years later of the George Floyd incident of 2020, without video camera proof.

Allegedly, Mr. Settles was stopped and arrested in Signal Hill for a non-working signal light and three hours later, this 21-year-old stand-out athlete, and future top draft choice for the NFL, was found dead, hanging in his jail cell, and the Signal Hill police allegedly said he'd committed suicide. There was all kinds of evidence that disputed their suicide complaint: multiple blows and brute force to his head and body – and yet the Signal Hill police officers were all acquitted.

So, needless to say, in 1982, I was terrified about going to a Christmas party in Signal Hill, especially during the Christmas holidays, knowing there would be "sobriety check points" throughout Los Angeles and surrounding areas. I mean, if you think Signal Hill is bad, Los Angeles and the infamous Chief Darrel Gates were ten times worse. Gates was the guy with his infamous "choke hold", about which he said, "The choke hold seems to break and cause more deaths in Black people than in normal people." Who says shit like that and gets away with it? Oh, I know.

It was ridiculous, and Johnny Cochran proved in a civil suit later that the Signal Hill police were guilty, and a multi-million-dollar settlement was paid to the family of the deceased.

Nevertheless, Dan's holiday party was mandatory, and I had to attend. So, I asked Tom, "my brother from another mother", if he would literally follow me in and out of Signal Hill that night. The plan was, if I got stopped by the Signal Hill police, Tom would also stop and get out of the car, like he's F. Lee Bailey, the attorney, and serve as my representative, my friend, and white translator to the cops to keep them from taking me to jail and beating my ass to death. This seems so ridiculous, almost laughable today, but that was a serious moment for me, because I know how crazy those split seconds can go so drastically wrong when you're a Black man in America—especially in the 1980s.

Well, actually nothing has really changed much since then when it comes to this reality. These events continue to happen today in 2021 and beyond, just as in the 70s and 80s. For more information, you can google Richard Prior in his 1982 *Live on Sunset,* where he talks humorously about the "choke hold" as a common occurrence in that era, if you want to understand the history of that abuse – one of the more popular ways the LAPD used to execute Black people in this country.

And yes, I, like most Black men and women in America, started having "The Talk" when my two sons were seven. I still have "The Talk", and they are now 21 years old.

So, Tom and I became weekend warriors. We would go to parties all over the city together from Hollywood to Santa Monica, to Marina del Rey, to Baldwin Hills, to Culver City, to Inglewood, to Compton, to Orange County. We partied. Often, I'd take Cynthia with me. She liked Tom a lot. I would have his back in those more predominantly Black party situations, and vice versa. It was a crazy time, and we were living life to the fullest. All the while, I was still working on my personal self-development, and so was Tom.

Tom told me about two local guys in Orange County: Mark Victor Hansen, co-author of *The Chicken Soup for the Soul,* and Jules Marine. Both were great motivational speakers and salesmen. I went to see them both, and they didn't disappoint. Tom knew my goal to be promoted into sales. I was starting to notice that many of our competitors were more advanced in Diversity and Inclusion than we were. I can't speak for the entire Roadway system, but at Gardena and Long Beach, we had diversity in operations but not sales. I can't speak for the entire country, either, but it seemed like we were far behind in D&I. I knew I would jump ship tomorrow if I could be hired by McClean Trucking and go into sales. I could care less if they were a smaller, niche carrier. All I know is that they have Mr. Hal Armstrong, a Black sales manager, and I would love to work for this brother. He is sharp to the max.

Also, I was hearing that Yellow Freight, Consolidated Freightways, PIE Nationwide, Willig, Delta, Time DC, Daylight, ABF, and Transcon are hiring people of color, including Black people. In fact, I was told that PIE Nationwide has a Black Vice President named Jay Johnson (aka: Big Jay) that is out-of-sight. Transcon has a Black sales manager, Clay Howard. I was so impressed, and I wanted my shot. I *like* seeing somebody who looks like me doing the job I want to do.

I'm now working the Inbound shift, and I love the challenge, but I hate how difficult it is to sleep in the daytime. I've been showing Tom the ropes on Outbound, and my biggest regret is that I miss Big Dewey. I no longer need him to threaten and do my bidding to get buy-in from the men, but I miss him as a person. He was such a good friend, and he helped pave the way for my success. I'm happy he's driving now and working days, and I'm eternally grateful for his support when I first started. What he was willing to do for me in less than 15 minutes was a game-changing experience for my career.

Things never got really bad once we split up the two terminals. Gardena is definitely smaller, but now we are faster and more efficient, and we have a good crew. I still have Mike as my lead and six or seven other great guys: Alex, Ken, Robert, Gary, Adolph, Jessie, etc. Also, I have a list of Casuals, including Mr. J.C. Carlos, on speed dial, who I can call in at a moment's notice.

Everything is going well, but moving at rapid speed, and before I know it, I exhale and realize that two-and-a-half years have come and gone. I've studied several spiritual and motivational books and lived and repeated two times now the 10 Scrolls from *The Greatest Salesman in the World*. Tom and I are the best of partners. Todd is no longer being a bully, and we're running a tight ship and making tons of profit. Even Dan has backed off and started to celebrate more of our positive victories than before. If I could be content with my station in life just as I am – it would be great, but I just can't. Being an Inbound Lead Supervisor is just not going to cut it much longer for me. I've been trying not to rock the boat, but I can't do this much longer. I'm ready to go into sales.

It's time I have a serious talk with Dan about the promise he made to me on my first day on the job back in May 1981. It's time for Dan and me to sit down and discuss my future. It's also time I know for sure how Dan feels about me and what he sees for my future – and when he will begin helping me move toward my next promotion. I hope our conversation is cordial and productive. It's been almost three years since I started working here, and I've done everything he's asked of me. Now, I'm ready for a new challenge: a promotion into sales. So, I'm going to shut up and listen and let Dan explain what he sees for me and what he's going to do about it. I seek the truth, and the truth will set me free.

And so it is.

CHAPTER THIRTEEN

THE KISS OF DEATH

"There is an old saying, 'No man is your enemy,
no man is your friend. Every man is your teacher.'"
- Florence Scovel Shinn

It's been said that you are not ready to tell your story if you are still playing its victim. If telling your truth still upsets you, makes you angry, weep, or become emotionally unstable, then you aren't at peace about the situation yet. So, I suggest that you wait to tell your story publicly, until you recognize that your messes have become your blessings. I know, for me, my lessons – good, bad, or ugly, have become my blessings. I have moved on and chalked them up as a part of my life's lessons, designed to prepare me for what is coming.

I wouldn't have attempted to tell this chapter of my story 30 years ago. I was not ready. I was still too close to the process. This may sound strange to many of you, but for almost the last half century, "The Key to My Success" has been my sincere practice of the Power of Forgiveness. I will explain more about this powerful technique in a later chapter, but for now, let's continue the story.

For the last two years, I had made it a routine to come into the office on my day off, at least once or twice every month, for the sole purpose of impressing Dan and Chuck, the new sales manager. Yes, that's right. Every month, I returned to the office, dressed to the nines, even though I'd be tired as hell from working all night and all week. I made it a faithful practice to go home, get all showered and cleaned up, put on one of my best three-piece suits and ties and return to work – pretending I forgot something, usually my paycheck.

I'd walk around in my three-piece suit, looking good, talking to Bill about his P&D strategy for the day, stopping to chat with Todd, and then, of course, giving attention to Teresa, the new office manager, and the other women in the office. I'd always make sure to talk with Dan, no matter how busy he might have seemed at the time. I'd pretend to be headed out to an all-day sales seminar, usually in Orange County, which would mean that I would be headed in that direction when I left the office, either by way of 91 Freeway or the 405 Freeway South. I'd usually flash a brochure of motivational heavyweights: Zig Ziglar, Earl Nightingale, Mark Victor Hansen, Jack Canfield, Brian Tracy, or Jules Marine, as a reference to the type of heavyweights I'd been listening to and following. I knew that neither of these guys, Dan or Chuck – nor any of the salesmen (Greg, Huckabee, Larry, or the others) – were familiar with these heavyweights. When I'd throw out their names, I could tell that to them, it seemed like a foreign language or a sport they weren't familiar with. I delighted in knowing and taunting them with what I knew was a vital ingredient for success in sales. At least I knew it was vital for me. Some of these sales guys were still relying upon their position as a privileged, white good ole' boy, to be their ticket to success in sales. I can't lie and pretend that it wasn't working for many of them, because in the climate of the 1980s, it still did. The winds of change were blowing, though, and thank God I was on the cusp of that change.

"Have you heard sales and motivational tapes by Brian Tracy and Earl Nightingale?" I would ask. "How about Zig Ziglar and Mark Victor Hansen?" They would just look at me, uncomprehending, so I'd continue.

I'd say to Chuck, "You ought to let your people go with me to Orange County and attend this seminar next week. This guy, Jules Marine, is fantastic – a local phenomenon, self-made millionaire. He's powerful! You go to one of his workshops and he's gonna beat that hammer on the podium to get your attention – and you'll be sitting up listening for the rest of the day. You know, he's got this workshop called "Selling is Easy". I love his approach to selling. He's good. Seriously, you should check him out."

Now I knew perfectly well that neither Chuck, the new sales manager, nor any of his people had ever heard of any of these motivational giants, but I just wanted to get them to see me as a "mover and shaker" in the world of positive motivational information. What can I say? This material just wasn't being studied by salespeople back in the day the way it is now. I was a serious student of the game, because I had nothing else, and no other roadmap that made sense. It helped shape me into who I would ultimately become, and for that, I'm eternally grateful.

Often on these visits, some of the office women would give me a cat whistle or some nice, friendly compliment as I paraded around in my brand-new suit. It wasn't offensive in those days to show true excitement over the opposite sex. I remember I was famous for the great neck and back massages I'd offer anyone who was feeling stressed and needed it. Most of the women would raise their hands, hoping to be selected, as if they were standing in line.

"Please, Tony, do me next!"

If I tried that today, I'd probably get arrested or get reported to HR for sexual harassment. But back in the 1980s, it was perfectly fine to be generous and helpful in alleviating stress among the staff, with an innocent neck and back massage. I was 30 years old, confident, and looking good, ready to take on the world. I felt that my future looked great, and that I belonged, just as I was. But the real purpose of this entire once-a-month drop-in was to elevate the consciousness of Dan and Chuck, so they'd start seeing me as a worthy and qualified candidate for sales; to see me differently than the way they usually saw me. I was simply trying to help them overcome their "unconscious biases" about me as a Black man, different from the way I assumed they saw me. I mean, here I was working all night, and by morning, I was tired, beat down, and haggard. I'm sure I never looked 100 percent my best after a long 10 to 12-hour shift. There is no substitute for good, restful, replenishing sleep, and I was so sleep-deprived that I knew my best personality was suffering. So, on my day off once or twice a month, I'd come in just to give them a glimpse… a reminder of an updated version of myself, the best version of me. I don't know if it ever paid off, but it was good for me to practice staying focused, and I did it religiously for over two years. Then, I'd go home and crash for a few hours before I began my weekend with Cynthia, Tom, Zach, and my other friends.

I was totally confident that I could be a great representative in sales for Roadway, as the face for the Big R, talking and solving problems with customers each day while expressing authentically me, the best version of me. I was on a mission to become a salesperson in transportation-logistics, and I had a message to anyone who was paying attention: "I'm ready, passionate, overqualified, polished, and prepared for this job. Hire me and you'll never regret it." I'd prepared myself and got myself ready, despite the odds. My confidence was permeating throughout my being, and if Roadway didn't recognize it soon, someone else was going to. And the rest would be history.

Well, when I stopped momentarily to exhale and acknowledged that 1984 was right around the corner and realized that the obvious fact was that it had been almost three years, and I was getting really tired. That's right. My energy, enthusiasm, and endurance were starting to fade, and I was feeling totally drained. The truth was that my spirit was feeling betrayed, and I was starting to question my original purpose for this entire commitment I'd made almost three years ago. As much as I'd grown into a man with tough skin, with spiritual enlightenment, strength, motivation, and leadership acumen, there were moments when I was questioning everything. I worried. "What If I get to the end of my life and find out I've climbed the wrong damned mountain, like Ivan Ilyich?"

I was so ready for a change. I was reminded of Leo Tolstoy's story in the book, *The Death of Ivan Ilyich*, about the Russian attorney and judge, who worked 50 years and hated his job. He also hated his wife, and most of all, he hated his life. At his deathbed, his last words were, as he looked up at his wife, "What if my entire life has been a mistake? Death is finished," he whispered to himself. "It is no more!" He drew in a breath, stopped in the midst of a sigh, stretched out, and died. I often thought of that story and questioned, "What if my life and everything I've been doing is a mistake?

All I knew in those days was that I was so tired that sometimes I didn't even feel like thinking. My body and mind were exhausted all the time, and I was feeling like a walking zombie. I've never been able to sleep well in the daytime, and just about when I was ready to fall asleep, it would be time to get up and go back to work. I needed coffee, cigarettes, and "No Doze" throughout the shift just to stay awake. All that stimulant kept me buzzing and floating in an altered state all night. The days that I was off, I was too tired to sneak around and interview with other companies. It was very difficult to put my best foot forward in an interview. I was honestly feeling like I needed to quit this job, just so I could rest up for two weeks to prepare for an interview where I'd be alive, afresh, and renewed.

I couldn't even begin a solid interview process with the competitors, because my mind and body were so tired. However, the other problem was that the competition would, undoubtedly, be more interested in hiring me for my operations experience. It's true – just as they'd said – my good Roadway training would be an appealing asset to the competition, so much so that it would be difficult to get another company to give me a chance in sales. In fact, it would be just as difficult for the competitor to consider hiring me in sales as it would be getting Roadway, my own company, to consider me as a viable sales candidate. Dan had made the promise years ago, and now it was seeming like a recurring dream I was questioning in my sleep. But, regardless, I was ready to confront him and have a real conversation about my future. I was ready to take a chance.

For three years, I had been carefully avoiding expressing even a hint about race or discrimination being a viable reason for being denied sales. Many people had warned me from personal experience and observation to never, ever play the "Race Card". It was considered by most as the "unforgivable sin" – "the kiss of death". If you were Black and wanted a serious, long, prosperous career in transportation logistics, you could not become known as a troublemaker, spouting off about racial injustices in the workplace. No one wanted then – and perhaps now – to work with that person, and you could be "blackballed" from the industry for a long period of time, or for life.

After leaving the Jim Crow South and moving to Los Angeles, I had vowed never to see racism as the elephant in the room that was denying my success. I vowed that I was in the land of the free: Southern California; and I chose to intentionally look beyond those racial potholes and blind spots, and never to have to see racism through the same lens as I had when I lived in the South. I had never looked at myself as a "Title VII Protected Class", and I certainly never saw myself as a member of a "privileged class" either. Also, I never liked the idea of being referred to as a "token". I truly felt that I was not only qualified, I was over-qualified and capable. Yes, my confidence was through the roof, and I felt that I belonged. This was my time. I was young, gifted, and Black, and all I wanted was a chance to prove that I could impress Dan and Chuck in the sales arena, just as I had amazed them with consistent, record-breaking performances for almost three years in Operations.

I hated the word "token" and the way it was often secretly discussed behind closed doors – whether boardrooms or bathrooms. However, I was certainly a part of the 1970s era when every college in America was clamoring to get their hands on the superstar Black athlete. I remember feeling like an expensive piece of meat when being recruited by all those Division One schools. These coaches were coming by the dozens to my little Oklahoma town to talk to me and my parents about my college future, and the possibilities of becoming a World Class Olympian track star someday. It all sounded and felt so good to be courted and pursued, and it certainly made my parents proud, too. But make no mistake – they wanted you to come to their university, but you had to deliver the goods, or you'd be gone and forgotten, with no athletic scholarship, in a New York minute.

As a family, we had never experienced this type of full-court college recruiting where the phone wouldn't stop ringing. Some coaches even parked and slept outside the house, waiting on the moment when you came outside. However, as exciting as all of this was, I would not be the first person in my family to go to college. That's not my story. I can't even pretend. In fact, in my family, including my extended family, a college education was a non-negotiable item for me and my sister. As a child growing up, it was understood early that in our family, you would be attending college. My parents and all my relatives were educated, and college graduates with advanced degrees were the norm. I was raised with the idea that education was the equalizer for your future. Moreover,

I knew I had to be two or three times better than my competition, just to be in the conversation and have a seat at the table of opportunity. So, that was fine with me, if the game was being played fairly. I knew that my odds were more difficult than the "privileged", but I had never felt that becoming a salesperson at Roadway was impossible. However, now I was having serious second thoughts.

Title VII and Title IX helped protect and level the playing field for Black people, women, and all people of color, based on race, color, religion, national origin, ancestry, sex, physical or mental disability, veteran status, and citizenship in education and in the business world. As they say, money talks and bullshit walks. So, when the federal government placed these demands and minimum requirements on the schools, colleges, universities, and the corporate world, it made a huge impact toward creating a more fair and equitable playing field for Black people, women, people of color, and others –at least for the time being.

As risky as it was, interviewing with the competition had become a necessary evil. I no longer trusted that Dan or Roadway had my best interests at heart, and I had to take the chance to see what else was out there for me. So, once I ended my morning shift, I'd go home and get all spruced up in my best suit and attempt to interview for a job in sales with the competition: Yellow Freight, ABF, Transcon, Leeway, PIE Nationwide, Willig, Watkins, and many others. There were hundreds of competitors out there to explore, and I was determined. However, it was risky. I knew that if one person from Roadway ever saw me driving my car in or out of the competition's facility, I'd be fired on the spot. But it was a chance I was willing to take. Yes, it was a scary ordeal, and I never did my best in the interviews, because, number one, I was too tired, and number two, I was too scared and self-conscious about being seen, knowing I would be fired immediately if discovered. The anti-trust laws and Roadway's rules, in general, were very clear, forbidding you from fraternizing with the competition. No exception to the rules.

What was starting to eat at my soul was the fact that I was finally starting to notice just how badly I'd been manipulated and lied to by Dan. I'd been patient, and it had come at a bitter price. It was becoming harder and harder to stomach the bizarre lies and racism that Dan was blatantly demonstrating in my face. Yes, I had said it, but not out loud: RACISM! I had tried so hard to ignore the elephant in the room for the last three years, holding out for hope's sake that my day was coming if I just kept my nose clean and did my job amazingly well. But now, I could no longer be silent and continue to pretend that I didn't see what I was seeing. Yet, despite the things that weren't right, there were a lot of things that were good.

I'd grown tremendously as a person during the last three years. We, as a company, had grown by leaps and bounds. I had created my own mental mindset foundation and formula for success, and I was ready to fly. I'd saved a few thousand dollars, approximately $20,000, and I was preparing to start looking for my first home in Southern California as a single man who desired simply to have a home with a backyard for his German Shepherd.

Yes, Cynthia had been right. A single person could purchase a home in Southern California if you got your mind and your money right, and yes, we were still together, but it was not the same. She was still a great lady, and she meant well, but her ties to Ray Duncan were no longer acceptable to me. Ultimately, our relationship would not survive long term, for I was becoming convinced that I could have a more exclusive relationship than the one I'd shared and endured with her ex-boyfriend, who continued to refuse to step out of the picture. I'd accepted it because of my impossible nighttime work schedule that prevented me from a normal social life except on weekends. Of course, she was still hopeful that we could all get along like a big, nice, blended family. But ultimately, I knew I was not going to stand for it. I was starting to get restless and notice other women and opportunities, even though I had not yet acted on any of it. No sir, this relationship would not work for me long term, and I only hoped and prayed that when the time came, Jamal would forgive me.

Over the last three years, I had completed the Scrolls not once, but twice, and I'd read so many books and listened to many tapes on positive motivation and salesmanship over and over and over. I had continued to get more involved in the church and was attending classes in eastern and metaphysical philosophy. I guess you could say that I was becoming a student of spiritual enlightenment. In two more years, I would receive my certification as a Spiritual Practitioner and Counselor. I was continuing to meditate daily and was truly on a solid spiritual path. I was becoming more about sharing more love and joy in the world and becoming the change that I wanted to see. I was now definitely a student of "the game of life" and how to play it.

I should mention one thing that had been so liberating for me was three years ago, back in 1981, when I had my big blow-up with Dan, I had sat down and written my resignation letter. That was the episode when he criticized me for not doing an "inbound Pre-set". Well, when I got home that night, I sat down and typed out my official resignation letter, which I proceeded to carry around in my car's glove compartment for the next three years. I knew then that I needed to learn how to control my anger, and I also knew that I was determined to learn how to do that. But, just in case I didn't make it to the finish line, I decided to neatly pre-type that resignation letter in advance, at a time when I was at peace, happy, joyous, and in a good space. I was able to articulate on paper how much I appreciated everyone and thank them for the wonderful opportunity they had provided me. It was a masterful letter that only needed my signature and the date. I kept this letter in its private envelope, neatly positioned and protected in that glove compartment, and when the day came when I finally did officially quit, I would, in fact, use that letter to give my two weeks' notice. The resignation letter remained an anchor; a symbol of my anticipation and preparation if things ultimately did not work out. Maybe that's a contradiction and an example of working with a dual purpose, but that's how I did it back then. It was my tool of survival.

During that three years, my life had been filled with a fast, constant rhythm, a sense of urgency, complete with critical, dramatic, and urgent events, one after another, both personally and professionally. This is the norm in the transportation logistics business, and this has become my life. I get to make decisions every night that could affect our company's bottom line by hundreds of thousands of dollars in profit and loss. What Dan has taught me, and what he preaches daily, is this one cold, hard fact. He had told me early on, "If you have to call me every night when faced with a major decision, then I don't need you. Make a damn decision, Tony, even if it costs me thousands, because I hired you to manage and make those decisions. If you have to call me, then you aren't necessary, which means that I don't need you."

So, rarely did I ever call him. I mean, the building would almost have to be burning down before I would call him. I learned to "make a damn decision", no matter what. It has served me well, even to this day. I will make a damn decision and live with it, no matter what.

Each morning when Dan would come in, his favorite thing was to walk the dock with me and ask a hundred questions to explain the status of each loaded trailer at the dock. I would literally do a practice walk each morning with Mike before Dan arrived, rehearsing and listening to how I sounded when discussing and explaining the thought process that went into building each P&D load. I would practice sound bites to create efficiency in my answers. Dan liked short answers that spoke clearly to the situation. I learned to anticipate his questions. Sometimes, the only answer I could provide was, "Dan, I know this decision at 7 a.m. looks like crap to you, but it was the best decision available at 3 a.m. this morning when I made it."

I would be amazed at how often he preferred that response over a more detailed, sophisticated answer full of multiple excuses. In his own way, I could tell he was proud of me as his protégé working on the dock, and as long as I kept my desire for sales at a minimum, he was good with most of my decisions. I think Bill had been my biggest fan and had been talking me up a lot to Dan. It had started as an experiment at Bill's request that all supervisors become "cross trained" and able to perform Inbound, Outbound, and Dispatch.   For the record, I loved the challenge of Inbound more so than Outbound, but I hated the hours. Becoming a full-time dispatcher—no way! Being a full-time dispatcher will shorten your life by ten years. It's a thankless job. You've got phones ringing off the hook, customers yelling at you on the phone, and drivers yelling at you via radio, simultaneously, all day long. Plus, ridiculous traffic and time restraints, and often customers with impossible, demanding situations that cause many delays, due to their own gridlock at the customer's facility. You are literally at the mercy of your drivers' performance out on the streets, without the ability to visually check them. You need them to answer their radios, and you need them to work at a fast pace to unload and be ready for pickups before the afternoon peak time. It takes a lot of coordinating, and the phones never stop ringing. That was pure hell. I would still take Inbound or Outbound any day over Dispatching. I don't know how Bill did it at age 68, year after year, with such ease, calm, and grace.

Becoming a "driver spy" was originally Richard's new job assignment, when we were still in Long Beach. The word had already gotten around to the drivers that he was the new "driver spy guy", assigned to sneak around and take pictures, exposing all the bad slug drivers and their bad habits. I could never have agreed to do that job, and I'm sure Richard was happy to be in Long Beach, relieved of that duty. Dan once joked with me, asking if I would like to be a "driver spy" when we got to Gardena and spend a couple of hours before and after work doing some investigating out on the street. He said he'd pay me extra to do it. I told him no thanks, not ever. I would NOT spy on those drivers.

He somewhat knew what my answer would be before asking, but he laughed, and then, deciding to sweeten the pie, jokingly said, "What if I promise to promote you to sales in one year from now for sure? If you would do 'driver spy' for a year?" That almost got my attention, but by now, I didn't believe or trust him. I replied, "Well, Dan, you told me it would take a couple of years to go into sales and I had to pay some dues. I'm okay with waiting and learning all I can about Operations."

For whatever reason, that moment between us was very warm and friendly and didn't lead to hostility. It was almost as if he was really starting to relax around me and open up a little bit. I thought that we could almost be friends, and we actually had some things in common, like growing up in the South. Of course, his life was different than mine, even though he told me of his positive encounters with Black people when growing up. (What, you loved your Black nanny and played on the farm with her Black children? Of course, as they got older, and when school started, things changed – and they eventually grew apart once they realized it wasn't cool to be friends any longer.)

Dan constantly preached over and over to me to always remain calm, composed, and flexible – and be able to turn on a dime when the circumstances at hand required it. Dan showed such calmness under pressure, but when things were going extremely well was when he would show serious irritation at the smallest errors. The only time I ever saw Dan get unhinged was when I was told by one of the office women, a lady he trusted more than the others, that one of his ex-wives had attempted suicide, unsuccessfully. On that day, Dan closed his office door and didn't resurface for hours. I was told he'd said practically nothing to anyone that day. Before I left to go home at the end of my shift, the door was still closed, so I left without doing our routine Inbound recap. Dan often said, "The one constant…the one guarantee…is that there will always be change." I guess that day's tragedy involving his ex-wife was the exception to the rule. However, I knew that tomorrow, he would bounce right back and continue to press forward, as if nothing ever happened.

The truth was that working for Dan was always challenging. He was the poster child for HARD WORK, SACRIFICE, AND A SENSE OF URGENCY. And if you worked for him, you'd better give 110 percent all the time, or you would probably not be at Roadway for any length of tenure. Dan was the type of leader always working toward making you stretch, which also makes you better, more efficient, more effective at doing your job, and which ultimately makes you a better leader and manager. You could never make him extremely happy, because he was never going to be satisfied with your performance, production, or success – no matter if you broke every performance record in existence.

In fact, the more you were able to achieve easily, the harder he would try to make your work life and workload a living hell. So, it was never going to be easy – get that out of your mind. Nevertheless, I had adapted quite nicely, and working for him did have its perks and rewards. I think it was my commitment to spirituality and positive motivation that had made the real difference in my ability to successfully cope with him and his management style. However, if I'm being completely honest, and before things fell irrevocably off the rails between us, let me just say for the record, that Dan had been by far one of my greatest teachers, for which I remain eternally grateful.

So, eventually, the day came when I arrived at the office on my day off, specifically to speak with Dan about my future. As usual, to impress him, I was dressed sharp-as-a-tack in my favorite three-piece suit. He insisted that we take a walk out onto the dock, where it was quiet, to be alone and also get away from all the nosey people with their big elephant ears. So, we took the long walk down to the far end of the dock, where we were completely alone. Our conversation then went something like this:

I began by asking him, "Dan, I need to know what you see for my future. I feel as if I've been doing a lot of things right and good; just as you want them. However, I need to know what you see next for me, and when."

"Now, Tony," Dan replied, "I've told you to just be patient. I've got big plans for you. I see you having your own terminal someday and going far – I mean even further than me. It's possible you could have your own terminal and someday even be over an entire region as a Vice President. I'm serious."

"Yeah, Dan, but there's just one thing. I've told you repeatedly that I'm not interested in going the operations route. I'm not knocking operations, because many people love it and thrive in this environment. However, I want sales, and you promised me that after I paid my dues 'in a couple of years', that you would promote me."

"Now I know what I said on your first day at work, Tony, but a lot has happened since that first day."

"Yeah," I replied. "You've hired four or five new sales guys. I can't even keep count any more. You've hired at least five guys in sales that never spent one day out on the dock. They never paid any dues in Operations."

"Tony, the bottom line here is supply and demand. We needed those guys in a hurry, and they had prior experience, and three of them even came through the door with large books of business and ready to go."

"Dan, I don't care what the excuse is. You promised me sales in two years."

"Tony, listen. You don't understand. I wish there was a better way for me to explain this situation. I know you've got your master's degree and everything, but that really doesn't matter. You see, where I grew up and where I'm from, Sales was always a white man's job. That's all I've ever seen. That's all I've ever known. So, you have got to be patient with me. It's not time yet for that kind of change around here."

I took a deep breath.

"Dan," I said, "did you hear what you just said? I can't believe I've worked for you for the last three years, and now you tell me how you really feel about me."

"Tony, now listen. I apologize for being so blunt, but I'm just trying to tell you as nicely as I can, the way things really are. Because this is reality where I'm from. Now, I've complied every single time when it came to hiring one of y'all, but I'll be damned if anybody is going to come in here and tell me where I have to place you. I'm still in charge, and this is my terminal, and I don't think you're ready. Hell, I don't think the customer is ready for you either. It's just not time yet, Tony. It's just not time. Sorry!"

"Dan, I think the only person who isn't ready is you. You do know that this is racism at its highest level. I mean this is out-and-out discrimination any way you look at it. I can't believe what you just said, but in 20 seconds, you just summed up what's in your heart about how you really feel about me and Black people in general. Basically, you're a damn bigot. That's the bottom line. You are a damn bigot."

"No, I'm not, Tony. I'm a realist. I'm not prejudiced. You just don't seem to know how hard it is, and you don't want to be patient and accept your place. I've got the perfect path for your future already lined up. You just need to be patient and believe in me. You can go far with my plan, if you stick with me, and make a lot of money along the way. I mean it."

"Dan, have you looked outside your window this morning or any morning around 7:30 to 7:45 a.m.? There's a Black man named Hal Armstrong that walks through the parking lot who is the sales manager for our neighbors at McClean Trucking. Have you not taken the time to look out the window as I have, and witness progress in America? I get to watch a Black man every morning stroll across the parking lot dressed to the nines in his three-piece thousand-dollar suits, and dream about what's possible for my future as well. If you haven't seen him stroll across the parking lot, you must be living under a rock."

"Yeah, I've seen Armstrong," replied Dan, "heard all about him, too, and personally, I'm not impressed with his body of work."

"You know what, Dan? The sentiment is probably mutual. Hal Armstrong may not be impressed with your body-of-work either, but he is one sharp, intelligent, professional Black man doing exactly what I wish to be doing someday soon," I retorted.

"Just keep in mind that McClean is a three-tier carrier compared to Roadway. We're the biggest and the best, nationwide. We are Number One."

"Dan, I don't care if McClean Trucking is a five-tier carrier and number 50 compared to us. All I'm saying is, that we are behind the times if you think that sales business can only be conducted by white men. This is southern California man, 1984! What year are you living in? You must think this is 1955, Montgomery, Alabama or something. I'm starting to see just how shallow and limited my future is if I choose to stay here and work for you. You'd probably like to keep me right here working on the dock as an Ops Supervisor for the next 40 years, until I retire or die."

"No, that's not true Tony. I really do care about you and your future, and I know that if you stick with me, I'll help you in ways you can't even imagine. After all, it's not just what you know, but who you know that will get you ahead in life."

"Sorry, Dan, if sticking with you means staying put in Operations my entire career, no thank you," I replied.

"I wish you'd go home and think about my offer and your future over the weekend," Dan said. "Just trust and believe in me, Tony, and I will prove to you that your future is going to be great. I promise."

"If believing in you means accepting Operations instead of sales as a career, then I can't, and I won't. This thing you said about sales being only for a white man is not only outdated, but racially charged by your own beliefs about the past. This is a new day, Dan, and you need to really think about what you just said, for this is total racial discrimination in every sense of the word. I'm sure you've heard about Title VII, the Civil Rights Act of 1964. Need I say more?"

Then, I walked off. I was truly proud of myself for not getting angry, yelling, and turning this into a real knockdown, drag-out confrontation, even though I had just broken the "unforgivable cardinal sin" and played the race card. I felt that, under the circumstances, I had no choice. Dan had started down that rabbit hole with his initial "sales as a white man's job only" comment, and I simply felt there was no alternative, other than to respond appropriately to his statements. Now, I understood why Dan wanted to take the walk on the dock, so no one could hear our conversation. He was well-aware that this could have become an angry, heated, totally ballistic exchange, as I reminisce about our 1981 confrontation.

But more importantly, by his choice of location, the content of our discussion meant that it was his word against mine. As much as this was not exactly a confrontation, but more of an honest, heartfelt discussion of Dan's unconscious biases, I still realized that I was treading in quicksand. For the rest of my career, I could be labeled and black-balled with the kiss of death as a troublemaker who plays the race card, even though I was simply responding to Dan's stated sentiments. In that moment, I was sure that my view was not the way the story would be told in the distant future, once I was gone.

In less than 60 seconds, Dan had summed up how he truly felt about Black people and women in general, and me in particular, and now, for the rest of my career, whether I stayed or went, I would have to push past Dan's toxic, haunting words about me and my people so openly expressed. I knew I would never succumb to his limited view of me in relationship to the world, no matter how it made me feel in that moment. I had honestly thought he was going to make an exception for me, because I thought he genuinely liked and respected me and my work. Yes, for that moment, I had been even willing to be his token. And I knew in my mind that I needed to take a stand. I knew it wouldn't be an easy decision, but I also knew that however it worked out would only be temporary – just an inconvenience that I would overcome. I decided to walk away. One foot in front of the other, just like I did when we had our blow up in 1981. And just like that, without another word spoken, this discussion was over.

While I was walking away, though, I realized that this time I was doing so feeling empowered and under control. I was not upset or angry with hearing Dan's truth about this situation. In fact, in a strange way, I was relieved to know where I really stood with him. I knew also that this would not be decided or settled in this moment, and that this was not the time to push or sweat it any further. After all, it was Friday. I decided to go back home and lick my wounds and rest up for the weekend.

However, I would be remiss not to mention that I did so with the full realization that this conversation had already gone too far and represented the "quiet before the storm". Next week, the shit would hit the fan. This I knew for sure, for I had now been officially labeled "the troublemaker", which meant that sooner or later, I would have to go.

CHAPTER FOURTEEN

GOOD TROUBLE

"My philosophy is very simple. When you see something that is not right, not fair, not just, say something! Do something! Get in trouble. Good trouble! Necessary trouble." – John Lewis

I once heard that when it's time for you to depart from a situation, if you don't go peacefully, if you don't go quickly, nature has a way of kicking you out. Sometimes slowly and gracefully; sometimes abruptly. Driving to work that Sunday evening, that's exactly how I felt. I was about to get kicked out of my job, and not gracefully either. Most likely, quite abruptly. I was certain of it. This week at work would inevitably be very different; tense, rigid, and uncomfortable for everyone. Last Friday morning's conversation with Dan was a serious one, the kind that could not easily be swept under the rug.

By now, the key personnel and top brass would know Dan's version of the story – not mine. And from his perspective, while he might get reamed for speaking so plainly to an underling, he would have had little recourse except to label me a troublemaker—a loudmouth—a hot-headed, angry Black man who had accused him of being a bigot. Naturally, the top brass and decision-makers would believe his version of the story.

Who I am as a person, and what I've accomplished here at Long Beach and Gardena would be irrelevant. After all, he's Dan Dixon, one of their brightest super-star managers. So, I can only assume the situation will be known and remembered as all my fault, and I'll be blamed 100 percent for the problem it caused.

On a spiritual level, however, it was beginning to dawn on me that I might have done what I came to do here, and it was time to move on. Indeed, as soon as I unlocked the door and entered the building on Sunday night, I knew unconditionally and immediately that it was time to go. Everything felt different, the way you know the movie is ending when the music starts and the credits roll.

As usual, no one was there that evening as I turned on the main office lights and coded the secret numbers into the alarm. I looked around and realized what a difference three years had made. I thought, "You've grown tremendously these last three years in this company, Tony, and no matter how you slice it, The Big R is responsible in part for a huge portion of that growth, maturity, and development—and no matter what happens next, you should be profoundly grateful. Thank you, God." I ended the thought with a silent prayer of gratitude.

It was almost as if I was already starting to say goodbye to the building and the many memories it held. The time was now 21:00, two hours before my men would be arriving, and for now, there was total quiet. I was alone and left with time to think. "The calm before the storm." And in this case, I anticipated that before the week was up, it would not just be a storm, but a full-blown tsunami.

In my mind, I was already preparing to leave. No other course of action made sense or soothed my soul. I could only hope that my leaving would clear the path for the next Black person – the way Earl had predicted three years ago, when on my arrival, he had told me I was his replacement. In a roundabout way, the cycle was continuing – one

Black person at a time, instead of two or three or even four. Yet, here I was, ready to exit the building with no real guarantees of my future. Still, it was time, and I was ready to go. No more mountains awaited my climbing in this place. I wondered briefly why the conversation with Dan had to become primarily about race. Why wasn't it about character, qualifications, commitment, dedication, excellent performance, intellect, collaboration, etc.? I guess it's really true: "people really don't quit companies, they quit bosses." And here I was, getting ready to quit Dan, almost like a disgruntled boyfriend leaving a relationship.

My mother, a deeply religious woman, used to say that "situations like this that are overwhelmingly intrusive and often appear hopeless in your life, represent a real test of your faith." She also used to say, "God doesn't put more on you than you can handle, Tony." At this defining moment, I couldn't see anything good about the situation as it related to me, except a huge test of my faith. I had given my all: blood, sweat, and tears for three years with the hope and implied promise of a promotion into sales, only to discover that the person who made the promise was psychologically incapable of following through on that promise, because of his own deeply rooted prejudices.

My thoughts once again circled back to what I knew, spiritually: that when it's time to go, it's time to go, and if I was smart, I'd choose to use that escape hatch wisely. Somebody would be left behind to explain, on a carnal level, what happened, why the relationship no longer worked, and why the person had moved on; but on a higher spiritual level, the ultimate choice was mine. The way I would choose to leave was mine as well. That was my reluctant conclusion – and today, in 2021, as I look back, it remains my conclusion. Today, there is no way for me to deny this revelation, because all the blessings and opportunities over the next 30 years came because I once found the courage to say, "I quit."

As I stated earlier, a few chapters ago, that human relationships basically fall into three different types: relationships there for a specific reason; relationships there for a specific season; and relationships there for a lifetime. As people come and go in and out of our lives, this is a useful idea to remember. Dan and I had managed to check boxes one and two quite easily. However, the third box – the one requiring a lifetime commitment – well, it's safe to say that, while his basic management teachings are definitely with me forever, our relationship had no way to survive the chasm created by that current chaotic national fight about basic civil rights.

The truth is that today, I am not bitter. In fact, I'm sincerely grateful to Dan, and today, I remember him as one of my greatest teachers. Maybe it was a "Freudian slip" that day, when Dan revealed his honest, deep-seated personal belief that was both hurtful and insulting to the listener, but it was one that needed to be revealed. I needed to hear his strong words of conviction about white privilege and people of color. However unintended, the confession of his deeply rooted values and beliefs became the push I needed to completely understand that it was truly over – and that there was no real future for me in that place at that time, if I were to stay with Roadway.

An important lesson here is that sometimes, there is a level of truth that needs to be revealed and expressed by the speaker, however unintended the revelation is. It happens to most of us, maybe to all of us, from time to time. When it does, most of us will stop, kick ourselves, and wonder in confusion, "Why on earth did I say that?" The truth is that it's very much like the analogy of a few chapters ago about the orange having only orange juice inside, and when squeezed, can only produce more orange juice. Why? Because that's all that's inside the orange.

Dan had a need to reveal to me privately what he felt in his heart regarding his unconscious, lifelong biases – not just about Black people, but about women as well. He saw sales through the lens of the Jim Crow South, and nothing in his Los Angeles-Southern California experience so far had changed his deeply rooted beliefs about race and white privilege. It must have been on his mind and heart, because with just a tiny squeeze from me, Dan could only express what was inside him – a racially biased position that was rapidly becoming unacceptable in the workplace.

It happened. He said it. Now it's over, but it's not forgotten. Not by Dan, not by the Top Brass, and definitely not by me. While I was still unpacking all this chaos, I was going through the motions of preparing for a big Sunday night shift. As I reviewed my loads and inbound strategy for the evening, I was keenly aware of an unfamiliar, intense, internal nervous tension, the kind that comes with the realization that I was in a bad position, a Catch 22. Because of that eight-minute conversation with Dan on last Friday, I could reasonably expect to get fired or be forced to quit sometime in the next two weeks. The writing was on the wall for me, and I could see no way for us to heal from last week's encounter. The urgent need right now was to find a pathway through it.

As I searched my soul for comfort, the words of Dr. Martin Luther King, Jr. and John Lewis came to mind. Dr. King had said, "There comes a time when silence is not an option; it's a betrayal." I realized that I would be blamed for being a troublemaker, so I might just as well make it, as John Lewis would have said, "good trouble...necessary trouble..." and do what I came here to do.

Still, I was looking for answers, so I kept asking myself, "why me?" The moment felt much bigger than me – not quite as big as the assassination of John F. Kennedy or the bus boycott of 1955, sparked by Rosa Parks' refusal to give up her seat to a white man – but big enough to know that I wasn't the first, wouldn't be the last, and wasn't alone. No matter that my days felt numbered – somewhat like the sacrificial lamb headed to slaughter. And then, I remembered something else I'd read: "When you replace your thoughts, 'why is this happening to me?' with a more spiritual challenge such as, 'what is this trying to teach me?' everything shifts."

Bottom line. I was not afraid of the ultimate consequences and outcomes in this situation, but the slow process of waiting for a story that hadn't yet been told was creating extreme trepidation, filling my heart and mind with all kinds of toxic thoughts. I just wanted it over – right now – so I could go back home and sleep for three days, uninterrupted. I could have walked out right then, not even having to say goodbye to anyone, sparing me the embarrassment that I knew was imminent.

Maybe this was just my own fear and depression seeping in. But management, with the behind-the-scenes "damage control" that had to be taking place, had no idea that I wasn't seeking revenge on Dan or anybody else. Truthfully, they just needed to relax. I hadn't spoken to Human Resources, nor an attorney, nor the Equal Employment Opportunity Commission (EEOC), not even my minister. While they were anticipating and preparing for the worst from me, all I still wanted was just to be promoted into sales. Realistically, however, I knew that my fate would be the opposite. I also knew, with utter conviction, that it was time to move on. No need to look in the rear-view mirror. *It is what it is*, I kept telling myself. My mother's wise words sounded again in my heart, reminding me yet again, "Tony, God will not put more on you than you can handle. So, keep your head up." Over the years, I cannot count the number of times my mother's words of wisdom have given me comfort and peace of mind, even in the midst of a storm. Metaphorically speaking, the storms were raging, but suddenly, I no longer felt alone. I began to feel restored, surrounded by a power greater than me, infinite and eternal, expressing love, energy, joy, peace, and strength. I took a deep breath and slowly exhaled.

God was not playing a joke on me.

Yesterday, I had begun a multiple revisiting of Scroll Marked 10: "A Prayer for Guidance". It seemed to be the only one of the collection that comforted me at that moment. Unlike the poem "Footsteps", where God is carrying you over the roughest parts of the journey, yet how quickly did you conclude, that you had been deserted, when noticing only one set of footprints? I no longer felt alone. I felt totally surrounded, perhaps by my guardian angels or whatever spiritual beings were protecting me. No, I was not hallucinating, but I was definitely not alone tonight in that room. The energy was too thick to cut. Something was definitely here that was soothing and comforting me in that room right then. Thirty minutes passed, and I was beginning to find my rhythm. I had just set up my inbound strategy for the shift, and then, to my surprise and dismay, in walked Todd.

WHAT? Why was Todd here on a Sunday night? Talk about an awkward moment! In three years, this had never happened – a manager showing up on my shift in the terminal, on a Sunday night. What was going on? Did Dan think I was so angry now that he couldn't trust me to do my job? Did he think I was going to burn the building down or steal the furniture and computers? For Dan to start micromanaging me now was an insult. Yet, it was also my wakeup call from management. In its simplest terms, the gesture was clearly saying to me, "Time's up, Tony."

Although the hierarchy chart showed Todd as my immediate supervisor, the middleman between Dan and me, I had never been officially required or told to accept him as my boss. And honestly, nobody seemed to mind. Dan had a well-known open-door policy, and my working relationship with him had been firmly established before Todd was even hired. Dan also had a personal hands-on interest in Operations he might not have wanted to relinquish.

Todd was his lieutenant to do his grunt work: motivate and harass the drivers, give warning letters, go to grievances, hire, and terminate people when necessary. So, under the circumstances, it was logical that he would show up tonight. Obviously, I had become a "subject of concern", and he was there on a specific assignment to watch me and deal with me accordingly. I decided to keep my head down, do my job, and avoid confrontation. If he wanted to talk, fine; otherwise, he could go inside the office and take a nap for all I cared.   Without even saying hello, he stood directly over me. "How many bills do you have tonight?" he asked.

Carefully, I ignored the intimidation in his attitude, voice, and posture. "I see about 250 so far, but that's not all of it," I replied, calmly. "We've got at least three more trailers that are due in before midnight."

"Oh, okay," he said, trying to keep it firm but upbeat. "Well, holler if you need anything. I'll be in my office. I'll see you later, Tony. I've got a lot of reports to do." Todd closed the conversation and turned away.

"Okay, fine," I replied, concentrating on the work in front of me. Here I'd been struggling to find my way through the toxic maze of relinquishing my relationship with Dan. But this brief conversation exchange had made it clear that change had already occurred. A new sheriff was in town. His name was Todd.

I had never disrespected Todd. I'd always found a way to talk to him and include him in conversation, and if he had left me a message to get him two warning letters on these two individuals, I made it a point to do it in a timely way. On the other hand, if I needed to take a vacation day or two, I'd always go directly to Dan and ask for a vacation. I mean, I had a relationship with Dan, even though it was awkward at times. He loved to walk the dock in the mornings. It was our morning ritual and bonding time, and we did it religiously every morning around 07:00 a.m.

So, with this history, I had always seen Todd's job as more significant in working with drivers and office staff, executing the administrative paperwork, rather than trying to corral me and the other Operations supervisors. That, however, was my unofficial off-the-record assessment. Now, the bottom line for this week was shaping up to be Todd, and his role had taken on new meaning and importance. In fact, in that moment on that Sunday evening, little did I realize that the next time Dan and I would speak would be in a big, formal setting with four other men.

Dan showed up about 7:00 in the morning, but he didn't come out to the dock. Instead, Todd replaced him in the walkabout with me. I remember thinking, "Okay, that's different."

For the next few days, Dan was totally off-the-grid, and we had no conversation all week, which was both strange and unusual. The change in atmosphere soon became obvious to Mike and my other workers, who were wondering why Dan had lost interest in walking the dock. Even Dan's memos directed me to get in touch with Todd if I had further questions or needed assistance. That whole week, my two administrative contacts were Todd and Bill. As far as I was concerned, Dan was MIA (missing in action).

It was a strange week. During my evening shifts, Tom knew I was going through "some stuff" and was incredibly supportive. We were still cool together as we worked in tandem on the dock, but since I had not confided any details, he had no clue about how serious the situation between Dan and me had become. I had told him my days were numbered, but he could hardly believe it, let alone accept it.

The biggest surprise of that eternal week came on Friday morning, beginning when Bill showed up early for the first time in almost two years. He said he hadn't been able to sleep, so he decided he might as well come in early. I could tell he was lying, and I could also tell that matters were reaching a climax, but since I was busy doing my job closing out my shift, I had no time to react. So, there we were. Both Todd and Bill were doing the walkabout with me as I explained the various P&D loads.

Everyone was carefully polite, and it was strictly business. Nevertheless, it was pretty obvious that today was "Judgment Day".

I didn't have long to wait before the terms of the "game" being played out hit me like a ton of bricks. It all made perfect sense. First, Bill had come in to take over and finish my shift. Second, behind the scenes, the stage was being prepared for the next act. Toward the end of the walkabout, I noticed three familiar faces – guys in dark suits and power ties—stepping up on the dock unannounced and walking toward the office. Top Brass had arrived.

All of this is for me, I thought. *They're here, and it's time.* Their arrival was far more subtle than the last time they'd shown up. This time, they didn't drive through fast and crazy, checking out the trailers in the yard and hunting for code violations. Instead, they acted like civilized human beings. They had driven in slowly, parked carefully, come up onto the dock, and walked into the office with great seriousness and dignity, not bothering to greet anyone. Damage control was taking over.

I finished my detailed explanation with Bill and Todd, and as they returned to their other work, I deliberately took a cigarette break at the far end of the dock, right where Dan and I had spoken last Friday. I needed a moment to get myself prepared for the inevitable summons that I knew would arrive on the PA system. And, as predicted, there it was. "Tony, please report to Dan's office ASAP," came an unfamiliar female voice – loud and enthusiastic.

I took my time and finished my cigarette. The die was cast, and what were they going to do if I decided to walk in slowly? Terminate me? As scary as the moment could have been, I felt invincible. I was empowered and in control. I had accepted my fate. As I walked slowly toward the office, I began silently repeating over and over one of my favorite mantras: "The God in me speaks, salutes, and responds to the God in you – and in every person associated with this meeting."

Then, I opened the door and walked in.

Once in the room, I took the "hot seat" facing the "firing squad" where everyone was waiting to pronounce my official sentence. I fully expected that it would be permanent "blackball" from the transportation logistics industry. Of course, they wouldn't actually say those words out loud, but they would certainly be inferred and quietly implemented.

"Come in and have a seat, Tony," said Nick Popoff, Regional Vice President for Operations.

"Do you know everyone here in the room, Tony?" asked Adam Clark, one of Popoff's assistants.

"Yes, I do," I replied.

To my surprise, even Todd was present. One of the three newcomers whom I'd met before, but whose name I didn't recall, I thought of as "Gentleman X". Under the circumstances, I didn't feel the need to waste time being officially introduced to him, since the outcome of the meeting was already pre-determined and thoroughly rehearsed before they arrived. I simply needed to pay close attention to what they had to say to me. I did notice, however, that Dan just stared at me without smiling.

"Tony, we're here to address a very serious accusation that I'm told you've made," began Popoff.

"Really? What accusation is that?" I asked, determined to make them put it into words.

"Well, I think you already know what accusation I'm talking about, but just so we're all clear about the topic and the reason for this meeting, I'm told you've accused Dan here of being prejudiced and racially biased," Popoff said.

"Yes, I did," I replied calmly.

"Tony, that's a serious allegation. You just don't go around accusing people of something so serious," he said.

"Well, my accusation of Dan is based on our conversation a week ago when he privately informed me that sales is a white man's job, and that I was not ready for it, nor were our customers ready to deal with a Black man in sales," I replied.

"Tony, I'm going to just cut to the chase and be really honest with you. We're not prejudiced. In fact, we just hired a new person in sales for Gardena, and he's Black. He's a good man, and Tony, I have to tell you that it's not you. His name is Samuel Bell, and he's starting next week right here in sales in Gardena. Now, what do you think about that?" Popoff's previously amiable manner had rapidly become harsh and intimidating, resonating with his disgust.

"Well, I actually know Sam, and you're right, he is a good man," I responded. "And so am I. I guess my loss is his gain. However, I had always thought and believed that I was going to be rewarded with a job in sales some day for my hard work and effort over the last three years. At least that's what Dan originally promised me when I began my career here," I said.

"Is there anything else you'd like to say, Tony?" Popoff asked.

"What do you need for me to say? Congratulations? Is that what you want me to say – that you made a great decision?"

"I guess nothing. That pretty much says it all," said Popoff.

"Well, congratulations! Looks like you've figured out a viable solution to this problem. I only wish that it could have been me heading into sales. However, while I'm happy for Sam, I'm also very hurt and disappointed at your decision. It speaks volumes about how you truly feel about me and my future, both personally, and as a Black man." I responded.

"Well, I'm sorry how this decision makes you feel, but do you agree that we are not prejudiced after all?"

"I agree that you are experts at damage control, and you've found a way to fix the problem," I said.

"Well, okay. That about sums it up." Dan spoke for the first time.

"Is this meeting over?" I asked.

"Does anyone else have comments or questions for Tony?" Popoff looked around the room.

"No," Adam replied, "I think we've covered everything."

"Tony, do you have any other comments, concerns, or questions for us?" asked Gentleman X.

"Do I still work here?"

Two of the Top Brass broke into smiles and laughter.

"Sure, you're still an employee here, in Operations, of course – as lead," Dan replied.

"Okay, that about covers it," said Adam.

"All right, the meeting is adjourned, and you are free to go back to work, Tony," Popoff said.

"Tony, it's been a long week. Why don't you go home early today? I'll get Todd and Bill to finish up your shift for you," said Dan.

"Sure. Will do. Thanks, Dan." That was our first verbal exchange since our fateful encounter the previous week.

And just like that, the meeting was over.

I walked out of that room and straight out into the parking lot, without looking back. I got in the car and decided to head for my safe haven at Santa Monica beach, knowing the silence, ocean waves, and saltwater air were what I needed to begin unpacking what just had happened, and restore a semblance of peace of mind. As I drove out of the parking lot gate, I thought I was holding it together, but once I was on the street, the assorted pile of pent-up emotions I hadn't even realized were there escaped.

My eyes filled with moisture, and tears started pouring uncontrollably down my cheeks. I felt like someone had just gut-punched me. The pain was so intense I could hardly breathe. I felt as if I'd attended a modern-day lynching. Those five men were on a mission to punish, destroy, and execute me. But I was still here, and I had not let them see my emotional meltdown, and certainly not my tears. However, those tears were so continuous and extreme, that I was literally blinded by them to the point where it was unsafe to continue driving. Twice, I had to pull over and stop, and there were moments when I absolutely could not see the highway in front of me.

The experience was so intense and profound that it immediately reminded me of the time a few years ago when I stood in my grandfather's church – the one he had helped build—for the last time, leaning over into his casket and using both hands to touch his face because I couldn't see him. My tears had poured down my face like a rain torrent, so profusely that I was temporarily blinded. Until this present moment, nothing had ever compared to that experience at my grandfather's funeral. Many years later, I looked back on the experience and felt as if I wasn't supposed to have seen him that one final time. Instead, I was supposed to remember him as my hero – strong, vibrant, healthy, and happy. He was truly my hero, almost equal to my dad.

In retrospect, it's obvious that these seemingly very different experiences with grief, pain, and tears left me with a great deal to unpack, and some of the unpacking and reprocessing has continued over the years as our conflicted land still struggles with the same old problems of civil rights and basic systemic inequality. But for that particular moment,

I recognized that the manner in which I'd handled Roadway's conflicted values had honored my grandfather and everything he stood for and projected – and in an odd way, I both understood something about the flood of tears and was comforted.

For now, however, in my safe space on a park bench at Santa Monica beach, I simply stopped, breathed, and let the wind, waves, and salty air quiet and heal my mind. Eventually, the healing waves did their work. My emotional energy was finally spent. Gradually, a measure of peace returned, although the final outcome was by no means assured.

I knew the meeting was over, but the clock was still ticking, and all I'd bought was a little time – time and space to come up with a plan. I knew that once that happened, I'd be okay. But then, I realized that another part of me was in full denial. Maybe I didn't hear them correctly when they said Sam Bell is coming to Gardena and going into sales. Maybe they said I was promoted into sales and Sam was coming to Gardena as my replacement in Operations.

With the invasion of that unwelcome, useless, wishful line of thought, I knew it was time to step back into something resembling reality. I was completely numb, with no appetite for food, although I knew that part of the denial was because I hadn't eaten properly since this mess started. My mind had been playing tricks on me, and I needed to call that game before I did or said something really stupid. Cynthia had offered to take off work early to come and be with me, but as much as I appreciated the gesture, I knew I needed space – to be alone for a while – to pull my own head together.

Truthfully, Cynthia wasn't the answer. We had been drifting apart for a while. She had made every attempt to be supportive throughout this hellish week, but her efforts had fallen flat. She and her ex-boyfriend, Ray Duncan, were in the middle of some big land investment deal in Palm Springs. She'd been terribly excited about it and its possibilities for an early retirement. Finally, Duncan had found a deal that had her full attention. There was nothing I could do now to re-write history. It was becoming obvious that we were approaching a fork in the road.

When I reached home, I found my answering machine full of messages. Six from family members – Mom, Dad, my sister Pat, and Cynthia—and fourteen calls from Samuel Bell. Here's an example of how Sam sounded.

"Tony, this is Sam Bell. What the hell is going on over there in Gardena? We need to talk ASAP."

"Tony, this is Sam Bell, I need to talk to you, man. Call me ASAP."

"Tony, they just promoted me to sales and told me I'm to report to Gardena first thing Monday morning. What the fuck? Can you believe this shit?"

"Tony, call me, man. I need to know how I got this job without even an interview. Hell, I didn't even apply for it. They called me into the office right as my shift was ending and told me I was being promoted into sales. At first, I thought they meant I'd be starting sales at the L.A. Terminal, but then they said no, you report to the Gardena terminal on Monday. What the hell is going on, man? Call me."

The messages were all nearly identical and genuinely concerning. Knowing he was walking into a potential bear trap, I eventually called him back and told him the entire story about how Dan and I had a spirited debate that led to a racially charged deeper conversation where Dan shared his honest views about white privilege.

"The conversation literally trapped me, and I unintentionally ended up playing the race card," I said. "Bottom line, I was trying to improve my personal condition, but it backfired on me, and now you are the benefactor of my demise. My days are numbered. That's real talk. So, good luck. I'll come by and speak to you and shake your hand on

Monday and welcome you to the team, but we shouldn't have any long, private conversations at work. Trust me. They will be very suspicious if we're seen talking, and it could turn bad for you very quickly, especially if they think we are sharing and comparing notes. So, I wish you well, my man, and I'll keep you informed regarding my next move. But we should mainly talk privately on the phone in the evenings. Okay?" I said.

As I began to come back to myself, I realized that this job had consumed me for the last three years. It was past time for me to come up for air, exhale, unpack, and begin processing all that had happened to me.

First off – I was not the enemy, and I had not become the "angry Black man in the room". I just wanted fairness and opportunity, but now I was being treated like I was the evil one. Sadly, the easiest path, the easiest solution for them would have simply been to promote me into sales, with a handshake, and let me rise or fall on my own ability, letting bygones be bygones. Before that fateful conversation, it would have satisfied all concerned. Instead, the damage control fix was in at the highest level, and I saw it and felt it. I knew they could never trust me again or believe that I would play ball and allow last week to be forgotten. That's sad, because the truth is that I'd have done so in a New York minute, if they'd just promoted me. Instead, management resorted to one of those classic cover-your-ass moments and there was absolutely nothing I could do to change it or stop what was about to happen. (And as I finished that thought, a quote from Catherine Ponder surfaced in my mind: "For every door that closes, another door opens.")

The bottom line was glowing like a guiding star: IT IS TIME TO GO.

Next: Sam and I met when we started working for Roadway about the same time as trainees in their management program. He was assigned to Los Angeles. I went to Long Beach and then to Gardena. We'd stayed in touch and often compared notes about how the training was remarkably similar at all the facilities. Roadway took great pride in creating "cookie cutter" prototype programs.

The first few days when Sam arrived at Gardena were both awkward and bittersweet for me. Everyone had known for years that my ultimate desire was to go into sales. So now, they had hired their first Black salesperson in Gardena – and it wasn't me. Naturally, everyone watched to see my reaction. I tried to be cordial and pleasant to Sam and everyone, but it was not easy. Inside, I was suffering like a dying man.

Then, one day after Sam had been there about three weeks, I woke to a realization of intense pride each morning when I looked out my window and watched those two Black men in sales stroll through the parking lot to their respective offices. True, pride was mixed with a healthy quantity of jealousy when I saw Sam in his suit and ties, and I secretly reminded myself that it could have been me – should have been me.

And yet, in a strange way, IT WAS ME! I was the one responsible for this moment at the Big R, because, clearly, I was the one who personally shook up that company's foundation with respect to Black people in sales. Technically speaking, I had made history – and all because I had created "Good Trouble". And even though someone else got the immediate benefit, I knew and understood that, because of me, this magical, special moment had happened. I found myself taking pride in this moment when history was made. I never wanted to be the sacrificial lamb. I never wanted to die for a cause. But it is what it is. Now, it is a part of my legacy, even if I'm the only one that someday remembers.

As the days wore on, I knew my time at Roadway was short, and eventually, I'd have to depart, but now, I was truly ready. I realized that, in a different way, I'd earned my stripes by paying the price of sacrifice that Dan so often spoke of. Maybe my type of sacrifice wasn't the way Dan envisioned it— three marriages and two divorces are not my style— but what happened to me qualified as a real sacrifice. Now, instead of promotion as promised, it was time for me to leave with a future no longer guaranteed.

I remember reading once, "Don't be afraid to start over. This time, you're not starting from scratch, you're starting from experience."

From the vantage point of the present, I can't really say when I actually quit The Big R. It's become a big blur. Three weeks or six weeks – or was it three months? But I know that I left shortly after Sam Bell arrived. I remember those months as being my time "down in the valley". It reminds me of people who get divorced and sometimes say, "Yeah, we got divorced last year in March, but truthfully the marriage was over three years ago." I knew for sure now that it was over for me that Sunday night: the moment Todd walked into the building. In my mind, I had officially quit, because when Todd walked into the building with a clear assignment to micro-manage and check me throughout my shift, the message was clear. It was over, and I was gone.

When the actual day came, though, it was extremely low-key and unceremonious. Dan wasn't there, only Todd. So, I walked in for the last time, dressed to the nines, and resigned. I knew they would not allow me to stay an additional two weeks and work, but to make sure, I told them I was starting a new job with a competitor. It was a lie, but I just wanted out. Then, I gave him the resignation letter in its envelope. The same letter I'd traveled to work with for almost three years. My final moments with Todd were very cordial. He wished me well, and I graciously accepted and wished him well, too. There was nothing negative about our final moments together. I walked away and felt real freedom for the first time in a long time. It was time to start a new chapter in my life. As I walked quickly into the parking lot, my mother's voice was again in my mind and heart: "Good things happen to good people, and you are one of the good ones, Tony. Hold your head up high!"

Yes, I cried again, but this time, tears of joy. As I drove out of the Roadway parking lot for the last time, I thought about my three-year investment in this company and how I had been so optimistic and hopeful that I'd have a long and prosperous future in sales. Quitting didn't ease my pain. I was still hurt and disappointed, but I was also celebrating my freedom.

I knew there would be spiritual work needed before I was truly free. I knew forgiveness and letting go were among the mandatory spiritual requirements, and the work wouldn't come easily. On a spiritual level, if I wanted to be free, the personal and professional emotional baggage accumulated in this relationship would require an emotional cleansing. But that work would come later – much later. Maybe starting this week, but not this day.

Right now, it was time to celebrate with a Jack and Coke. Driving down the 110 Freeway headed home, I began to reflect on Dr. King's last speech when he spoke about the mountaintop experience and his glimpse into the promised land, even as he predicted quite correctly that he might not get there with us. Still, he shouted out that promise with total confidence and conviction that we, as a people, would get to the promised land.

And that's when I rolled down all four car windows, and like Dr. King, I, too, began shouting at the top of my lungs: FREE AT LAST, FREE AT LAST. THANK GOD ALMIGHTY, I AM FREE AT LAST! That's how I felt in that moment, with tears of joy streaming down my face.

FREE AT LAST – FREE AT LAST –THANK GOD ALMIGHTY, I AM FREE AT LAST!

CHAPTER FIFTEEN

THE PRICE OF SACRIFICE

"A man is great not because he hasn't failed,
a man is great because failure hasn't stopped him."
- Confucius

Yesterday, I may have quit Roadway Express, but I haven't quit my dreams. I am more determined and obsessed with my future career in sales and achieving my personal goals than ever before. "'No one' and 'no thing' is going to stop me. The only person who can stop me is ME." In the silence of night, lying sleepless in bed, I boldly declare this truth. I reflect with pride on the hard work, commitment, and persistence I've proven to myself and others, from blind faith, while I worked for Roadway over the last three years, hoping I would receive the ultimate prize. Softly, from memory, I utter the words of the Scroll Marked 3: "I will persist until I succeed." Oh, how that particular scroll has inspired and sustained me through many long, challenging nights at work!

Last night, Cynthia and I, and a few of her friends, stayed up late socializing and unofficially celebrating my newfound freedom. The party was over several hours ago, yet I'm wide awake, unable to sleep. All this bottled-up, unfamiliar energy seems to want to explode and express itself.

It's a different energy – intense, yet comforting. It's early morning, and yet, my thoughts are reflecting a mixture of ideas, from excitement about the unknown, to fear regarding the facts.

Bottom line, my reality is that I am no longer gainfully employed, and I NEED A BETTER PLAN!!!

Then, in the next few breaths, I no longer feel afraid or remorseful about my decision to resign. As I breathe deeply, I feel better; light-headed and free, as if I'm being led or pushed by a force greater and stronger than I am. This burst of energy feels like a sudden electrical shock wave, emotionally overwhelming, and I'm compelled to get up and start moving about. I'm restless, and I need to do something. Like cry out to the heavens, or like a baby desperately needing milk and screaming for his mother. And for those of you who are biblical scholars, I consider, for the first time ever, the reason why Jesus cried out on the cross, yelling, "My God, My God, why hast thou forsaken me?" And yet, in the next breath, he uttered in peace, "but nevertheless, Your will, not mine," as He made the ultimate sacrifice, and gave up the ghost for all mankind.

It seems, at birth, that we've all been given the natural instinct to cry out. It is the universal sound that places our plea in the category of "High Alert" – and top priority. So, who, or what, is it that we cry to? Baby eagles, in danger, will cry out for help, and their mother will quickly swoop down to protect them from harm. Are we humans any different from that bird, instinctively and involuntarily crying out for help—even if we do not believe in such a power? It seems to me – and I could be wrong – that in our deepest and darkest moments of trouble and need, the universal sound, the one that gets the attention of all interested parties, is not the name of God, Buddha, or Allah, but instead, it is the instinctive, involuntary, universal sound of the cry for help. Hmm…

I mean, why didn't my plan work? Why did it have to turn so badly for me on that one conversation with Dan? Why did things get so heated and racially charged that day out on the dock? Why couldn't we have kept it lighthearted? Why did things turn so sour and horrible for me afterwards? Why was I not just given the promotion into sales, instead of Sam Bell, like I was promised? I was promised the chance, and then denied it. Why, why, why??? It all seemed so simple. Why couldn't we have just made amends and lived happily ever after? Why me, God? Why do I have to make the sacrifices for the greater good of my people? I mean, when do I get my shot? Why are other people getting theirs, with all the benefits from my sacrifices? Hell, Sam Bell didn't have to read one damn book on salesmanship, but he got the promotion, without even asking for it. Why are others reaping benefits from my loss, my embarrassment, my personal crucifixion?

"Nevertheless, not my will, Your will be done…" I think this is the first time I've ever acknowledged the fact that I am mad at God. I'm upset and feel betrayed. I worked so hard to get prepared, mentally, emotionally, socially, and spiritually. I just KNEW everything was going to fall into place. I thought that I had this personal relationship with God that was indestructible.

Stop it, Tony! This negative self-talk is a prescription for more failure and disaster. You are NOT a victim, Tony! *You are not a victim!* CANCEL, CANCEL, CANCEL WHAT I JUST THOUGHT AND SAID! I TAKE IT ALL BACK! I continue muttering to myself, pacing back and forth in the bedroom, secretly wishing Cynthia would wake up, talk to me, comfort me, as she lies there in bed, sound asleep.

Then, without pre-meditation, I am inspired to raise my right hand, proudly making the high Black power sign, re-enacting the scene at the Mexico City Olympics in 1968, when Tommy Smith and John Carlos raised their black-gloved fists up to the heavens. I don't know why that scene has come to mind, but here it is, and I am emboldened instantly. I was in the eighth grade at the time, and other than watching my idol,

Muhammad Ali yell, "I am the Greatest," this was one of the most exciting, and daring statements by two Black, American athletes that I had ever observed. And that impression has never left me. I remember pondering the question, "Would you have done that, Tony, if you were there?" I honestly wasn't sure, but after watching that, and along with tens of millions of people, earlier mourning the murder of Dr. Martin Luther King, Jr., just a few months prior to the 1968 Olympics, I had realized, maybe for the first time, that anyone is capable of doing almost anything for a cause, including dying. I recall being angry and scared at the same time, as I watched in horror the aftermath of Dr. King's assassination. And, I remember thinking, *If they will kill Dr. King, we Black people are all doomed.* And then, there were those brave, Black fists raised in power and hope.

Everything in that year of upheaval seemed challenging and problematic. The 1968 Chicago riots at the Democratic Convention, the assassination of Bobby Kennedy, and of course the ongoing Vietnam War controversy. Everywhere you looked, 1968 seemed to be consumed with protest, drama and death. Fairness for my people was a concept reserved for a later time. In 1968, nothing seemed to be going right in our country.

But I remember watching these two world-class athletes as the situation unfolded. Each second seemed like minutes. Here were these two Black men standing boldly, right there on the Olympics Awards Stand, representing the United States of America, on international television, with their hands and Black fists held high. I gasped and my first thought, as a teenage Southern boy, was, "Ooooooo, y'all are in big trouble now. They will crucify y'all for this." Yet, I couldn't pretend that I wasn't pulling for these two men. I, too, had dreams of being an Olympic track star one day, so how could I not be supportive of my Black brothers?

Today, as I look back at that time and the climate that was our country in 1968, the 30-year-old man in me clearly understands the significance of that moment – including John and Tommy's desperate need to "cry out" and start some "good trouble" for the greater cause. And yes, today, I believe that I, the 14-year-old boy that I was then, would have been bold and brave enough to stand with Tommy and John, and seize that iconic moment.

As I bring my full attention back into the room and this moment, I ponder again my own unemployment predicament, and without considering a possible audience, I start to yell out loud my daily affirmations – the ones I know by heart. Never before have I allowed anyone, at this point in my life, to hear me speak aloud my affirmations. They were—and remain—my autosuggestions or self-suggestions – that are the real truth about me. Over time, they had become so personal and sacred to me that I had published and copyrighted them. I felt that no one could say my affirmations with the cadence, compassion, and emotional conviction like I could.

Specifically designed to increase my faith in me, they are uniquely mine, even if others have said some version of them, too. Now, this morning, I am feeling so energized and liberated that I have stopped caring about the other people in the house. Utterly caught up in the moment, I have become totally bold, indifferent to my surroundings, which, obviously, include Cynthia and Jamal. In retrospect, it was really selfish of me, especially considering the fact that I was aware that Cynthia would not understand at all. The moment reminds me of the 1976 movie *Network*, where the anchorman, Howard Beale, reporting on world conditions, becomes so upset that he tells his listening audience to go to their windows, open them, and yell loudly, "I'm mad as hell and I'm not going to take it any longer!"

Anyway, my emotions are all over the place, and in this moment, the need to yell like the man in the movie overwhelms me – and I must let the world hear my truth. So, with my fist in the air, symbolizing Black power, just like Tommy Smith and John Carlos did, I yell, "I am bold! I am proud! I am unafraid! I am daring! I am loving! I am kind! I am handsome! I am beautiful! I am rich! I am a genius! I am happy! I am healthy! I am free! I am whole, perfect, and complete! My mind is the mind of God! My eyes are the eyes of God! My ears are the ears of God! My body is the temple..."

Suddenly, Cynthia wakes up, sits up in the bed, and shouts over the racket I am obviously making. "What the HELL are you doing? You're scaring me, Tony!"

I can hear the note of fear in her voice and realize, at some level, that I probably shouldn't have made so much noise.

"Baby, I'm just saying my affirmations!" I reply, trying to laugh it off and smile at her. "It's the kind of thing I do when I'm alone, and it's helped me so much become more positive and spiritually grounded – and SANE. Why, I wouldn't have lasted as long as I did at Roadway if it weren't for these affirmations and my spiritual approach to life!"

I smile confidently and give her a big, playful bear hug. Cynthia isn't exactly reassured. I can feel her body stiffen, even though she isn't pushing me away.

I realize suddenly that I had never, ever uttered – let alone performed with emotional conviction – my affirmations in public. In the moment, I hadn't stopped to consider how this unexpected outburst might scare someone badly, especially if they'd been asleep. (Looking back at my behavior from years later, it seems totally childish and unreasonable, but at this time of struggle to become a man, I was "consumed in spirit", as the old wise folks would say, and it just felt so good to release my pent-up emotions. The perfect way to jump-start a Saturday morning after quitting an otherwise good job.)

Knock! Knock! Someone is banging on the bedroom door.

"Is everything okay, Tony?" asks Jamal. His voice is calm and reassuring – but maybe a little scared, too.

"Yeah, Jamal! Everything's fine. I'm just doing my morning affirmations. You remember how I like to get down sometimes and yell out loud, right?"

"Yeah, man, I remember, but this time you woke me up, scared me half to death!" he replies.

I stop dead for a moment, remembering that day three years ago when Ray Duncan stood over me with a concealed weapon, yelling at me at the top of his lungs, "Go and fix some shit!" – and Jamal had slept right through it.

"Funny, Jamal," I think, "none of Duncan's cursing, swearing, and horrible threats woke you up that day, or at least you didn't come to my rescue. Still, you were much younger and smaller, way back then, but I could have used the help."

I take a deep breath. "I am so sorry, Man. Come on in and check things out. We're cool and your mom's cool, too."

"Nah!" Jamal says, reassured. "I trust you, man. I know you wouldn't hurt her. I'm going back to sleep, okay Mom?"

"Okay, Baby, sorry about the noise," Cynthia says in a carefully normal voice, apologizing for me and my big mouth – and glaring sternly at me.

"Sorry about that, J," I quickly add. "It won't happen again."

Cynthia looks at me in disgust. "You've never done anything like this before, Tony. What's going on with you, anyway?"

"I'm so sorry I frightened you," I say, somewhat sheepishly. "But I think it's time you get to know the spiritual man in me – the real man that I've been reluctant to show you. Because the truth is, I'm a BAAAAAAD,

BAD MAN, and I know it." I joke, imitating the words of my childhood idol, Muhammed Ali, when he shook up the Universe, knocking out the world heavyweight champion, Sonny Liston.

Cynthia smiles at the reference and falls into my arms. "Okay, yes, you're a bad man, Mr. Tony, a.k.a. Muhammed Ali."

"No, Baby, I'm serious. I'm a BAD, BAD MAN. A force to be reckoned with In the Universe, and I'm on a special assignment. I've got work to do here, in this life. Do you know that my personal efforts and sacrifices have made history for Sam Bell and many other African Americans in the future – the ones who join Roadway Express? Because of my sacrifice, their career path will not be as nearly impossible, as it obviously was for me."

"Yeah, that's great, Tony," Cynthia says. "You're a bad man all right. You're a bad man with no job, remember?"

"Well, thanks for bursting my bubble this morning. I'm on a natural high. God is in charge of my life. You don't understand, this is where I get my strength and courage."

"Tony, no offense, but most people try to get a new job before quitting their present one."

"Well, I'm sorry that you don't support my program for freedom and prosperity. Maybe we should just agree to disagree," I say, walking away enroute to the bathroom.

Later that morning, we are having breakfast, and I hit Cynthia with another big surprise.

"Guess what I want to do, Baby! I'm ready to buy that house. I'm ready to meet your realtor friend, Doris Harper. Please call her for me. I'm ready to talk some business."

Cynthia looks at me like I've been smoking weed. "Man, have you lost your damned mind?"

"No, I've never been as clear-headed as I am right now."

Cynthia just shakes her head. "You want me to call Doris and ask her to waste her valuable time showing you homes in Los Angeles when you don't even have a job anymore?" Her voice is rising again, and she looks at me in disbelief.

"Baby, my unemployment situation is temporary. Not having a job at the moment doesn't define me. I'm still who I am, with or without a damn job. I know my worth, my strength, my gifts, and my capabilities. You promised you'd help me when I was ready. Well, I'm ready. You see, I don't need a job to look at houses, but I do need to look at houses to build my buyer's mindset. Bottom line, I need to see, feel, and touch those potential houses to believe that my burning desire can literally cause the home that's right for me to materialize in my reality."

She is beginning to tune me out, but before she can, I have one more point to make. "Remember – it's done unto you as you believe. As a man or woman thinketh, so is he (or she)? Whatever man can conceive and believe, he can achieve. Are you starting to get the message?"

Cynthia just looks at me, and the frown is still there.

"I want to meet her," I persist. "I think she'll understand where I'm coming from."

"Tony, what I said was that you could buy a home in Los Angeles without being married. I never said you could buy a home without having a job. There's a big difference, as you well know."

"Okay. But – would you please just call her? Let me talk to her, and I won't bother you about it again."

Reluctantly, Cynthia picks up the phone and the conversation unfolds like this:

"Hi Doris, my boyfriend, Tony is here, and he's got this crazy idea that he'd like to start doing some house hunting. The only thing is that right now he doesn't have a job. I'll just let you talk to him. His name is Tony, and he's been dying to meet you." She hands me the phone.

"Doris!" I say. "Finally, I get to meet you via the phone. I've heard all good things about you and your ability to perform miracles. In fact, Cynthia told me two years ago that if you can't help me get a home, no one in L.A. can."

"So, tell me, Tony, what is your ultimate goal here and what are your concerns?" the voice on the other end of the phone inquiries.

"Well, I've got about $20,000 saved up, but at the moment, Cynthia is right. I don't have a job, but what I do have is a whole lot of faith. Doris, getting a new job is not my concern. I'll get another job when I'm ready, but what I need most is to start the process of believing in the infinite possibilities of purchasing my first home. And I can't successfully do that unless I'm actually on the ground, exploring and going through the paces. Many people have told me it's damn near impossible as a single person, to own property in Southern California, but I don't want to accept that mindset. I need to be taken seriously, which means I need a confident real estate agent who is comfortable representing and working with me. Cynthia has spoken of you often and so highly and has said numerous times that I don't have to accept the mindset about single persons purchasing homes, and that you are the one special lady who can help me. Doris, I need you to help me make this dream come true. I know what I want, and now I need to see what is out there, so I can better understand what I can have."

"Well, Tony, that's quite a speech, and between you and me and our faith together, I believe we will find you your perfect home!"

"Oh, shit! I knew you were a true believer in infinite possibilities! That's exactly what I'm talking about!" I can scarcely contain my excitement. We both start laughing. "I just knew you were special and would understand me," I finished.

"Listen, Tony, I do understand you, and I'm going to help you all I can to get your new home, if you're willing to do everything I say."

"I promise you I'll follow your instructions to the letter."

"Good. Then we can get started today? Do you want to look at some houses?"

And with that, our journey together begins. Cynthia is astounded that a busy woman like Doris would spend time with a single, unemployed man-with-a-dream. And for a moment, I wonder – is she working with me because I'm single and so damned good looking? No. She's much older than I, older than Cynthia, too. Plus, she talks all the time about her beloved husband. I don't pick up a "cougar vibe" from her at all, but I do pick up on a spirituality akin to my own. Over the next months, Doris and I will become such good friends that Cynthia's concerns about our intentions rise once again.

"Does Doris like you beyond a client?" she asks, the doubt in her eyes similar to what I'd seen before when her sister Janelle was visiting us three years ago for Thanksgiving.

"Hell no, Cynthia!" I sighed.

"Do I need to be worried?" she persisted. "Because nobody in their right mind, especially a professional like Doris, will take a person with no job out every damned weekend just to look at houses."

"Listen, Baby," I try again. "Doris understands something called 'divine timing', and when it's time, I'll get a job. I promise." I smile playfully and continue. "This little mini-vacation has been just what I need to get my priorities straight. When I was working, I was too tired mentally and physically and too emotionally upside down to even think about buying a home. Now I'm free to think, and my mind is soaring with possibilities."

And with that, Cynthia shakes her head in disbelief, but the doubt is gone from her eyes.

And I know, just as clearly and deeply that I'm back on track. What I needed was a "smart time out". I needed to get my mindset right, my spirit aligned, my imagination working effectively, and all in concert to excite and ignite that burning desire for a home. Bottom line – I needed to get my belief system, my consciousness, and my personal vibes moving at a faster pace.

Every weekend for an entire month, Doris would pick me up in her brand-new fancy Mercedes Benz and drive me around, showing me neighborhoods and various homes in my projected price range. I grew to love her style, professionalism, and humility, and we always had a good time. Not surprisingly, it soon emerged that we share and practice the same religious philosophy, even though we attend two different church locations. We would stop for lunch, and we would even pray together. Something Cynthia and I had never done consistently, except for special holiday occasions. Cynthia continues to believe that this can't possibly be a legitimate business relationship. Finally, I tell her as politely as possible that she needs to look in the mirror and consider that's how I feel 90 percent of the time when it comes to her business partnership with Ray Duncan.

Next, I start looking at dogs, visiting shelters, looking for German Shepherd breeders in the newspapers, and talking to friends. I know the time is here to make this process complete, so I make it a daily spiritual ritual to meditate for 15 minutes while visualizing on playing with my new German Shepherd in my own backyard of my new home. So, I now know that I have solid, workable plans, and three initial immediate goals. #1 Get job. #2 Buy home. #3 Get dog. I am ready!

And suddenly, it's one month since I walked out of Roadway, and I receive an unexpected – totally out of the blue – phone call from Anderson Huckabee, a former Roadway colleague, who had been one of the top corporate sales guys during my time there. He primarily handled the larger, one million plus accounts. I'd always liked and respected Huckabee, because he seemed to be more serious and focused than the others. His professional style and demeanor were different—maybe a little dry, but on point. He was a more serious type than the others, with little time for socializing and small talk. A hard worker, who didn't appear to rely solely on his "privileged status" for sales success. As far as I knew, he didn't indulge in the heavy drinking, smoking, and partying, like most of the good ole' boys of that era. At the big secret swim party years ago, he drank sodas – but it was during the day and business hours, and perhaps that was because he operated with a different set of rules. In any case, I am shocked and flattered to receive his phone call.

He starts by telling me he's left Roadway and is now with P.I.E. Nationwide, where his new title is Director of Hawaii and Puerto Rico Sales, a very specialized new start-up program covering exclusively Hawaii and Puerto Rico. He expects and has been hired to expand and grow the program. He tells me that things are very different at this company, and as the new director of this program, he has more leverage than he ever had at Roadway. "That's actually why I'm calling you, Tony," he says.

"Well, I'm definitely listening. I'm glad you called, and I like the way this is sounding," I reply.

"I'm calling to see if you'd be interested in coming aboard as an Outbound Supervisor for P.I.E."

"Damn, just when I thought you were calling me to offer me a job working for you in your Hawaii-Puerto Rico sales department," I say, with a chuckle.

"Nope, sorry. Tony, right now, I'm a one-man show. I'm starting this from Ground Zero. Eventually, I'll be hiring salespeople, but not yet. First I have to prove that this program is going to work and be profitable."

Wow sounds like the same old same old, like I just walked out of. But then that little voice says, "Tony, you better shut up and listen…." So, I did.

"How did you get my phone number, Man?" I asked, intentionally going off-topic. "I mean, I know damn well Dan Dixon didn't give it to you."

"Actually, it was Sam Bell – and he told me to tell you hello, and to thank you again for everything," he said.

"Nice guy. Glad he broke into sales. So, you want me back in the same type of situation I just left? You know Dixon promised me sales, and instead of honoring his promise, they gave it to Sam, which is why I chose to leave. Huckabee, here's the bottom line, I want to go into sales. That's always been my goal and I feel like I've paid a LOT of dues to get there. I think you remember that about me if you don't remember anything else!"

"I do remember that, and what they did to you was foul. I also remember that you were incredibly good at your job in Operations and the men loved you, and they worked their asses off for you. Your production was through the roof!"

"Dan never appreciated me for what I did for the terminal, or the company, for that matter," I said, regretfully.

"But Tony, he actually did appreciate you more than you'll ever know. He just never told you about the full impact you were making. It was his style – he intentionally withheld his compliments to you and others. But, with all due respect, I just don't have a sales job to offer you today. However, what I DO have is this position that I think would be a perfect next step for you, if you're thinking about, or planning to return, to the industry. Are you currently working anywhere else?" he asked.

I'm sure he already knows the answer, but I reply, "No, not yet."

As he continues talking, he tells me they need someone special – someone with industry experience and maturity. Someone with demonstrated excellence in dealing with the Teamsters, because of all the confusion going on currently between his company's recent merger with Ryder Truck Lines and P.I.E. Nationwide. "If you'll come aboard, Tony, and work for a year or so in Operations, I promise you that I will do everything within my power to get you a position in sales."

Damn, I was just offered a job without an interview. They must be desperate as hell.

"Listen, Huck. I'm only interested in this position if it provides a clear, definite pathway for me into sales. Almost a guarantee, because you know I've heard this promise before."

"You know there are no guarantees in this business, Tony. Hell, I could get hit by a truck tomorrow, and I can't give you something in writing, but you have my word. If I'm here – and by the way – I do plan to be here – I will get you a promotion into sales in two years or less. That's the best I can promise. What do you think?"

"Well, I'm definitely interested, but a one-year promise, followed by an immediate promotion into sales would sound much better."

"I promise, Tony, to do my best to make it happen sooner – but I can definitely promise you that it won't extend past two years," he reaffirmed.

"Okay. I'm interested. So, what happens next?"

"I need you to come by and speak with a few other people here at the Carson terminal. It will be conducted as an official interview, so dress to impress, but between you and me, unless you are falling down drunk, you will get the job. We need someone like you to start ASAP. So, I'm not worried. I know you'll impress these people. I've seen you all dressed up in your three-piece suits before, many times. There will be only me and two or three others present in the interview, and I'm certain they're going to like you. Can you meet with us either tomorrow or Wednesday at 10 a.m.?"

"Let's make it Wednesday at 10:00," I suggest. I am trying not to sound too desperate, and I need a day to get my head prepared for battle.

The truth is that this phone call seems perfectly scripted. It has happened in "divine timing". It is time, because I now need a job for a couple of critical reasons: #1 – I am running low on my allocated cash flow. #2 - I need to show gainful employment that specifically reflects the transportation industry, because I have just found my perfect home and it is time to make an offer. This is divine timing – and my plans are now working in divine order.

So that Wednesday, I keep my appointment with Huckabee and three of the P.I.E. operations managers (Frank, the terminal manager, Herb, the assistant terminal manager, and Andy, the regional vice president). It is a warm, friendly environment, nothing like the last "crucifixion meeting" I'd had at Roadway. I can tell they are desperate and needed someone with my experience to come aboard a month ago. So, I agree to their quick offer, pending their verbal agreement that I would be promoted into sales in two years or less. All four men agree. I explain that sales is my ultimate goal, and I will not accept the position without a clear pathway leading to a promotion into sales. (My dad always said, "if you don't ask, you don't get – so I asked!—and got!)

We shake hands and agree on a fair starting salary, more than I was making at Roadway, and we agree that I will start the following week.

Whew! This job has happened so fast and so effortlessly that my head is spinning. These four men meet with me one time and in effect, hire me on the spot, without displaying an ounce of intimidation towards me. Compared to how long it took with Roadway, I can hardly believe it – but it is exactly what I need to get back into the game – fast.

Yes, I am back - well on my way to starting a new life in my new home with my new German Shepherd puppy, and even though it's a verbal agreement, this time, I have a solid promise (in front of witnesses) of a promotion to sales in two years or less – a promise that seems honest, legitimate, and official. I feel that I am truly back – with a fresh start and a new attitude. I've learned a lot through this ordeal, and I'm still here – and still loving all things logistics.

"What I want, wants me!" Florence Scovel Shinn.

CHAPTER SIXTEEN

FORGIVENESS;
THE SECRET SUCCESS INGREDIENT

*"Whether you understand it or not, whether you believe it or not,
there is no substitute for the power of forgiveness. It is the elixir
that attracts and turbo-charges divine right action for your
ultimate success and happiness."*
- Tony L. Harris

The unexpected opportunity to join P.I.E. Nationwide so soon after I walked out of Roadway, and never looked back, opened a new chapter and a new opportunity to reach for my ultimate dream. Moreover, it's been a "textbook example" of success principles in action, even though I'm still working as a Lead Supervisor on the Outbound dock.

It's after 4 a.m. Saturday morning, and we've finally finished a very tough Friday shift. My feet and I are extremely tired and glad it's over, although I know I won't be able to sleep yet. My men moved over 550 bills. This type of work isn't for the faint of heart. Even with this new high potential opportunity to go into sales someday, I hate the swing shift lifestyle, but remain unable to change it. Most weekends, I find myself questioning every spiritual principle I've embraced the last few years, because the one thing that still eludes me is my rite of passage into transportation-logistics sales. Why can't I make this promotion a reality?

I'm beyond ready to start working daytime hours, like most people do, especially my friends.

On the other hand, just six months after starting this new job, I closed on my new home – just as I'd predicted and planned for. It wasn't easy. My credit approval was refused three times, but neither Doris nor I lost faith. Together, we made it happen in record time. Cynthia and Jamal were immensely proud and happy for me. I was surprised to learn, though, that with my success, I'd lost a few folks I'd considered friends; folks jealous of my success, who showed their spite in ugly, negative behavior toward me.

Also, a week before closing on my house, I'd attracted my beautiful German Shepherd puppy. His name is "Atman", which means "the true self". No longer a puppy, he's now a whopping 96-pound beast of a guard dog. As I reflect upon those days, he is sitting at attention right beside me, for not only does he know all my meditation drills quite well, he also knows my expectations for his behavior when I close my eyes to meditate. He is a very spiritual animal and one of the smartest dogs I've ever had. Atman is a special breed of German Shepherd, mixed with wolf; something other dogs seem to detect, respect, and fear. Even as a young puppy, I saw some fierce Rottweilers and pit bulls cower respectfully in his presence. I'd never seen such respect given to an individual dog by his peers.

Yet, even with these obvious blessings, I'm not completely happy. I'm still working nights and still can't sleep well in the daytime. My sleep deprivation continues, making it hard to appreciate my home and my wonderful canine friend. Nothing in that respect has really changed and won't any time soon.

Don't misunderstand – the atmosphere at P.I.E. is a big step up from Roadway, but it's still a Teamster environment. What makes it different, but similar in terms of hostility, is the merger of two companies

– Ryder and P.I.E. – each with its own culture and computer systems. It's a bit like the Hatfields and McCoys, complete with constant feuding and blaming each other for every mistake. It's a lot to manage, but as a nighttime Outbound Supervisor, I'm definitely and openly appreciated – and obviously needed much more here than I ever was at Roadway. Still, the bottom line is that the players' names have changed, but the end game remains the same. Since P.I.E. is also a Teamster Union Barn, poor performance from Teamsters and Casuals result in the same warning letters, grievances, suspensions, and terminations that were routine at Roadway. It is what it is.

As much as I've grown in some areas of my life, I've not yet been able to meet my original goal: promotion into transportation sales, and daytime working hours. Until I accomplish these goals, I won't have fully succeeded. I've never changed my mind, nor wavered from the original goal. And in meditation, I constantly ponder why it's taking so long. What lessons do I still need to learn? How much longer do I have to wait? How much more will I need to sacrifice to reach my dream job in sales? I must be doing something wrong. Please, tell me!

Often, my meditation sessions start out this way, but then as the spiritual ritual takes over, I've learned to stop. "Okay, that's enough," I tell myself, firmly. Then, I begin to relax into a pleasant inner peace that soothes and comforts me. The thing is, at some level I KNOW what the problem is – and it's NOT that I wasn't born a privileged white male. It's that I'm having trouble trusting the two-year timeline, and the promise that Huckabee and the other three men made to me.

The betrayal of the promise at Roadway still haunts me, I guess – and besides, two of those four men have left the company. I'm beginning to become anxious about who will be leaving next and whether the promise will leave with him. Soon, I'll complete my first year at P.I.E. and so far, there's been no mention or follow-up conversation about the promise made in that first and only interview. By intentionally not putting any pressure on Huckabee or any of the others from that interview, I'm trying to be patient and not repeat the negative episode like the one I had with Dan Dixon.

And, I need to keep remembering that, by agreeing to a two-year maximum commitment to work the dock, I also made a commitment to them, although I certainly hoped something would transpire sooner. I must also remember that this is not Dan Dixon, and this is not Roadway – and actually, it's nowhere near being close to two years at P.I.E. – more like several months. I must be willing to go the distance and fulfill my promised commitment. A promise is a promise.

I relax, let go, and let God bring the peace and tranquility of something greater than I. From my meditation-induced sense of peace, I remember that Frank Richardson, my terminal manager, along with Huckabee are the only two men left, who made the promise to me, and fortunately, I get to see Frank almost every day. True, he's cut from the same cloth as Dan Dixon when it comes to management style. They're practically brothers from another mother. But – I'm much better dealing with Frank than I ever was with Dan. It appears one metaphysical truth may be that I've attracted and created a remarkably similar situation. Lesson not learned? Maybe.

I know that I must work on my inner self continually not to let Frank rattle me. So much of his complaining and criticism are ego-driven and senseless. And, if I'm being honest, on most days, I KNOW I'm more qualified and prepared to do his job as Terminal Manager than he seems to be. As much as Dan got under my skin, I never felt I could do his job better. However, my Roadway training truly was the best and is paying off. Which means I have Dan to thank for the confidence and competence that I daily demonstrate in my job. As long as I secretly and seriously make it a point to stay in my lane, control my anger, and not raise any concerns in Frank Richardson's mind that I'm a potential threat to his ego, I'll be okay. I've learned the hard way that a threat to a privileged ego creates nothing but turmoil and destruction.

Huckabee is still here too, and honestly, he is my only real hope that my trust in a sales future is not misplaced. While I could certainly find a way to remind him of the promise, I've wisely chosen to keep working hard, smart, and patiently. Truth is, I'm a little afraid to inquire. So, I make it a point to try to impress Frank every day with my new ideas and thoughts about efficiencies and innovations. Overall, things are going quite well, and I don't want to mess them up. I'm getting along with practically everyone, and I love what I'm building and accomplishing. Most importantly, I never want to experience with Huckabee, Frank, and P.I.E. what I experienced with Dan Dixon, Todd, and Roadway's Top Brass. For now, I choose to be quiet, keep doing my best, and remember that it's premature for management to be promoting me. If I were to confront any of them about the promise and they were to start acting like they have amnesia, I might go postal on them. Not really, I'm totally kidding... because I KNOW I'm so much more chill now. I've changed, a lot. What a difference four years can make!

Today, I'm on a spiritual path most can't touch. I'm literally months away from becoming a certified spiritual counselor at my church. In fact, once I complete my teaching assignment at our youth church and pass my oral and written exams, I will be officially awarded and crowned "Certified Spiritual Practitioner and Counselor with all the rights to counsel, wed, bury, and pray for people, as well as speak in the absence of the minister of the church, if and when asked." This might not be a big deal for most of my readers, but it is for me – and also for this particular church and the church movement at large. I am becoming a Big Deal, at least at this particular church. Unfortunately, it is not enhancing my relationship with Cynthia, that's for sure. If anything, it's going in the opposite direction. She's simply not a fan of the philosophy. But that's something that will have to be settled another day.

Meantime, I'm confident and ready for whatever is about to happen in my life once I receive my spiritual practitioner credentials, while remaining hesitant and downright confused about what, if anything, I should do or say in my career, regarding "the promise". I'm beginning to think I need my own spiritual practitioner to coach me on this sensitive topic. I'm definitely grateful that I have time, and for now, I'm staying in prayer about the whole thing, instead of reacting.

Not long ago, while doing my time at Roadway, I was so over-confident that I sometimes allowed that confidence to get in the way, and I'm sure that confidence was perceived by some as arrogance or ego, instead of authenticity. Well, I've changed, and I've grown. But I do think that, in the next month or so if I don't hear anything, it may be time for me to check in with Huckabee and inquire about his promise to put me in sales.

Lots of changes at P.I.E. are coming down the pike. We've hired a new West Coast Regional Vice President of Sales that Huckabee will now report to. But my biggest most exciting highlight, (aside from watching Florence Griffith Joyner, aka: "Flo-Jo" compete in the 1984 Los Angeles Summer Olympics) was meeting Jay Johnson, the Black Vice President of Corporate Sales, aka "Big Jay" or "Mr. Big Stuff". Wow! This man is intoxicating. He's perhaps one of the highest-ranking Black executives in the entire transportation-logistics industry in this year of 1985. My thought on my first encounter with this impressive, sharp, and articulate 6'5" Black man was, "When I grow up, I want to be just like you."

Everyone seems to love this guy. They say he's fantastic when facilitating a sales presentation. When he walked into the office the first time, he literally took up all the air in the room – as if a celebrity had just graced us with his presence. I'm told he rules Home Depot and Walmart, two of our largest corporate accounts, like Superman. They do whatever he says and will give him first choice over all the competition on any lane of freight he prefers, as well as first refusal on those lanes that are undesirable for our company. I'm told that this Black man is masterful at his job and will not take any shit from anyone, not even the Home Depot and Walmart executives. His legendary rockstar status dates all the way back to the mid-1960s and 70s. It's hard to believe that a Black man was even in transportation sales back then, but that's the way the story goes. Well, after all this is Southern California, so maybe it's really true. Some say he was a former boxer and actually fought or sparred against Sonny Liston. He certainly looks fearless, like he could whip somebody's butt with one hand, while holding a cup of coffee with the other and not waste a single drop. And in his spare time, he's got the audacity to run (first African American) for mayor of his city.

And there's talk about a new woman manager, Nancy Porter, who's coming from San Antonio, Texas to be our first Woman Sales Manager in the history of the company. She'll be domiciled here in Vernon, California and I'd love to work for her. This I know for sure: I'm going to do whatever I can to impress her when she arrives, so I can join her sales team. It's amazing and exciting to see all this good Title VII Diversity and Inclusion stuff finally happening all around me. But, what about me?

(Dang, I've gotta get off this merry-go-round!) I pause and remember the words of Les Brown, The Motivator, from the first time I ever heard him speak. My favorite part of his entire speech was when he highlighted, in detail, the life of the Chinese bamboo tree and its five-year growth process. I remember how he challenged the thinking of each of us that day. In his huge, impactful voice, filled with conviction, he suddenly looked in my direction, and asked the audience, "So, did the bamboo tree grow 90 feet in six weeks, or did the bamboo tree grow 90 feet in five years?" (Five *long* years. I remember thinking, *Damn, that's a long time.*) Sounds like my situation I've got right here at P.I.E.—but 90 feet, now that's impressive.

What Les Brown went on to say was, "The bamboo tree grows 90 feet in five years, because, you have to know that, at any time, if the growers had stopped cultivating, fertilizing, and nurturing the bamboo seed and its process, the tree and all its potentiality would have died." He paused, allowing the audience time to think and process. I remember thinking, *I am like the bamboo tree.*

Today, I repeat the thought in my mind as I contemplate my reality, and once again feel the presence of God. *Please, God,* I silently ask, *Reveal to me the truth that will set me free. What will it take?*

Little do I know that I am about to find out.

During my Spiritual Practitioner and Counseling Certification Training requirements, I had recently been pre-selected to work with a young woman named Tiffany, to team-instruct our youth—ages 13 to 17. It was just Irish luck that I'd been assigned to that youth class of approximately 40 very excited kids, rather than our younger pre-teens. Tiffany, a young woman I hadn't previously met, was, I understood, a regular teacher who preferred to teach youth classes most Sundays, rather than attend the regular adult church services. I had been told that we would be teaching from lesson plans prepared by one of the assistant ministers – a four-week program dealing with a specific spiritual topic. I realize that this class is scheduled to begin tomorrow.

I WILL NEVER FORGET THE FIRST DAY, WHEN WE ATTEMPTED OUR FIRST ASSIGNMENT!

First, as I look around the room, I see the boys who will be my personal responsibility – and then there is the shock of meeting Tiffany. Beautiful, competent, extremely easy on the eyes, and she looks really familiar. As I search my memory, I realize that I've seen her on television. Wow! Well, after all, this is Southern California!

Oh, my goodness, I'm all in – but I'm not sure what is going to be more intriguing: Tiffany, the lovely Hollywood actress, our youthful and energized students, or the topic – FORGIVENESS – surely one of the most difficult spiritual concepts to practice, and hopefully, to begin to master. One thing is for sure: it's going to be an interesting four weeks!

So, after a quick introduction, we begin! Tiffany and I do the first example for the class, to break the ice, and also to show them how to do the exercise:

"FACEOFF – DYADS"

Tiffany sits at the table across from me, looks deep into my eyes, and starts confronting me, as if she's known me for a lifetime. In this role-playing exercise, she begins calling me Marcus, her ex-boyfriend. And the conversation goes something like this:

"Marcus, you were always so jealous, and you never really wanted me to do well. You never believed in me, and you tried to destroy my self-esteem. You KNEW how much I wanted to play that part in the movie with Eddie, and how it could have changed everything for my career. But your jealousy wouldn't allow you to support my dream. You just wanted me all to yourself, so you kept digging and digging, trying to sabotage the entire audition and steal my confidence. And I almost let you get away with it."

She went on at great length, telling me how much I had affected her acting style and career in the early years, because I didn't believe in her – which caused her to doubt herself even more. She started crying – I mean real tears – and I wasn't sure if she was acting or was playing full on – but I found myself getting emotional, just feeling her hurt and sadness. Man, I just want to hug her so badly! But talking and touching aren't allowed from the perpetrator. Then, her personality becomes strong, and she ends the dialog by saying, "But I forgive you, Marcus, and I let you go free. I wish you the best in life. And now, I want you to release me, too, from your mental, spiritual, and emotional grip; it's time for you to let me go free too, right now. Everything between us is over and done with – and cleared up now, and forever."

As we complete the exercise, everyone starts applauding and yelling for us – well, really, it's for Tiffany, because I didn't do anything except listen and maintain sincere eye contact. But she almost had me in tears, too, and ready to apologize for Marcus's dumb ass. In retrospect, it felt good to roleplay with her, because I instantly felt a strong sincere connection... like kindred spirits, or maybe even soulmates. Oh well, perhaps that's just wishful thinking.

Next, after everyone settles down, we explain the instructions in more detail – and I can see the kids getting both scared and excited at the same time, because soon it will be their turn.

SO, HERE ARE THE INSTRUCTIONS

Pick a partner. Next, the partners will sit quietly, facing each other in their chairs until it is time to begin. DO NOT TALK OR LAUGH while waiting.

Now, Partner A and Partner B will each have 60 seconds to begin thinking about one particular event or situation that happened to them, one that was painful and difficult to overcome. After deciding on the situation and the actual person you need to forgive, you will tell your partner the person's name. (Example: Say to your partner, "Hi – your name for this exercise is Jonathan!")

Now, it's time to begin. Note: Partner A will play the victim first, like Tiffany did, and Partner B will play the Pretend Perpetrator, like I did. Then, they will switch.

(WRITE ON A WHITEBOARD AS A CLASS REMINDER)

The three things you are to do in this faceoff:

1. *Acknowledge the event or situation.*
2. *Confront the person. (Discuss their actions and how they made you feel.)*
3. *Begin saying appropriate words of forgiveness to your partner. REMEMBER: Talking and touching are NOT Allowed from the Perpetrator.*

Partner A will do this exercise for three to five minutes, maximum.

Note: This exercise is happening simultaneously with all the Partner A's talking. The room may become filled with lots of noise, talking, laughter, and tears. Partner B becomes your "Pretend Perpetrator" for this first exercise and will not speak nor touch you – only maintain good, sincere eye contact.

(SWITCH – PARTNER B's TURN!)

As we switch to Partner B and start moving faster through the drill, the kids are catching on. I notice, though, that Kevin, a 16-year-old, quiet, young man isn't participating. Indeed, he refuses to do the exercise when it becomes his turn. I walk over and ask him to just try and say the appropriate words, even if he doesn't mean it. I try to explain that the first step in forgiveness is to simply acknowledge the situation and confront it – and then find the appropriate words of forgiveness to say to the pretend perpetrator.

"You aren't expected, initially, to mean it – but only to just say it," I tell him.

"Yeah, but you don't understand what she did to me. I can't forgive her." He repeats this over and over again, like a broken, scratched vinyl record. I continue to try for another five minutes to get him to participate.

All the while, the other kids are finishing up, filling the room with energy, laughter, tears, and noise – and drowning out Kevin's attempt to explain why he can't and won't do the exercise.

I simply cannot get his buy-in and participation. This is hard for me, because I'm not used to failing when it comes to working with young people. Finally, out of respect, I conclude that forgiveness really is not easy for this young man. It must be a really bad situation he's dealing with, and he's just not ready.

Meantime, we break into four small groups of eight to ten and have a sharing and group discussion session. In this small group situation, it is easy to get the kids to talk about the exercise and how it made them feel. Tiffany and I casually walk around and listen in, allowing the kids to facilitate their own discussion, without direct supervision from us. To my surprise, many express a sense of relief from doing the exercise; a feeling of peace and closure. Somehow, just getting the opportunity to say it, get it off their chest, even though they are pretending and saying it to a random person, still affords them, at minimum, peace of mind, and for some, closure. Many are crying, and some are laughing uncontrollably as they discuss some of the critical moments of relief. What is the most interesting is how free everyone seems to be after sharing the experience – as if a weight has been lifted off their shoulders. And then there is Kevin, who I have been watching out of the corner of my eye – and wondering what type of trauma was making this exercise so difficult and painful.

Wow – time flies when you're having fun, and before I know it, it's time for the class to end. I can't stop thinking about Kevin, though, and what his lifelong burden may be, that won't allow him to experience the joy, excitement, and obvious benefits that many of his peers are expressing.

To finish up, Tiffany reads from the lesson plans, and then hands me the homework assignment for the week. While I am reading it, she goes first and explains the instructions to the girls, then turns it over to me to do the same for the boys, quietly remarking that she has some doubts about whether the boys will want to follow through.

So, here's the assignment for the week:

Each student is to pick one person in their life that they need to forgive, and send, via U.S. Mail, a genuinely nice gift – anonymously - to that person. Choose a person who is still alive. The gift must be of value and special. And it must be something you, yourself, would love to receive. If you don't have something at home to send, and if you are planning to purchase something, then, you must keep your purchase reasonable.

Everyone agrees that $25 is a reasonable dollar amount. Personally, I have no idea how much disposable money kids have these days. And I think, *What an interesting exercise this is*, and I try hard to sell it to the boys. I mean, I go overboard, emphasizing how powerful this exercise is going to be. I even say, "For some of you, this one exercise may change your life forever. What is it worth to you to let go and forgive? If you know that forgiveness will change your life in a positive way for the better – forever?"

Then I say, "For others of you, the exercise may give you the peace of mind you've been seeking. Some of you may find your authentic voice and find a way to speak up and speak out for the very first time." And I look directly at Kevin.

Then, I continue, "Here's the bottom line: You're not forgiving your enemies to free them. You're not giving them a pass or a pardon. You're doing this to free yourself from them – to break this invisible cord that binds you. So, trust us for one week and do this exercise – and then next week, we'll share notes and evaluate our results. Is that fair?"

Well, 90 percent of the young men raise their hands, agreeing that it is fair, and they will participate. I don't get an up or down reaction from

Kevin, but he is looking directly at me as I talk, and I can tell I finally have his attention.

And just as I am acknowledging and thanking those willing to participate, I am suddenly hit, like a ton of bricks, with a realization: _What I've just been talking about to these young people is actually a personal message to me._

And I realize that I need to do this homework assignment, too – maybe more desperately than the kids. And in my mind, the name spins round and round: Dan Dixon, Dan Dixon. Dan Dixon, DAMN…Dan Dixon. THAT'S who's wrong with me, and that's what's missing. I need to forgive Dan Dixon. That's what's holding up my stuff – my promotion – keeping my life stuck in the mud. That's my answer to this problem.

I'm so struck by the fact that this is the solution to my problem that I can hardly wait for class to end, so I can go home and start wrapping my gift for Dan. I need to forgive Dan Dixon, and every fiber of my being tells me that this is my long-awaited answer. And I know exactly what gift I want to send him.

HOMEWORK RULES

The gift must be sent anonymously, so you must type all the relevant information without leaving your name or a return address. Also, if you live in a certain city that the perpetrator will recognize, you must drive across town to a different city and mail the gift, to throw their suspicions off the trail. You must take away any suspicion or possibility of them figuring out who sent the gift.

I had just purchased a brand new 12-cassette album of Napoleon Hill's classic, _Think and Grow Rich_. I had only taken the sealed, clear wrapping off, but all 12 cassettes were brand new and untouched inside. This cassette tape album had cost me a whopping $79.95, and I had definitely wanted to keep it for a lifetime – but because I wanted to keep it so badly, I know that its value also makes it the perfect gift for Dan. So, this is what I sent to Dan Dixon on this Sunday afternoon: a 12-cassette album of Napoleon Hill's *Think and Grow Rich*. I type my note, which simply says, "To Dan Dixon, one of my greatest teachers ever. Thank you."

I put the note inside, wrap up the package, and drive to the main post office near LAX Airport and mail it. I feel fantastic about the possibilities. I'm so excited, just driving to and from the post office, that I decide to spend the rest of the afternoon at Redondo Beach, just sitting and listening to the ocean waves. Somehow, I feel the need to recognize this moment as my official completion of forgiveness, and my new experience of freedom.

I estimate that Dan should receive the gift no later than Tuesday or Wednesday, since it is only going about ten miles to Roadway's Gardena office.

Wednesday afternoon, I arrive at P.I.E. around 3 p.m., my usual time to report for work, and I begin planning and preparing my evening Outbound shift. I'm checking with Dispatch to get a sense of the number of outbound bills we'll be picking up today, when suddenly I look up and see John Paul Hardaway, the new Regional Vice President of Sales, walking into the Dispatch office. He comes over and interrupts my conversation with the two dispatchers. He says, "Tony, can you spare a moment and stop by my office to talk before you start your shift tonight?"

"Sure, John, I'll be by in five minutes, if that's okay," I reply.

"Perfect," he replies, walking away.

Well, I cannot lie – my curiosity has been aroused. What could John Hardaway possibly want with me on this quiet Wednesday afternoon? My pulse is beating 210 beats a minute. I am on high alert, but I maintain my cool as I walk casually into his office.

John is on the phone when I arrive, and the conversation seems more personal than business – like maybe talking to your wife about one of the kids or being reminded to pick up items from the store on the way home. The only other time I've been invited into this man's office since he arrived two months ago, was to discuss certain special customers that needed special attention, and the best ways to expedite their freight when their shipments were delayed.

So, I'm wondering if this is the same scenario as the last time – you know, more special favors for special customers, or— just maybe, just perhaps, because of the forgiveness work I did on Sunday, could this meeting possibly be about something else?

With his left hand, he gestures me to take a chair while he finishes his conversation. I sit down and try not to look directly at him, as if eavesdropping on his private conversation. What on earth could this request be about?

Then, he hangs up the phone, looks at me, and smiles; slaps both hands on his desk simultaneously, sits up real straight and tall in his chair, and says, "So, I understand you're ready to go into sales, is that right?"

Whoa! "Yes sir, you heard that absolutely right," I reply.

"Well, we're ready for you, too – and we've got just the right spot for you in downtown Los Angeles. You're going to start your sales training next Monday. I've got you set up to ride with several of our sales reps in the district. I don't have your complete itinerary set up just yet, so I'll have to fill you in on the rest as we go. How does that sound?"

I am speechless, trying desperately to hold back happy tears.

"Oh my, it sounds incredible," I stammer.

"Great! I was hoping you'd be pleased."

"Yes, I'm speechless – literally speechless – I am so pleased! Thank you, John. I'm going to make you proud," I manage.

"Okay, that's great, and I believe you will. Now, I've got a few more things to cover. I need you to fill out these forms tonight, so we can get you your company credit card. Once you complete these forms, just leave them in my mailbox. Also, tomorrow is Thursday, and that will be your last day working the dock."

"Really?"

"Yes. I need you to attend a play on Friday night at Saddleback College with the rest of your new sales team. We're having drinks and dinner starting at 5:30, and then we're all going to the play together and support Frank."

"Frank? You mean Frank Richardson is in the play? I never knew Frank wanted to be an actor," I said.

So much for first impressions. I'd never seen Frank as a right-brain, creative person. Maybe he's been acting all this time, pretending to be a tough Terminal Manager. I remember the time he kicked a trashcan over in a fit of anger in the dispatch office and started cursing at the dispatchers for having so many missed pickups that day. But I also remember thinking that it seemed as if his heart wasn't in it, and I'd wondered if he was pretending. I mean, I've seen people in this business get extremely upset, like Popoff, or Dan, of course, and Ronnie Luster, or the time David and I had our faceoff, and many others—too many to name. So, compared to my previous Roadway experiences, Frank's actions on that day seemed very pretentious.

"Oh yes! It's his second love – maybe his first – so we're all going to be there to support him," John smiles. "And this will be your big opportunity to meet the whole sales team in a social setting. So, remember: you'll be with us Friday night at Saddleback College, and we've got other people already assigned to take your place in Operations. After Thursday night, you, Mr. Tony Harris, are officially in sales."

I nod and simply say, "Thank you."

"Now, next item. Do you have someone who can drive you to work around 2 p.m. tomorrow, so you can pick up your new company car?

"Yes, I do," I reply.

Great, this company car will become both your personal and business vehicle. We swap them out every two years or 100,000 miles, so take care of it, and treat it just like it's your own. You'll need to drive it home tomorrow night, after your final Outbound shift ends.

"Yes sir," I reply with overwhelming respect, out of habit.

"Great, so come in early and go see the shop mechanics. They'll be expecting you. They have three cars out there to choose from, but truthfully, if I were you, I'd only check out the one that's brand new. They all look the same except different colors, and they all have low mileage, but the brand new one would be my choice. You'll see the difference," he says.

"Wow! Am I on *Candid Camera*?" I start smiling and laughing uncontrollably. "I'm not sure I can take much more, John," I say.

"I assure you, this is not *Candid Camera*," John is smiling.

"Well, then I'll definitely be here tomorrow at 2 p.m."

"Great! I'll let the shop know to expect you. I want you to know, Tony, that I have an open-door policy, and I'm here most days. If you have any questions during work hours or after hours, just call me, okay? That's my policy, and it won't ever change. However, as information, in about three weeks, you're going to be meeting your new sales manager. Her name is Nancy Porter. She's from San Antonio, and she's a fireball. You're going to love her style, because she's really good. I'm sure you will learn a lot under her direct leadership. She already knows about you, and she's extremely excited to meet you. Anyway, that's just a heads up for you to be aware of. But for now, what questions do you have for me?"

I have been wearing a full, thick beard for some time, fine on Outbound, but a "no go" for almost all sales reps, so I ask John,

"What about my beard? Do I need to cut it, because I'm willing to do that?"

"Well, we typically don't want salespeople wearing beards – they need to be clean-shaven, but since you're going to be calling primarily on the Jewish community in downtown Los Angeles, many of them wear beards, too. So, we're going to make an exception in your case and see how it goes. So yes, it's okay. You can keep your beard, at least for now."

I cannot believe what I'm hearing. I'm walking on cloud nine, like I'm in *The Twilight Zone*! How can this be? I just sent off my forgiveness gift to Dan on Sunday, and I'm already seeing this return on my investment?

And in that very moment, I silently declare, *From now on, forgiveness has become as essential as breathing is for me."*

"What other questions do you have for me right now?" John asks.

"That's all for now. Thank you."

"Okay. Have a good evening, and congratulations, Tony. Welcome to the sales team. I'll see you tomorrow."

WOW! CAN YOU BELIEVE IT? I can barely breathe, as I take in the transformation that I have witnessed in my life over the last two days. I have just had a fantastic and unforgettable weekend, 48 hours of celebrating my official promotion – Sales Executive for P.I.E. Nationwide, with my newly adopted professional sales family. As I reflect back, Friday night at Saddleback College was so euphoric, practically the equivalent of having an out-of-body experience, as I witnessed myself floating around the room, while enjoying a mixture of fun, excitement, business discussions, camaraderie, and lots of laughter throughout the night. The majority of the P.I.E. Southern California sales division personnel were in attendance, and they all seemed sincere as they welcomed me into our sacred and somewhat exclusive sales fraternity, like I was their long-lost brother returning home. Anderson Huckabee was there, of course, and welcomed me with open arms into my new family of transportation sales. I am so grateful to Huckabee and more importantly, I'm so glad that I took a chance and trusted him.

I'm also quite impressed with our female sales representation. I count only five or six at our dinner tonight, but they are all very stunning attractive women, three of which once worked in their past lives as flight attendants for the airlines. Who can forget the Continental Airlines' commercial, "We move our tails for you"? Also, one sales lady is African American, named Amaya, a beautiful cross between Jane Kennedy and Venessa Williams. Man, she is absolutely drop-dead gorgeous and sexy. This woman can take your breath away when she smiles. I can only imagine what her customers are thinking whenever she stops by. (Little did I suspect from this innocent first-time introduction, that one day she and I would become the best of friends and trusted partners, while developing the #1 and #2 top revenue producing terminals in the history of P.I.E. Nationwide)

But no staring or roving eyes tonight from me. No no no, I've got my baby with me, the one and only Ms. Cynthia as my special guest, and I am giving her complete admiration, attention, and respect. After all, she has been with me through thick and thin for almost five years. Plus, I must admit, Cynthia is quite beautiful and sexy her damn self - tonight, as she parades around in her tight-fitting red skirt and that modest slit on one side, revealing just the right amount of her sultry lightly tanned redbone skin. Yes, Ms. Cynthia knows how to enter and work a room. She came to play, and she is not holding back. I mean she is hanging with this P.I.E. crowd as if she's known them for ten years. So, to put it in perspective, I'm quite impressed with Cynthia's charm and charisma over everyone in attendance tonight, and it's moments like this that I value her so immensely. If only my beautiful, sweet lady in red would embrace and support me in my newfound spiritual evolution, commitment and journey. Our relationship would have a real chance, but never-the-less, she's still been good to me and good for me. It's been almost five years now, and still I have many unanswered questions about our future. But one thing is for sure: we have an undeniable connection. I can only wonder, if push comes to shove what the future holds. I mean, if you were me, what would you do? Who would you choose, if you could only choose one from these top candidates? Cynthia, Amaya, or Tiffany? Just kidding! CANCEL, CANCEL, CANCEL THAT THOUGHT!

Speaking of customers, a handful of the sales executives actually brought customers to the event as their special guest. But if I'm being honest, it almost seemed like some of them were on a secret date together, like David and Kim were at the infamous Roadway swim party. Some of them, I'm noticing are really touchy feely, acting quite familiar and comfortable with one another, and to my biggest surprise, Naomi, (a former devoted Roadway customer) is here as one of Huckabee's special guest. I guess there's no real loyalty in this business after all. This is my first-time seeing Naomi since our meeting years ago, when I did a ride-along with Larry. But tonight, it's just a cool and casual greeting between us, without a hint of flirtation or fireworks. No, tonight Ms. Naomi is off limits and definitely no longer my type, even though she still looks good, but after meeting the beautiful Amaya tonight, everything has shifted. And No, I am not the only Black man in the room, either. Out of sixty or more people in attendance, there are four of us, plus Jay Johnson, aka: Mr. Big Stuff. Not a bad ratio percentage, representing people of color for 1985.

Also, in case you're wondering: yes, I totally forgot in last week's meeting with John Paul Hardaway to ask about a salary increase. I was too overcome with joy to think, however, turns out I received the promotion and a raise without having to ask. It was all inclusive, a part of the package deal. Truth is... I would have said YES to the job, with or without a raise. I thank God that John and P.I.E. were both operating with integrity, because for someone like me who was too emotional to remember to ask for a raise, I could have left several tens of thousands of dollars on the table over the next few years.

Lastly, I must admit, Frank Richardson is a better actor than Terminal Manager, or maybe it was all the alcohol that I consumed that made him appear so great at his craft. I thoroughly enjoyed his performance in the play; however, I was just so damn happy; it really didn't matter. All I know for sure is that I felt like I was finally home, validated, and accepted. It was a very surreal and authentic moment, almost too much to take in, even for Cynthia, my beautiful lady in red.

By the time I get to church on Sunday, my entire life has changed so drastically that I am not the same person. At the class, I definitely – and selfishly – feel or assume, that I have more to share and talk about than most of the kids, because in less than one week, my entire life has changed forever, with this one forgiveness homework assignment.

I am about to be proven wrong. Because, once I start to focus and pay attention, I recognize the room is awash in excitement. So many kids are raising their hands, wanting to share their wonderful results – and here I am dominating the conversation and trying to overtalk everyone in the room. But I'm so excited, I just can't stop sharing what has happened to me.

And then suddenly, I realize I'm forgetting about Kevin. Kevin – who has just stood up and started talking! Loudly, looking dead at me, making eye contact! I finally manage to close my mouth and listen. Kevin is clearly talking directly to me – making eye contact, and his voice is strong and confident.

"I believe you, Man," he says. "I believe everything you're saying because of what happened to me. I mean, something really good happened to me on Friday this week. I mean, I really can't even believe it!"

This silent, withdrawn young man has had a reawakening. Thankfully, I am now giving him my full attention.

"Tell us, Kevin. What happened?"

"Well, like I told you last week, I didn't think I could ever forgive my mother, because when I was younger, she did some things that I felt were unforgiveable. But then I decided I should send her a gift anyway, just in case the exercise worked. So, I did. I sent her an anonymous gift, just like you said. I sent her a music jewelry box. I told my grandmother, who I've been living with for the last five years, what I was doing, and she helped me pick it out and mail it. I hadn't seen my mother in over two years, but Friday, my mother came by unannounced, for the first time in a long, long time. And she asked me to forgive her and come and live with her. She said she'd changed, and she really wanted us to try again to be a family. I couldn't believe it. She cried, I mean sincerely cried, just like Miss Tiffany did, and asked me to forgive her.

"So, I did, but first I did that exercise that you tried to make me do last week. I acknowledged, and then I confronted, and then I forgave. We both started crying and she hugged me so tight I could hardly breathe. She kept crying, repeating over and over that she was so sorry for what she did. If we'd not been doing all this forgiveness stuff in class, I would never even have spoken to her when she stopped by. I would've bounced, the moment she came – without even speaking to her.

"Now, I've got both my mother and my grandmother in my life again. She has no idea who sent her that gift, but she took me shopping and bought me all kinds of brand-new clothes. I couldn't believe it. I had no idea she had this kind of taste. So what do y'all think, guys? How do y'all like me now?" he finishes, turning around and modeling his new clothes and Air Jordans.

Everyone starts applauding and yelling.

"I mean, look at me! I'm so happy today! I didn't realize how angry I was at her, and how much I was missing her. My grandmother is incredibly happy for us, too. She says she's not losing her grandson; she's gaining back her daughter."

"Wow! That's fantastic news, Kevin! That's the best news I've heard all day!" I say.

Tiffany is getting very emotional, and with tears in her eyes, inserts herself into the conversation. "Let's all give Kevin another round of applause!" she says.

It's taken everything for me to hold back my tears on hearing this young man's testimony. I am so happy for him and his breakthrough. It has put everything back into perspective for me. I walked over to him and gave him a handshake that turns into a big, sincere, man hug – with both of us crying, and hanging on for dear life.

So, that's my story.

Tomorrow, I begin my first day on the job as a professional transportation sales executive for P.I.E. Nationwide, and I can't wait. And yes, I'm sure that many of you will say, "Come on, Tony, it was all just a coincidence – get over it. Becoming a transportation sales executive was bound to happen for you sooner or later. Forgiveness had nothing to do with it – it's luck."

I could say it was luck or a coincidence, too, if that was the only great thing that ever happened to me over the next 40 years. But – once I started implementing forgiveness techniques as an essential part of my lifestyle, good stuff continued to happen – frequently—and I could always point to my sincere intentions and actions from "My Forgiveness

Toolbox," to better understand and confirm what I did to create and attract my good results.

Bottom line: It takes faith to forgive. You can't make such a huge investment of time, energy, sincere effort, and even money, to try to release your past mistakes, past events, and problem people, unless you are operating from faith. But good results for your highest good will be your outcome if you do. My closing words for you, if you made it to the end of this book, is to always remember that "as a man or woman think and believe, so is he or she."

THE END

EPILOGUE

Once I left Roadway, my career at P.I.E. Nationwide, Inc., hypothetically grew 90 feet, almost overnight like the Chinese bamboo tree. First, my promise was granted, and I got promoted in only a few months, from Operations Supervisor to Sales Executive, and after a successful two-year run, and earning numerous raises, bonuses, and awards, including "Salesperson of the Year," I was then promoted again, from Sales Executive to Sales Manager. Then two years after that, I was promoted again from Sales Manager to District Sales Manager, where I led and coached the #1 (Long Beach) and #2 (Orange County) top revenue producing terminals in our company, out of 350 terminals, systemwide. Looking back, I find my growth and success to be remarkably like that of the Chinese bamboo tree, because of adding this one essential secret ingredient: forgiveness. And the rest, as they say, is history. Thank you!

The Chinese Bamboo Tree...
If you take a little seed, plant it and fertilize it for years,
nothing happens.
However, during the fifth year,
the Chinese bamboo tree grows 90 feet in six weeks!
"I AM Like the Chinese Bamboo Tree."
...Tony L. Harris

TO BE CONTINUED – STAY TUNED FOR VOLUME 2

ACKNOWLEDGMENTS

I would like to express my deepest gratitude to my editor, Betti VanEpps-Taylor. It was Betti who helped champion my proposal to write this book. And it has been Betti who has held my hand and mentored me throughout this incredible writing process. Often she understood intuitively, before I did, what I was trying to accomplish with this book, and gently and firmly kept me on the straight and narrow, demanding that I and my voice remain transparent, vulnerable, and authentic. Bottomline, she has been an ideal editor, friend, and mentor. Without her, this book would not have seen the light of day.

I would also like to thank my graphic designer, Aaron Ray. We've been on this journey together for several years now and I truly appreciate you for your excellence in creativity and style. You are tremendously gifted and have always been able to understand me and my vision, and for that I am truly grateful.

Also, I would like to thank my publisher, Michael D. Butler and his entire staff at Beyond Publishing. Your professionalism is magnificent, and I truly have enjoyed the process of getting to know you and working with you.

Lastly, heavenly thanks and gratitude to my mom, Louisteen Harris, my dad, Leveorn Harris, and sister, Patricia Harris-Cook. Thanks for believing in me and encouraging me to always be my best self. Also, there is a very long list of other people to thank who have assisted me on my journey; too many names to mention in this space provided, but you know who you are, and I sincerely love you and appreciate you

CPSIA information can be obtained
at www.ICGtesting.com
Printed in the USA
LVHW081609010622
720199LV00004B/307